Rowdy Joe Lowe

ROWDY JOE LOWE

Gambler with a Gun

by

Joseph G. Rosa

and

Waldo E. Koop

University of Oklahoma Press
Norman

by Joseph G. Rosa

Age of the Gunfighter: Men and Weapons on the Frontier 1840–1900 (Norman, 1995)
The West of Wild Bill Hickok (Norman, 1982)
They Call Him Wild Bill: The Life and Adventures of James Butler Hickok (Norman, 1964; second edition, 1974)
Alias Jack McCall (Kansas City, 1967)
The Gunfighter, Man or Myth? (Norman, 1969)
Colonel Colt, London (London, 1976)
Wild Bill Hickok, Gunfighter: An Account of Hickok's Gunfights (Norman, 2003)
Wild Bill Hickok: The Man and His Myth (Lawrence, KS, 1996)
Wild Bill Hickok: Sharpshooter and U.S. Marshal of the Wild West (New York, 2004)

With Robin May

They Call Him Wild Bill: The Life and Adventures of James Butler Hickok (Norman, 1964; second edition, 1974)
Gunsmoke: A Study of Violence in the Wild West (London, 1977), published in the United States as *Gun Law: A Study of Violence in the Wild West* (Chicago, 1980)
Cowboy: The Man and the Myth (London, 1980)
Buffalo Bill and His Wild West (Lawrence, KS, 1989)

By Waldo E. Koop

Billy the Kid: The Trail of a Kansas Legend (Kansas City, 1965)

ISBN: 978-0-8061-3962-3 (paper)

Library of Congress Catalog Card Number: 89-40221

The paper in this book meets the guidelines for permanence and durability of the Committee on Production Guidelines for Book Longevity of the Council on Library Resources, Inc.

Copyright © 1989 by the University of Oklahoma Press, Norman, Publishing Division of the University. Manufactured in the U.S.A. First paperback published 2008.

*To the late Nyle H. Miller,
for whom Rowdy Joe was his
favorite frontier character,
as Nyle was one of ours.*

Contents

Preface	*page* xi
Acknowledgments	xv
Introduction	xvii
1. Rowdy Joe	3
2. Frontier Roustabout	11
3. Newton: The Wickedest Town in Kansas	38
4. Wild and Woolly Wichita	61
5. Red Beard	73
6. Gone to Texas	93
7. Interlude at Leadville	119
8. Denver: A Sporting Life	129
9. With His Boots On	151
Bibliography	173
Index	179

Illustrations

Ellsworth, Kansas, in 1867	*page* 13
Wild Bill Hickok, Texas Jack Omohundro, and Buffalo Bill Cody	15
Joseph Geiting McCoy	40
Newton, Kansas, in 1872	41
Billy Brooks	55
Douglas Avenue bridge	83
Rowdy Joe Lowe	108
Rowdy Joe Lowe and an unknown lady	136
Joe Lowe's Colorado marriage license	138
Lena Larson	139
Thomas Lowe, Joe Lowe's son	140
Joe Lowe's deed to a cemetery plot	141
Bat Masterson	156
Undertaker's bill for burying Joe Lowe	161
Joe Lowe's daughters, Elizabeth and Anna	163
Joe Lowe's double-action Colt Army revolver	169

Preface

I first heard of Rowdy Joe Lowe nearly forty years ago; but it was not until I read the section devoted to him in Miller's and Snell's *Why the West Was Wild,* published in 1963, that he became more than just a name. Later, during an exchange of information on other subjects with Waldo E. Koop, I learned that he had been researching Lowe for some years. By the late 1960s, however, when other projects intervened, Mr. Koop's research had come to a halt. He then offered me his material if I would be prepared to continue the research and write a book. I agreed, provided it was a joint effort. I then became sidetracked myself by other projects, which will explain why it has taken so long to produce the present volume.

When reviewing the material that Mr. Koop had made available to me, I discovered what proved to be a major breakthrough: a clue to the whereabouts of Joe Lowe's family. Thanks to a friendly postmaster, I was then able to contact his surviving daughter. Once she had recovered from the initial shock of learning (from faraway England) of her father's Wild West reputation, she passed my letter to her son, Edward Dunbar. He was so intrigued to learn of his grandfather's past that he and his wife decided to visit the scene of some of Joe Lowe's exploits. When the couple reached the Kansas State Historical Society at Topeka, they were welcomed by the director of the society, Nyle H. Miller, who, having assured them that I was a bona fide character, also provided them with additional information on Rowdy Joe. Mr. Miller later recalled that even before Mr. Dunbar introduced himself as Rowdy Joe's grandson, he felt that he knew him because he resembled Joe.

Some time later, Mr. and Mrs. Dunbar visited England and met me. It was a nail-chewing moment, for I had no idea how the family might react, both to the news of Joe's past and to an individual who was digging into it. To my great relief they could not have been nicer. In fact, they were so impressed by the material that they had already seen, and by my additional information, that they offered to cooperate in any way they could. Mr. Dunbar then explained his mother's reaction: she and her sister, Elizabeth, had never been told anything of their father's past. She herself was only four years old when he died, but ten-year-old Elizabeth had been old enough to remember him and some of the things that went on around her. On his return to the United States, Mr. Dunbar allowed us (and the Kansas State Historical Society) access to available photographs and other family documents, which helped considerably toward the completion of this book.

Sadly for me, Waldo Koop's active involvement in the book came to an end following illness; but with his agreement and encouragement, I continued the research, adding new material that enabled me to write the book on my own.

Once I began following Joe's trail across Kansas, Missouri, Texas, and Colorado, I soon realized how elusive he was despite a lot of contemporary publicity. Later references to Rowdy Joe Lowe in books, magazines, and newspapers were based mostly upon hearsay, so I concentrated on contemporary material. Consequently, the bibliography is restricted to books, magazines, and newspapers that have a direct bearing on the subject or related events rather than a passing reference or repeated fiction.

According to his Civil War enlistment papers, Joe Lowe was born at Tampa Bay, Florida, but this information proved to be erroneous, for Joe was born elsewhere. There are still gaps in Joe Lowe's story. For instance, it is not known with certainty what happened to Rowdy Kate Lowe, but I was able to find evidence of Joe's two legal marriages. It must be said that were it not for the problems I encountered with several state organizations, more of the gaps in Joe's and others' lives might have been filled also. Although Great Britain has no such restrictions, in some states of the United States it is now difficult for researchers to gain access to old personal records without proof of a relationship to the subject.

At my request, Mr. Koop agreed to remain as coauthor, for without his initial enthusiasm and research, this volume would not have been possible. However, any errors or omissions in the text are mine.

JOSEPH G. ROSA

Ruislip, Middlesex, England

Acknowledgments

Many of the people and the various institutions that assisted in the compilation of this book are acknowledged in the notes, but we would like to express our special thanks to the following:

The Lowe family, especially Joe's daughter Anna, his grandson Edward Dunbar, and his daughter Mrs. Christine de Vies, who were most helpful with additional information; Mr. Jean D. Baker; the county clerks and staffs of the district courts in Ellsworth, Kansas, and Tarrant County and Tom Greene County, Texas; Paul and Penny Dalton; Mrs. Eleanor M. Gehres and Mr. Philip Panum, the Denver Public Library, Western History Department; William ("Bill") Ellington; the late Richard L. Lane; Robert Knecht, assistant curator, Manuscripts Department, and Nancy Sherbert, curator of photographs, Kansas State Historical Society; Nyle H. Miller; Gary Roberts; William B. Secrest; Joseph W. Snell; Ms. Kay Wilcox of the Denver Public Library, who kindly supplied me with all she could find on the trial of Emmanuel Kimmel; and F. W. Wilson, M.D.

To all those mentioned and to those whom we may have inadvertently neglected to include, our grateful thanks.

J.G.R.
W.E.K.

Introduction

The frontier world of the gunfighter, the cowboy, the soldier, and the Indian has been explored many times. Indeed, this route has become well worn. But the twilight world of Rowdy Joe Lowe and others of his ilk who earned a living or a reputation as gamblers or as keepers of saloons, dance halls, and brothels, together with the innumerable characters associated with them, has not enjoyed such wide coverage. But to suggest that they were a breed apart would be stretching credibility to the limit. Rather, one should accept that they were a necessary evil in a male-dominated society into which few respectable women ventured. Yet without such tough characters as Joe Lowe, whose exploits shocked even his hard-boiled cronies, the West would have been a much duller place.

Naturally, Joe Lowe's prowess with a pistol and the number of men that he killed has increased with the telling, and it was even claimed that he started a graveyard for his unfortunate victims in Texas. In truth, he was by no means as "pistoliferous" as some would have us believe — he killed only two men, wounded several others, and blinded one poor unfortunate by accident. As for his rowdy reputation, some described him as gruff (when drunk) or vindictive (when provoked), but usually amenable and friendly. But it was generally understood that Joe Lowe never shot at anyone without provocation or in self-defense.

Like many of his contemporaries, Joe had several mistresses and is credited with a number of wives, although we have found no evidence to support the claim that he married seven times. His first "wife" was the redoubtable Rowdy Kate, whom he met at Ellsworth in the late 1860s, but no record of a legal marriage has emerged. Then came Mollie (or Mary) Field, whom he married at Fort Worth in 1876 and later divorced in order to marry his last wife, Lena Larson. At the time of his death it was claimed that Joe treated his wives and other ladies with much consideration. Unfortunately, that was not true, for when he was in his cups he tended to abuse his ladies, occasionally finding himself in court as a result. But once he sobered up, he always regretted his actions, freely admitting his liquid weaknesses.

The pistol played a prominent part in the lives of Joe Lowe and his generation, but so did law and order. Communities soon realized that a good police force and properly enforced ordinances proved less deadly than the six-shooter and very much more effective. Having passed stringent ordinances, town councils empowered police to enforce them and to supervise the collection of taxes and fines imposed upon the saloon set. City fathers, whilst bemoaning the fact that such individuals polluted the landscape, were not averse to extracting hard cash from them in exchange for official sanction to practice their trades. Consequently, expensive licenses were granted to saloonkeepers and dance-hall proprietors, and heavy fines were imposed upon those who fostered or promoted prostitution. During the cattle-driving season (May to October), the coffers of Kansas cowtowns bulged with cash extracted from what some called "the evil in our midst" and others described as "the locusts of lechery." Of course, these enforced contributions eased the tax burden of ordinary citizens, who otherwise would be considerably out of pocket — an irony not lost upon those who had to pay up. Some, like Joe Lowe, rebelled and refused to pay, which only delayed the inevitable. Pay up or be shut up was the rule. Thus the "politics of economics" took on a character all of its own.

Our look into the smoke-filled saloons, brothels, and gambling "hells" at some of those who prospered or perished amongst the pasteboard pirates, pimps, and like characters is an informal glimpse at a way of life that paid scant heed to morality, yet in its way was both dangerous and exciting.

1

Rowdy Joe

Rowdy Joe Lowe was a character, undoubtedly a character. Among western gunmen and gamblers his name ranks high, as does his reputation for violence. But like other noted western characters, there were two Joe Lowes — the man and the myth — and it is this curious mixture that today is confronted by those who seek the real man.

Joe Lowe gained his name and fame (or ill fame) for rowdyism as the proprietor of several saloons and what were politely called dance halls spread across the West from Kansas to Colorado. These places were very much in the public eye, earning a reputation for depravity and wickedness that owed more to the notoriety of the proprietors and the attention they received in the press than to what actually took place in them.

Contemporary descriptions of Joe Lowe noted that he was heavyset, of dark complexion, with a black mustache and black hair, worn long but not shoulder length. His army records state that his eyes were hazel and that he was five feet eight inches tall.[1] By the time Joe appeared in the cattle towns, he favored a frock coat and sported fine boiled white shirts with jeweled studs, the whole adorned by a top hat, generally called a stovepipe. On the few occasions he rode a horse, Joe used a California-type saddle.

In character Joe Lowe was as controversial as his name. To some he was a tough customer, a man to be avoided. Others, however, described him as a peaceably disposed individual unless aroused — a description which would fit any one of a half-dozen noted gunfighters. Joe carried a gun in his earlier years and on occasion used it, but later he was wont to go unarmed, which, considering his reputation, was thought to be courageous if foolhardy. A contemporary newspaper noted that "he values his spoken word in a commercial transaction more highly than many more reputable men do their spoken oaths."[2] And it was generally understood that anyone's secret was safe with Joe Lowe. His failing, however, was drink, and when in his cups he could be vicious. General David Cook, a noted policeman and detective, recalled that Joe "never was a quarrelsome man, though in the early days of Denver, I have taken shooting irons off him many a time." On one occasion, Cook recalled, Joe got into a fistfight with some fellow saloonkeepers. When the battle was over, and on the pretext of giving one of them "a kiss for his mother," Joe bit off the end of his nose. This act disgusted the onlookers and "sickened the strong men around the bar-room."[3]

Despite his reputation for violence, many people recalled that Joe Lowe also had a kind streak. This was appreciated by a young man in Wichita who had the misfortune to fall from his mule and be knocked unconscious. When he came round, he was in Rowdy Joe's place and was being looked after by one of the girls. When the young man's fiancée found out where he had spent the night, she refused to listen to his explanation and promptly broke off their engagement.[4]

Joe Lowe's contemporaries were not alone in their curiosity concerning his activities. Long before he became aware of his grandfather's nickname, Joe's grandson plied his mother and her sister, his Aunt Elizabeth, for stories about "grandfather Lowe." His grandmother rarely mentioned him, and only his Aunt Elizabeth knew anything of her father's later exploits:

My aunt told me at one time my Grand mother would prepare huge dinners for Joe's friends (good or bad) and many prominent people from Denver. At these dinners they did a lot of gambling at cards, it seems that the one big thing in Joe's life was that he loved to gamble. She told me that Joe and his friends used to go out in the backyard and shoot their names on the side of the barn.

From what I can gather, Joe was the person who could furnish you with any kind of entertainment you wanted, prize fight or dog fight. He seemed to have all the connections of this sort, if it couldn't be done in Denver it could be done at Joe's ranch.[5]

This reference to Joe's sporting interests, in particular dogfights, is borne out by the contemporary press. In his later years he organized a number of them, and on one occasion the police broke up a meeting at Joe's roadhouse on South Broadway in Denver, an area known as Cottage Grove, and arrested eleven men. Others escaped (some of them, it was alleged, members of the police force and fire department), and one man who was chased for half a mile gave up only when shots were fired at him.[6]

Joe Lowe had many affairs with women, and it has been claimed that he was married seven times. One lady, however, more than any other deserves our attention. This was the one remembered by the old-timers as "Joe's woman," whom he met at Ellsworth and who became known all over the West as Rowdy Kate. She was the ideal partner for Joe Lowe and was almost as tough as he was. It has been reported that they were married, but no evidence has come to light to support such a claim.

Kate Lowe was described as an "unfortunate of more than ordinary attainments, and a woman who in her earlier life was good looking." When Joe was in his cups and she upset him, he would abuse her "most shamefully" and Kate promptly had him arrested. But once he sobered up Joe was always sorry and would ask for a continuation of the case. Kate then arranged to pay the costs and have the case dismissed. Peace would once more reign over their "mansion until Joe would thoughtlessly take on more red liquor."[7]

Joe's devotion to Kate was manifested on several occasions, but never more so than when he killed a man named Sweet who molested her. His reputation as a killer, however, was firmly established following the now legendary shootout between himself and fellow saloonkeeper Edward T. ("Red") Beard at Wichita in November 1873. From then on, Rowdy Joe was a man to be reckoned with.

For a man of reputation, curiously little is known about Joe Lowe's origins. His last wife, Lena, was quite vague on the subject. She claimed in 1899 that he "was born in Florida in 1842. While he was a boy his parents removed to Missouri." His first wife, Mollie (who believed herself to be his sixth), also stated that he came from Florida but could not remember the name of the town, although Joe himself had often mentioned it. However, a search of available records failed to establish any link with Florida.[8]

Even Joe's age when he died was uncertain — some reports claimed that he was seventy-two. In 1969, his surviving daughter, Anna, recalled: "I was very young when my father was killed, and I do not know anything about his life, as my mother never spoke about him. I never knew where he was born, his birthday or how . . . old he was when he was killed."[9]

Missouri was the place favored by the old-timers who mulled over Joe's origins, but a census return in the 1870s and a newspaper report of the 1890s claiming that he had been "born in the 1850's in LaSalle, Illinois" were closest to the truth:

> LaSalle, at the head of the navigation on the Illinois river, where the traffic coming up the river from St. Louis and the south was reloaded into the canal boats on the Illinois-Michigan Canal, and with a motor power of two or three mules, was taken to Chicago and to the other numerous towns located upon this canal. Perhaps this was Joe's birthplace; it was on the canal, and his early education and environment along the canal left their impression upon him as it did upon many another youth born and raised along the same canal.[10]

That comment was either inspired guesswork or written by someone who had a good knowledge of Joe's earlier life, but even Joe got it wrong.

Late in the 1840s somewhere in New York state, Thomas Lowe, his wife, Susan, and their young son, Joseph, gathered their meager belongings together and headed west toward Illinois. They were among thousands trekking into the state, and eventually they stopped in Dimmick Township, LaSalle County. Here Thomas settled to the life of a farmer, and two more children were born to the couple. According to the census enumerated on October 31, 1850, Thomas Lowe was thirty-three, born in England, and a farmer worth one hundred dollars. His wife,

Susan, was twenty-six and had been born in Ireland. His son, Joseph, was then five years old and had been born in New York state; his two daughters were Anna, two, and Elizabeth, three months, both born in Illinois.[11]

LaSalle County at that time was still part wilderness. It is now the second-largest county in the state, and its 1,152 square miles encompass a lot of territory and a lot of history. In order to settle the area, early residents had to come to terms with the Indians. Sometimes this was achieved peacefully, sometimes there was bloodshed. By the early 1830s the influx of settlers into the rich, fertile land gave the Indians cause for alarm. Some accepted the white man's arrival as inevitable, whilst others resented it. A major cause of conflict was the treatment of the Indians by many of the whites who despised them. As more people arrived and the Indians were pushed farther away from their hunting grounds, their anger increased. Among those who bitterly resented this incursion into their lands was Black Hawk, the venerable chief of the Sac and Fox tribes. In his youth he had fought for the British during the War of 1812, and while he had respect for the white man, he did not wish to abide by the treaty made in 1804 between the Fox tribes and the federal government. This soon led to trouble.

In 1832 war broke out between Indians and whites, and when hostilities ceased in August, such was the feeling amongst the whites that Black Hawk was banished to Iowa. Shabonna, a chief of the Potawatomi tribe who had tried to help the whites when young men from Black Hawk's tribe had gone on the warpath, was denounced by his own tribe and treated badly by his ungrateful white allies. The end of the Black Hawk War also meant the end of the Indian wars in Illinois. The land was now ripe for settlement.[12]

Within a short distance of Dimmick was the village of Homer, later renamed Troy Grove. It was here on May 27, 1837, that James Butler Hickok was born. Whether the future "Wild Bill" and Joe Lowe were aware that they were onetime near neighbors is uncertain, but according to Hickok's nephew Howard, his Uncle James had once been forced to throw a bully from Peru fully clothed into a stream for ill-treating a youngster who could not swim. The Hickoks, like most people in the area, were well acquainted with the young men of LaSalle and Peru and their unsavory reputations.[13]

According to Henry S. Beebe, writing in 1858, Peru was located on a bluff, a narrow strip above the Illinois River, on which were built the stores and warehouses. "The street under the bluff," he noted, "was generally avoided by the more orderly and quiet citizens. This became the rendezvous of all the congregated rowdies and ruffians. In the night it was almost entirely given up to them. Orgies and revelry were always in order." These rowdy activities, coupled with the financial panic of 1837, which affected the economy of the state for some years, gave both LaSalle and Peru a bad reputation. No explanation has been offered for Joe Lowe's colorful nickname of "Rowdy Joe." It has long been assumed that he earned it because of his antics in the Kansas cowtowns, but perhaps it had been fastened upon him in his youth.[14]

The Lowes apparently did not remain in Illinois very long. Perhaps they did spend some time in Florida — it seems odd that Joe should have memories of the state if he had not been there — and then made their way to Missouri as Lena Lowe later claimed. This latter possibility makes sense, for he enlisted in the Union Army in a Missouri regiment. His father is reported to have died during the war, and a check of available records has failed to establish any service by Joe Lowe, either as a "government teamster" (his given occupation on enlistment was listed as "teamster") or in any other capacity prior to his entry at the age of twenty into Battery B of the Second (New) Missouri Regiment of Light Artillery at Rolla on February 25, 1865.[15]

According to official records, Battery B had spent a lot of its time during 1864 on the march or in changing its equipment. It took part in the defense of Jefferson City, Missouri, during General Sterling Price's abortive raid and later, in October 1864, became involved in a frustrating river trip to Rocheport, where the troops were soon in action destroying a sawmill occupied by Confederate guerrillas. The detachment returned to Jefferson

City and remained there until the November, when it was ordered to Rolla and then to Franklin, Missouri, when Private Joseph Lowe and other recruits joined it.

Battery B remained at Franklin until the Civil War ended on April 9, 1865. While other enlisted troops were contemplating their mustering out, the army had other plans for Battery B. It was ordered to remain at Franklin and, in between polishing equipment, marching, and drilling, was told to prepare for a western campaign. On June 11 orders were received to mount and equip the battery as cavalry, and with other batteries it was ordered to Omaha, Nebraska Territory, where it arrived on June 20.

Joe Lowe now experienced his first known frontier contact with Indians when the regiment became part of the Powder River Indian Expedition, organized to stop Sioux and Cheyenne raids against the whites as they passed through Indian hunting grounds on their way to the Montana goldfields. The expedition was under the command of General Patrick E. Connor, who had already established a reputation as an Indian fighter against hostile Bannocks and Shoshonis in 1863. Battery B was part of the right column, which left Omaha on July 1 and marched up the Platte River to the mouth of the Loup, then followed the latter stream's north fork to its head and cut across to the Powder River, a distance of about 900 miles. The Powder was followed to a point within a few miles of its mouth, and then the expedition went up to Fort Connor, where it arrived on September 20, having marched in all a distance of 1,250 miles through largely unexplored country. There had been fights with the Indians on September 1, 5, and 8, but no serious casualties were sustained.

From Fort Connor the regiment marched to Fort Laramie, arriving early in October. After a short rest it was ordered to Fort Leavenworth, where it was joined by the other companies, then to St. Louis for mustering out, arriving there on December 12. Official records disclose that the regiment had marched 3,535 miles, by which time the raw recruits had become seasoned but very tired campaigners. On Christmas Day, 1865, Private Joseph Lowe became a civilian and, like many thousands of others, he must have looked beyond the festivities and wondered how he was to survive. There was little employment to be found in the East, so Joe turned to the West.[16]

Notes

1. Muster Roll, Battery B Second (New) Missouri Regiment of Light Artillery.
2. Wichita *Weekly Eagle,* January 16, 1873.
3. *Rocky Mountain Daily News,* February 13, 1899.
4. L. C. Fouquet Scrapbook, Wichita Public Library.
5. Edward Dunbar to Joseph G. Rosa, December 1973.
6. *Rocky Mountain Daily News,* April 28, 1898.
7. Wichita *Eagle,* February 15, 1899.
8. *Rocky Mountain Daily News,* February 13, 1899.
9. Mrs. Anna Cappelle to Joseph W. Snell, May 13, 1969.
10. Wichita *Eagle,* February 15, 1899.
11. Census of Dimmick Township, LaSalle County, Illinois, enumerated October 31, 1850, 289, 577 (copy supplied to Joseph G. Rosa by Miss Margaret E. Mills, May 15, 1969).
12. Robert T. Burns, *A Link to the Past: The Saga of LaSalle County, Illinois,* 24–26.
13. Joseph G. Rosa, *They Called Him Wild Bill* (2d ed., 1974), 15.
14. Henry S. Beebe, *History of Peru,* 87.
15. Muster Roll, Battery B; Annual Reports of the Adjutant General of Missouri, 1864–1865.
16. Ibid.

2

Frontier Roustabout

The Civil War was over, but the battle for survival had only just begun. The industrialized East, which had kept the Union so well supplied during the conflict, now faced a slump and unemployment was rife. In the South, still reeling from defeat and yet to suffer the indignity of Reconstruction, the future looked even bleaker. So it was to the West that many of the returned soldiers from both sides turned for survival. Even the threat of hostile Indians failed to deter would-be settlers, for there was the promise of work on the soon-to-be-built railroads, which in turn would mean settlements and cities spread across the nation.

Joe Lowe's movements from his demobilization at St. Louis in December 1865 until he appeared on the plains are obscure. When he enlisted, he had directed that his bounty be "credited to Jackson Township, Monroe County Mo.," but no trace has been found of any members of his family in the township or surrounding area. It was later claimed that soon after the war he located a claim on land near Fort Riley, Kansas, and from there moved to Fort Harker. And there is also the story that he worked for a time as a clerk to a paymaster. Considering that Joe had great difficulty in signing his own name, the latter information is incredible. But his experience as a teamster prior to or during the war most probably led to employment by the military, and one old-timer claimed that he had known Joe in that capacity. Charles Schafer, post quartermaster sergeant at Fort Leavenworth from 1865 to 1867, described his first meeting with Joe Lowe:

This was in 1867. . . . This cowardly scoundrel was really as yellow as they make them, but got away with his bluff until he tackled the regulars. For some act, he ran away before we could find him. Went west to Fort Harker where I again saw him. He was driving a six-mule team.

Having left the service July 27, 1867, [I] came west to Ellsworth, where I bought a house and lot. My job was to see that supplies were loaded and unloaded under my supervision. Joe had the wagonmaster hoodooed, and did about as he pleased. He was driving a team, and should have taken his turn, but when the wagonmaster told him to drive up to the platform, he refused. I saw the wagonmaster was afraid so I took a step toward Mr. Rowdy and he came all right. He was discharged and came to Ellsworth where he murdered a man by shooting him in the back.[1]

Schafer later lived in Wichita where he again met Joe Lowe, but the pair had no further difficulties. His allegation that Joe shot a man in the back at Ellsworth is not verified. Possibly, he was referring to the shooting of "Red Beard" at Wichita.

Similarly, recollections by others claiming that Lowe was an army scout as early as 1865 have not been verified. The only scout named Lowe found in the records was one Samuel Lowe who was employed by the Quartermaster's Department and who served with the Seventh Cavalry in 1867. Possibly this was the man later confused with Joe Lowe when it was reported that he had once scouted with Buffalo Bill. But it is to Ellsworth that we must look for our first authentic sighting of Rowdy Joe.

In 1864 the military established a post on the Smoky Hill River where it crossed the Santa Fe stage road. The fort gave protection to travelers on the Smoky Hill Trail to Denver and was on the route of the Union Pacific Railway Company, Eastern Division (the UPED) when it began building west in 1866–67. Named originally after 2d Lt. Allen Ellsworth who established it on November 11, 1866, it was later renamed Fort Harker, in honor of Brig. Gen. Charles G. Harker, who was killed during the Civil War. In January, 1867, the post was relocated on a site about three-quarters of a mile northeast of the old one. On the 23d of that month what would soon blossom into the city of Ellsworth was also laid out on the north bank of the Smoky Hill River, about four miles from the fort.[2]

Southside Main Street, Ellsworth, Kansas, photographed by Alexander Gardner in September 1867. The place was hardly three months old (having been re-sited following a flood), yet it was growing rapidly. Courtesy Kansas State Historical Society.

The prospect of the UPED's passing near Fort Harker prompted a number of businessmen to consider establishing a point from which supplies could be dispatched to most of the western military posts. A corporation was formed on January 15, 1867, and by April the Ellsworth Town Company had been established. It was fortuitous that the military authorities also upgraded Fort Harker to a status equaling that of Forts Leavenworth and Riley, and the temporary buildings were soon made permanent. The townsite was laid out about a mile west of the fort on a flat strip of land close by the Smoky Hill River. By late May and early June a number of temporary structures had sprung up, and the town was booming. On June 8, however, the normally placid Smoky Hill River rose and flooded the place, compelling the residents to move to firmer ground to the northwest. By July the new site was legalized and Ellsworth was in business.

According to the Junction City *Union* of July 6, however, Ellsworth still had problems. A report that Indians had attacked

Ellsworth was refuted when it was learned that the trouble concerned the denizens of "that classic portion of the town known as Scragtown, which is the lower end of the city," who were "compelled by the recent flood to find a more secure place to ply their vocation. They accordingly pitched their tents on the top of the hill, or as a narrator called it, a 'beautiful plateau.' What would be known as 'nymphs du pave,' in Manhattan or Leavenworth, but at Ellsworth 'nymphs du prairie,' were the innocent cause of a melee in which two stage drivers lost their lives at the hands of a gang who claimed prior possession of the premises. We understand that one or two were also wounded. This incident in an unlawful institution, we learn is all the foundation there is for the report that the Indians had taken Ellsworth."

The presence of the railroad and the economy that accompanied it suffered a setback when the tracks moved farther west and Ellsworth was no longer an end-of-track boomtown. An attempt was then made to persuade the government to withdraw its support from the proposed Kansas-Pacific extension of the UPED to Denver and instead sponsor an "Ellsworth and Pacific" route to the Pacific via Santa Fe. The proposition was turned down, but Ellsworth residents were mollified when it was learned that the army would use Fort Harker as a main military supply base rather than Fort Hays.[3]

The Kansas legislature also named the county Ellsworth. Governor Samuel Crawford appointed several county commissioners, and E. W. Kingsbury became acting sheriff pending a proper election. Ellsworth boomed. A contemporary newspaper noted that the place had two lawyers, two doctors, and one justice of the peace and that Kingsbury also fulfilled the offices of deputy sheriff, constable, and mayor.[4]

Stories of violence and murder continued to excite or cause alarm. On July 7 it was reported that a man named Thomas Wallace was "stabbed in the left lung" during a drunken spree by an unnamed ruffian and died about an hour later. The sheriff of Saline County happened to be on hand and quickly arrested the murderer, but "had great difficulty in keeping the prisoner from the violence of the people. Wallace was a foreman of a grading party on the railroad."[5]

James Butler ("Wild Bill") Hickok, John B. ("Texas Jack") Omohundro, and William F. ("Buffalo Bill") Cody, photographed late in 1873 or early 1874 when they appeared in Cody's theatrical combination. Hickok, Cody, and Joe Lowe were familiar sights at Fort Harker in the late 1860s. Joe was in Leadville when Texas Jack died there in 1880. Claims that Joe once scouted with Buffalo Bill have not been substantiated. Courtesy Joseph G. Rosa collection.

Violence, however, took a backseat when there was an outbreak of cholera at Fort Harker. The first victim was a laborer in the Quartermaster's Department. Later a woman and two children died, and her husband the day after. It was thought that the family had eaten poisoned berries picked on the Smoky Hill, but when others succumbed and the disease was confirmed, the authorities did their best to contain it. All manner of rumors spread. One claimed that Wild Bill Hickok, then a government scout, had died, and Deputy U.S. marshal B. Searcy, later a policeman in Ellsworth, came perilously close to death but recovered. Thanks to the strenuous efforts of the post surgeon, aided by a number of soldiers and civilians, the epidemic was contained; but an estimated 120 lives were lost. Many of the victims were buried in the recently laid-out post cemetery.[6]

Ellsworth held its first election on August 10. Kingsbury ran for sheriff, and Wild Bill was reported to be running for marshal. Whether Hickok actually did so is moot, for on August 6 it was noted that J. E. Hudson and U. E. Thurman were standing as "constables" and after the election a note appeared in the county commisioners' records, dated September 5, stating: "Resignation of Fred Drought as Constable accepted. C. B. Whiting [Whitney] appointed."[7]

Ellsworth, meanwhile, continued to expand. Inevitably, the saloon and gambling business flourished, and it was here that the city had problems. By September the county commissioners were so concerned about the increasing violence and the role played by strong liquor that they met on the second and passed a number of ordinances. Licenses to act as dealers (for anyone selling more than one gallon of liquor or other intoxicating fluids) were sixty dollars per annum. Wholesale and retail dealers were not allowed to sell more than one gallon at a time. Anyone selling the stuff without a license was liable to prosecution. Licenses were provisionally granted for three months, but when there were requests that the fees be reduced and paid quarterly, the commissioners had a rethink. As a result, retailers had to pay one hundred dollars quarterly and wholesalers sixty. It was further ordered that liquor dealers who were engaged in other mercantile business were to pay fifteen dollars a year, whereas those whose mercantile business was exclusive of liquor dealing paid twenty-five dollars. The effect this had upon the saloon population is uncertain, but the commissioners soon learned that enforcing such legislation had its problems.[8]

By September 1867, with a population estimated at twelve hundred, Ellsworth's violent reputation still inspired many rumors. Leavenworth resident John Hancock was reported killed in a violent row over a woman, but soon afterward he reappeared in Leavenworth and "denied the rumor." Some people claimed that newly founded Hays City was far more violent, for nobody "sits down to a social game of cards without laying a revolver upon the table and loosening his bowie knife in its sheath. The place is reported to be similar to California in '49. If reports are true, they must be 'real purty' places to live in." But detractors of Ellsworth remained adamant that no "fouler birds ever congregated around the putrid carcass of a departed ox than those which frequent and tenant the brimstone scented dens of this modern Sodom. A decent traveler would be far safer among the thugs and brigands of Italy than in association with these murderous and larcenous desperadoes." After noting that he had been "reliably informed" that four men had expired in two days and yet another had been shot through the heart in broad daylight, one editor conceded that there were some decent people in the place, but even they were reluctant to go out at night. As for the authorities, he assumed that they had tried but failed to stem the violence.[9]

Despite its conflicting press, Ellsworth was indeed a rough place. On October 3 the vigilance committee hanged one Charlie Johnson and a man named Craig from a tree near the railroad for reasons not disclosed. The citizens took umbrage at the allegations in the Leavenworth press of wholesale murder and mayhem, but the *Daily Conservative* insisted that its reports were true. On October 10 it cited a story published in the Lawrence *Tribune* which claimed that passengers from the West spoke of "quite a panic among the thieves, rowdies, gamblers and other flash characters of Ellsworth. A notice was found on the bodies of two men hung [sic] there last week, stating that such would be the fate of all rogues, and a heavy migration is taking place in consequence. The Vigilance Committee avow it is their intention to keep up operations until the moral atmosphere of the place is purified."

Among the many visitors was a man said to be a member of a "Peace Commission" who was very concerned over the cleanliness of his room, especially the "presence of bed bugs and fleas" in the sheets. His fellow commissioners pulled his leg a little and he retorted: "D – n the bed bugs, why don't you make peace with them?"[10]

The county and city elections took place on November 5. Hickok, still a familiar figure in the city and at Fort Harker, was one of the five candidates for sheriff. He polled the highest number of votes within the city (155) but received little support from the rest of the county. Kingsbury was reelected with a twenty-eight-vote majority, and Whitney was again elected constable.[11]

Despite the election and the promise of law enforcement, violence continued unabated, much of it racial. Early in March 1868 a "Mexican bummer named Chaves, formerly of Kansas City," was shot and killed in an Ellsworth saloon. He and a number of other Mexicans entered the saloon and Chaves remarked that "Americans did not like Mexicans." He then drew his pistol and opened fire, shooting one man in the arm, who promptly drew his own pistol and shot Chaves dead. "Let 'em kill," remarked an editor who was well aware of the still prevalent disdain of Mexicans by Americans, particularly Texans. But Mexicans (or "Greasers," as they were disparagingly called) were a common sight at Ellsworth, where many of them worked as teamsters at Fort Harker, and later Mexican vaqueros came up the trail from Texas with the Longhorns. One writer noted that

society at Ellsworth is of the roughest kind, boiled down. The Greasers are rougher, and the soiled doves are roughest. A single instance will illustrate. One of the latter was playing cards for the drinks, with a novice in Western life. Between her "coral" (I believe that's the word) lips a fragrant Havana (?), before her a glass of forty rod whisky. Lying across one end of the table watching the game was a genuine "greaser," dressed in a buckskin suit, Mexican spurs, Navy revolvers, bowie knife, and long hair. Across the opposite was a Texan similarly dressed. The fair damsel, not succeeding in her efforts to find a passage through her cigar for the smoke, which would naturally come from the ignited end, threw it down, and turning to her "feller" said, "Jim give me a chaw." Jim deliberately drew out an enormous plug of black "navy" which she coolly inserted between her teeth of pearl, and biting off a chew, continued the game. "Pah," we turned away in disgust, wondered how womankind could fall so low.[12]

A further spate of lynchings included that of a Negro who was "suspected of attempted rape of a nine-year-old girl." By December the county commissioners again considered the cost of licenses for saloonkeeping. It was decided that the fee for a dramshop license was to be increased to $250 per annum and grocers' licenses to $150. On December 6 it was also noted in the commissioners' minutes that Kingsbury was no longer sheriff. It was recommended to the governor that C. B. Whitney assume the office, but no action was taken.[13]

Where was Rowdy Joe Lowe during Ellsworth's violent first formative year? If he was employed by the Quartermaster's Department as Charles Schafer claimed, then it would explain his appearance in the Fort Harker post sutler's journal covering the period November 14, 1867, to November 30, 1868. Joe Lowe appears amongst a host of noted purchasers (including Hickok, who bought sundries from stock for $33.50, and Captain Miles W. Keogh, Seventh Cavalry, for assorted wines, whiskies, and cigars). On April 4, 1868, Joe Lowe paid $2, the balance on a pair of pants; on the fifteenth he laid out $4, the balance on a coat; and on August 13 he purchased two undershirts for $3.50.[14]

The same record reveals the name of Joseph Lane as the purchaser of a coffee mill, knives and forks, spoons, plates, a coffee pot, and a butter knife for $8.55. Evidently, this was the Joseph Lane who partnered with a man named Hill in the running of the U.S. Saloon before Joe Lowe became its proprietor.[15]

It has not been established when Joe Lowe took over the U.S. Saloon, but by early 1868 he was well entrenched. A description of the place was left by Peter Robidoux, a French Canadian who spent most of his life in the United States and died in Kansas in 1927. He recalled that early in 1868 he had saved enough money to fulfill an ambition to visit the West. He arrived at Ellsworth on a mixed train (passenger and freight), having taken a whole day to get there from Kansas City. He arrived at 7 P.M. and spent some time at the depot pondering his next move — he was now down to seventy-five cents, having invested the bulk of his money in fares. Eventually he ventured across the street to the U.S. Saloon. "It was a big one," he recalled, and was

about 125 feet deep. I took a chair in a corner near the front where I could watch everything. It was getting interesting. Soldiers from Old Fort Harker were coming and going. The dames and gamblers were there. Yes, and there were Indian scouts, teamsters, bull whackers and citizens of all sorts promenading the streets, as well as the dance hall. The orchestra was playing melodious tunes and the ball was on. Drinking, gambling and dancing were in full blast, all of which was a new picture to me, and there I sat looking on.
Every now and then groups of long-haired men wearing high-heeled boots, and spurs, red underwear, cartridge belts full of cartridges [this is obviously included for effect because metallic pistol cartridges were very rare at the time], scabbard[s] at side with [a] pair of six shooters, and bowie knife would come; call for drinks, and as they went out, bang, bang, bang would ring out from their guns. Poor Pete, sitting there in the corner, would jump every time a gun was fired, and say, believe me it was some new experience for Peter.
Long after midnight the crowd began to thin out. About 3 o'clock the barkeeper tapped me on the shoulder, saying "Kid, wake up. We are going to close up." I knew this meant get out. He was a fine-looking fellow with black hair and black mustache, white shirt and glittering shirt studs. With me it was quite different, I was 2,000 miles from home and friends. I was broke, hungry, tired and sleepy. I asked the price of a bed. "One dollar," he said. There was no choice, no need to argue, so I just turned my pocket inside out to show that seventy-five cents was all I had. He accepted and led me the way up to "drunkards' heaven" where there were about fifty single cots containing that many drunk men. I lay there with fear and trembling until daylight, then got out quickly by the outside stairway, thanking God I was spared once more.[16]

Disregarding the description of six-shooter salvos, Robidoux's pen picture of the proprietor of the U.S. Saloon makes it clear that it was Rowdy Joe Lowe. Unlike his Hollywood counterparts, Joe also served behind the bar when it suited him, which was the best way to get to know one's clientele.
The first reference we have to Joe Lowe's involvement with

the law in Ellsworth is found in Justice of the Peace Michael Newton's papers. Lowe first appeared before him in April 1869, then again in July. On April 15, Henry Irwin charged Lowe and W. D. Howe with "destroying property and throwing filthy water upon him," but Irwin failed to appear in court and the case was dismissed.[17]

An important reference to Joe Lowe — possibly the first written evidence of his nickname of "Rowdy Joe" — came to light when we examined the records of a hearing before Justice of the Peace James Miller. Joseph Brennan, a saloonkeeper, was charged with the murder of Thomas Atkins (no relation to the celebrated scout and guide). Atkins was well known and respected as a wagonmaster who had friends in Ellsworth and Lawrence. On the night of April 6, 1869, there was a dispute between himself and Brennan over a business matter. Atkins threatened to "kill Joe Brennan before he slept, if he had to get a double-barrelled shotgun to do it."

By the time Miller came to examine the evidence, it was very controversial. Witnesses said that Atkins claimed that Brennan, while dining with several others, including his partner, John S. Park (who occasionally served as a deputy U.S. marshal), made insulting remarks about him. Brennan denied the allegation. Later, after a confrontation in Brennan's saloon (when Atkins was quickly disarmed), Atkins toured several other saloons, where he attempted to secure another pistol in order to "kill the Irish son of a bitch before morning." He even asked Joe Lowe for one but was refused. He then made his way to John Hawks's St. Louis Saloon, described by a witness as "this side of Rowdy Joe's." Here Atkins tried to persuade the bartender, Henry Allen, to lend him his pistol for two dollars. When Allen refused, Atkins offered to exchange his watch for the gun, but this, too, was refused. Tom then asked for a cigar; as Allen turned to get the box, Atkins made a grab for the pistol behind the bar. At that moment, Brennan, who had been severely shaken by Atkins's threats against his life, appeared in the saloon, pistol in hand. Allen stated that Brennan's first shot grazed Atkins's "neck and passed on through a picture hanging behind the bar." Three shots were fired, during which time Atkins tried unsuccessfully to get behind Allen. Two soldiers who had been in the bar minutes before and heard the shots rushed back and one of them placed his uniform blouse under the wounded man's head. Chauncey Whitney, who earlier had warned Tom to go home and sleep it off, ran in and arrested Brennan, who was taken to Joe Lowe's saloon and given a drink of water. Atkins was removed to the marshal's home, where doctors fought for his life, but in vain. Brennan evidently was acquitted on the evidence presented before the magistrate, for a search of court records has revealed that the case never came to trial. Later, he was again in trouble when he and Miles Brennan (possibly a brother) were charged with stealing seventy-one mules and two horses from C. E. Musick on July 28, 1869. The outcome of that complaint is not known, for the court records disclose only the initial charge. Joe Brennan remained in business as a saloonkeeper at Ellsworth for some years.[18]

The testimony at the Brennan hearing disclosed not only an early use of the name "Rowdy Joe," but also the statement by W. D. Howe that "Joe Lowe" was "the teamster who works for Charley Seibert." We think Howe was referring to J. Charles Seiber, who served as county sheriff from 1869 to 1871. If Joe was employed by Seiber as a teamster — presumably in a part-time capacity — it suggests that, saloon ventures aside, Joe continued to follow his original calling at least until the late 1860s.[19]

In July 1869, Joe Lowe again appeared before Justice of the Peace Michael Newton. On the seventeenth, James S. Bush, Joseph Lowe, and W. D. Howe were charged on the affidavit of a Mrs. Hohneck, who testified that she saw the defendants take "John Doe" into a saloon and rub something into his face. This may relate to a report in the Junction City paper, which declared that "Friday night of last week [the sixteenth], a man was found drugged and robbed in Ellsworth by fellows known as Jim Bush and Rowdy Joe, the people got after them and in a few days secured the robbers and about seven hundred and fifty dollars of the money. They turned the money over to a pal named Howe who was also secured. The parties were permitted to leave the country." On Monday morning Bush was brought into court by Sheriff E. A. Kesler, but Joe Lowe failed to answer his bond, and following another appearance on the twentieth, J. S. Bush was released, having pleaded not guilty, and Ben Erlick, who had been Joe's bondsman, was arrested. A later entry in the records indicates that Joe was returned to custody and the "case dismissed by the complaining witness." But where Joe was before he was "returned to custody" is a moot point. One possible answer is found in the journal of Major George Armes, who noted on July 19 that "yesterday Mr. Boyd [Alexander Boyd?] and his men came from Ellsworth and brought with them Wild Joe, who had robbed a man of $11,000 [sic — $1,100?] the night before. Lieutenant Schellabarger [Jacob Henry Shellabarger] appeared before the court today. I was notified to hold myself in readiness as a witness, but was not called." If Armes's Wild Joe was in fact Rowdy Joe, it is an understandable error, considering his reputation. As for Howe, court records indicate that he did not appear to answer the charge, and no further action seems to have been taken.[20]

Another of Ellsworth's colorful characters cashed in his chips on August 3 when William Seamens, a policeman, popularly called "Apache Bill" or simply "Patchy," was killed when attempting to arrest an unruly Texan who had fired his pistol indiscriminately in a crowded dance hall. The Texan shot Seamens through the lungs, and he died shortly afterward. Apache Bill was described as about thirty-five or forty years old, five feet ten inches tall, "tough," an expert shot, and renowned as an army scout — although when he once succeeded in losing his way in bad weather, causing great suffering to troops, his reputation suffered. It suffered even more when, late in December 1868, he and Alexander Boyd were arrested and charged with the theft of government mules and horses. Their trial took place on May 20, 1869, at Topeka. Seamens was discharged for lack of evidence, but Boyd was indicted and a motion for a new trial was granted. It was later erroneously reported that Apache Bill had been "sheriff of Ellsworth County" when he was killed. His reputation in Ellsworth, however, was good and his loss greatly felt. The Texan who shot him "escaped having been followed as far as Wichita."[21]

The date, sometime in the late 1860s, when Joe Lowe first met

Kate (whose maiden name has escaped the record), with whom he was to share the next seven years, is not known. According to the 1870 census, "Kate Lowe" was nineteen years of age and Joe was twenty-four. Both were said to have been "born in Illinois." Many assumed that the pair were married, but no record of their union has been found anywhere. The conclusion is that Kate was Joe's common-law wife. Although Joe described himself as a saloonkeeper in Ellsworth, the census enumerator thought otherwise. He wrote before their names (in red ink) "house of ill fame." It is curious, how, in defense of decency, morality, and Victorian prudery, those old-time scriveners delighted in colorful descriptions of the "ladies of the night." One finds such enlightening comments as "ceiling expert," "horizontal worker," "diddles in the dark," and other meaningful descriptions.

The evils of the saloon, gambling house, and dance hall, however, were not lost upon local society. By 1870, Ellsworth was determined to make things difficult for those involved. In April, Ordinance No. 1 warned citizens against discharging any gun or pistol within the following limits, to wit, "on the North Bank of the Smoky Hill River East of the Round House on West of a point 600 yards of the East of the Rail Road switch in the Eastern portion of the town, and south of the North line of the town which is about 100 yards from the foot of the Hills." Any contravention of that ordinance would be punished by a fine of not less than ten dollars or more than twenty, and drunkenness merited a fine of not less than five or not more than ten upon conviction. As for disturbing the peace, such as causing riotous and unseemly behavior or shooting off a gun or pistol, this could mean a fine of not more than twenty dollars and not less than ten. Similarly, policemen caught in houses of ill repute, gambling, or drinking while on duty would be fired. As for "deadly weapons," it was unlawful for anyone to carry "about his person any gun, Pistol, Dirk, sling shot or other weapon, within the limits of the Corporation." On conviction one could pay a fine of not less than five dollars and not more than twenty dollars. The problem, of course, was trying to enforce such ordinances.[22]

A major problem faced by the county commissioners was suppression of "houses of prostitution." It is important to note, however, that suppression really meant the imposition of fines or certain restrictions rather than closing such places, which would have been nonproductive. For the town councils of most of the so-called boomtowns, whether they were noted for freighting, as railroad terminuses, or as gold-seeking or cattle towns, relied more or less on the revenue from these establishments to run the towns.

Any person who was charged with keeping a house of prostitution or an assignation within the corporate limits could expect to pay a fine of not more than fifty dollars and not less than twenty-five. Inmates of such places, if convicted, were fined ten dollars. When there were disturbances in any of the saloons, especially at night, the police were empowered to close them down, and should the proprietors fail to conform with the order, they faced a fine of not more than twenty dollars and not less than ten. These sums may seem paltry by today's standards, but when repeatedly enforced, they proved costly. For the record, one of the fifty citizens eligible to vote at the trustees election on April 4, 1870, was Joseph Lowe.[23]

Joe's activities during the summer of 1870 were peaceful, for it was November before his name again came before the public. That month he petitioned for a renewal of his saloon license, which was granted, and it was noted in the county commissioners' records that "every Saloon Keeper" was to give "Bonds as required by Law." That same month, however, Joe was also in trouble with the law: he was accused of stealing a mule. According to justice-of-the-peace records, the crime occurred in Sedgwick County:

The State of Kansas
Against
Joseph Lowe   Criminal Action 35

Comes now T. L. McAdams this [?] day of November 1870, and after being sworn according to Law deposes and Says that one Joseph Lowe on or about the 12th day of October A. D. 1870 at and in Said County of Sedgwick and State of Kansas, then and there being, did feloniously Steal take and carry away One Slate Colored Mule of the Value of One

Hundred and Seventy five Dollars the personal property of Thomas J. McAdams.
November 1870 State Warrant issued returnable forthwith.

Served this warrant by arresting Joseph Low alias Rody [sic] Joe at Ellsworth City, Ellsworth County, Kans and bring him to Wichita, Sedgwick County Kansas before Justice Van Trees Wichita J. P. Kans this 17th day of March 1871. . . .

W. N. Walker Sheriff
J. C. Seiber Deputy

The fees and expenses involved came to $40.75. Joe's appearance in court was a wasted effort, for McAdams failed to appear to testify. The case was dismissed, and McAdams paid the costs of the action, $49.40. It is a curious fact that on several occasions when Joe Lowe was charged with various offenses, witnesses failed to appear. Cynics may well suggest that some kind of "persuasion" was applied; if so, there is no evidence to support such a suggestion.[24]

Some weeks before the hearing, Joe and fellow saloonkeepers Nick Lentz, Thomas Dowd, and John Kelly were the subject of discussion by the county commissioners. Later, on January 26, 1871, it was ordered that C. B. Whitney, who had just resigned as constable, make his last act that of closing their saloons if they did not immediately present bonds required to allow them to stay in business. Lentz, Dow, and Kelly complied, but Lowe failed to do so. On January 30, the clerk was ordered to notify Joe that either he produce acceptable bonds immediately or his saloon would be closed. Reluctantly, Joe paid up. He was next heard of in April when he visited Topeka, where he was registered at the Tefft House. J. C. Seiber was also registered at the hotel on the same day.[25]

Joe soon returned to Ellsworth, where his presence was recorded by Edward Judson Dodge, who reached Kansas from his native Wisconsin early in May. He recalled that he was in Junction City on May 12 and left there on the thirteenth, arriving at Ellsworth on the fourteenth. He described the place as "one of the roughest and most desperate cities of Kansas." Having secured a room in one of the city's best hotels, the next morning he wandered about to look the place over. When the breakfast bell rang, he walked back to his hotel and sat at a table alone:

Presently another gentleman walked in and took a seat directly opposite me, placed a heavy revolver by his plate, and inquired of the waiter what kind of meat he had for breakfast. "Beef and pork," said the waiter. At this the boarder swore and said, "That will not do for me; I will have a piece of a man," and suiting his action to his words, he gave me a terrible demoniacal look, but only for a moment. I met his gaze with a steady countenance, and he quailed. He got up, and with revolver in hand, stepped to the door, and shot dead the milkman, who was just then passing and whom this fiend had never seen before. In five minutes a crowd had gathered about, placed a rope around his neck, run him across the street, and stood him upon a barrel under a tree, with the rope thrown over a limb.

LAST SERVICE

As the mob came up, "Rody Jo," [sic] a German who was keeping a saloon nearby, inquired what they were going to do with that man, saying that their prisoner owed him $2 for whisky, and they must make some arrangement to pay that before they fixed him. They frankly told Jo that their prisoner had killed a man without cause and they were going to hang him for it. Jo simply said: "Hold on, I won't let anybody hang midout I say somethings," and at the same time ran into the house and brought out an English Bible, and undertook to read a verse in English; but made a poor job of it, and throwing the Bible down on the ground, said it was "no use making so much fuss and trouble over such a little thing as that" and immediately ran up and kicked the barrel from under the wretch and sent him swinging into eternity. And the executors of the law and just adjourned to the nearest saloon (Rody Jo's) to congratulate each other on their prompt, willing and ready way to punish crime.

No evidence of a lynching involving Joe Lowe has come to light, and we suspect that the story was hearsay. Dodge died on October 10, 1910, at age eighty-seven. An examination of his source material (if it still exists) might reveal further information.[26]

In June 1871, Joe ran afoul of the United States Army, but we have to go back two years to explain why. Prior to April 1869, James Stitt and Manley B. Gilman were employed as government scouts at Fort Dodge and were highly regarded until they joined a gang of horse thieves. Arrested and sent to Fort Hays, they were handed over to the civilian authorities for trial, but when no evidence was offered against them, they were released. On June 6, when ten bay geldings were stolen from Company I, Seventh Cavalry, stationed near Fort Hays, the two were suspected immediately, and when they appeared at Topeka they were promptly arrested.

Gilman was found guilty and sentenced to four years in the state penitentiary, but Stitt was acquitted. Soon afterward, he and John Schooler became involved with Lewis Booth of Butler County and the pair sold some mules at Abilene which had been stolen some months before. All three men were arrested. Schooler and Booth were given bail, while Stitt was tried and found guilty. Meantime, Booth continued his rustling, and early in the November he and his brother George were shot dead by vigilantes. Jack Corbin, government scout and former partner of Moses Embre ("California Joe") Milner, was found at the house and lynched despite his claim that he was on a mission for the military in pursuit of a wanted man.[27]

In June 1871 it was learned that Schooler and Stitt had been involved with Ellsworth's Sanderson family, whose horse-stealing activities were well known. The Sandersons had many friends in the saloon set, one of them Rowdy Joe Lowe. John Sanderson and his brother Jonathan had made several appearances in the district court at Topeka. John had murdered a man named Thomas Reynolds in 1868, and when he was arrested at Junction City in August 1870 he had managed to get hold of a shotgun, wounding two officers before being overpowered. He was taken to Humboldt Creek for a hearing before a magistrate (and accompanied by his two brothers Jonathan and George), and it was decided that he should stand trial. A lynch mob then appeared and removed the prisoner. He refused to admit his guilt and was shot dead. His two brothers were persuaded to sign a document saying they would leave the area for good and were released. When Deputy U.S. Marshal Charles Seiber, who was also sheriff of Ellsworth County, learned that George Sanderson was in Ellsworth and that there was a warrant out for him, he and two assistants went to George's home to arrest him. Seiber's warrant charged George with stealing government property (mules or horses). Mrs. Sanderson met them at the door and said her husband was in a back room but if Seiber attempted to enter he would blow Seiber's head off. Seiber promptly turned about, ordered his two unarmed assistants to keep watch, and set off to fetch his revolver. Sanderson ran out of the house, six-shooter in hand, pushed the deputies aside, mounted his horse, and fled across the prairie. Seiber organized a posse and after a lively chase captured Sanderson and placed him under arrest. Sanderson was taken to Topeka, where he was indicted and bail was set at two thousand dollars. Later, however, the court ordered it raised to four thousand dollars and Seiber was ordered to rearrest Sanderson. Again bail was met and Sanderson freed. When he returned to Ellsworth, Seiber was attacked by Sanderson and James R. White, who beat him over the head with an army revolver. Only the intervention of citizens prevented serious injury.[28]

Seiber then went to the commanding officer at Fort Harker and requested military assistance in capturing Sanderson, White, and a man named Jackson, an employee who had aided Sanderson's earlier escape attempts. Backed by a squad of soldiers, Seiber surprised the trio at three o'clock in the morning, arrested them, and took them to the post's guardhouse. Here he learned that a number of citizens (including Rowdy Joe Lowe) had applied to the local court for a writ of habeas corpus to secure the prisoners' release. Again the army came to the rescue and under Special Order No. 84, dated June 12, 1871, Second Lieutenant Henry Quimby, one noncommissioned officer, and six privates of the Fifth Infantry were detailed to escort the marshal and his prisoners to Brookville. The Quartermaster's Department was instructed to provide transportation.

At Brookville, Seiber learned that a party of fifteen or twenty "roughs" from Ellsworth, led by Rowdy Joe Lowe, was en route to secure the release of his prisoners. Immediately the troops were placed on alert, prepared to resist any attack. "It was not long before the cowardly desperadoes came in sight, but seeing the soldiery they retired to a neighboring saloon to take on some courage generating fluid." News of the events at Brookville were telegraphed to Fort Harker, and Captain J. A. Snyder and a detachment of troops were ordered to Brookville. They arrived just "before the desperate gang got sufficiently drunk to dare an attack on the marshal, and at 4 p.m., the marshal got off with his prisoners and arrived in this city [Topeka] yesterday morning." The trio were released on two thousand dollars' bail and departed for their "happy hunting ground." The editor noted that "this is the first case under the new Ku Klux law relative to resisting United States officers, and the penalty is a severe one, but not too severe for such desperadoes as these, who infest our frontier caring neither for life nor property."[29]

News of Sanderson's capture and the excitement it generated reached New York, where on June 2 the *Times* cited a report in the Leavenworth *Commercial,* which told how the citizens of Brookville, enlisted in the service of the United States, had resisted the invading force and how, after a "short, sharp, and decisive conflict," strategy won and the miscreants were conveyed to Topeka and "the war is over." On June 19, however, B. H. Bristow, solicitor general and acting attorney general, addressed a letter to Secretary of War William W. Belknap in which he deplored the events in Kansas:

I learn that on the 12th instant, at Ellsworth, in the State of Kansas, Captain Snyder, of the United States Army, at the request of the United States marshal for the district of Kansas, arrested three men on the charge of obstructing and opposing the said marshal while attempting to execute a process of a court of the United States, and assaulting him while so engaged, and that while the parties thus arrested were in custody of Captain Snyder, under the direction of the marshal, the probate judge of Ellsworth County issued a writ of *habeas corpus* commanding the said Snyder to bring before the said judge the bodies of said prisoners, together with the cause of their detention. It is stated that the "proper return in writing" was made to this writ, and that the prisoners were not taken before said judge, but were afterward turned over to the United States marshal by Captain Snyder, whereupon the probate judge issued process of attachment against Captain Snyder. Upon this state of facts General Pope desires to be informed whether or not this process shall be obeyed. It further appears, from the correspondence before me, that on the 15th instant General Whipple advised General Pope that the process need not be obeyed.

You are pleased to state that these facts are submitted to the Attorney-General for such suggestions as he may have to offer from which I conclude that you desire the opinion of this department touching the legality of the action of Captain Snyder, and the instructions given by General Pope.

It was determined that although the judge had the right to question the marshal's actions, once it was established that the prisoners were in the custody of the United States, the judge could proceed no further.[30]

Unfortunately for Seiber, his problems were far from over. In October 1871 he was arrested in Ellsworth and committed to jail, charged with assault with intent to kill. "As near as we can ascertain the facts," declared the editor of the Topeka *Record*, "the arrest was caused by some of the Sanderson gang whom Sheriff Seiber [he had resigned from this position in July 1871], as United States Deputy Marshal [*sic*] had been active in hunting up. We presume Mr. Seiber will be discharged upon examination." He was charged with misappropriation of government property: the theft of mules. Seiber asked for and was granted a new trial. Sanderson, meanwhile, stood trial at Topeka and was acquitted, which brought the reaction: "Great trouble has been caused by a failure on the military authorities selling condemned animals, to duly brand the same as government property."[31]

Early in 1872, Seiber was reported to have been shot by Deputy U.S. Marshal A. B. Barnes at Wichita. Charged again with stealing horses, Seiber had resisted arrest, and it was noted that "he will hardly die, such men are hard to kill." George Sanderson offered himself as a witness for the prosecution, which did not sit well with Seiber. In May, Seiber was granted a new trial and released from jail on his own recognizance for five hundred dollars' bond. An examination of existing trial documents has revealed that no further action was taken.[32]

Rowdy Joe Lowe, meanwhile, was also involved in a shootout, but this time as a material witness. Early in July 1871, bad feeling between Richard Cavanaugh (sometimes spelled *Kavanaugh*) and John T. Snyder, a deputy sheriff and constable, came to a head on the morning of the eighteenth. Cavanaugh later claimed that witnesses had heard Snyder say Cavanaugh had better watch out for himself or he would fix him so that he would not trouble anyone else anymore. That morning, both men were in the barroom of the Larkin House. Snyder is reported to have informed Cavanaugh that he had a warrant for his arrest and that he was to come with him. Cavanaugh, who was tending bar, told the officer that he had to get a relief first. Snyder then struck him over the head with his revolver, inflicting a severe wound. As Cavanaugh reeled from the blow, Snyder grabbed him and dragged him across the street to the office of Michael Newton, justice of the peace, who examined his wounds and arranged to have them dressed by a barber. At that time there was no warrant for Cavanaugh; but later, when Snyder went into Little Jake's Saloon, where Cavanaugh was sitting on a table, he produced one and Cavanaugh handed over five dollars of a fine and said he would get the other five. He then complained to Snyder about his earlier beating and Snyder retorted: "If you don't like it you can help yourself." Cavanaugh then suggested that they have a drink and part as friends. Moments later, however, Snyder pulled his pistol and Cavanaugh drew his. Witnesses said both shots sounded as one, "for it was impossible for one man to have fired two shots from one revolver so quickly as those two shots were fired." The two men then clinched and were pulled apart by Rowdy Joe Lowe and Chauncey Whitney.

Snyder was helped across the railroad tracks, where he collapsed and was at first left for dead. Whitney returned to the place where he had left Joe Lowe in charge of Cavanaugh and both participants' pistols. Witnesses' statements that the two shots came so close together that they must have been fired from two pistols suggested that both men had fired at each other almost simultaneously. Whitney, however, was of the opinion that although both pistols (one was a .36-caliber Navy and the other a .44-caliber Army revolver) had five of the six chambers loaded, he did not think one of them had been fired. At least the telltale grease and traces of burnt powder common to percussion weapons was not present on one of them, which suggested that it might have been cleaned and reloaded.

At a preliminary hearing soon after the shooting, Joe Lowe was subpoenaed to attend but was not present; later it was stated that he was then in Sedgwick County. In spite of another subpoena, dated September 15 and directed to the sheriff of Sedgwick County, he still had not made an appearance. When the case came to trial in May 1872, however, Joe was on hand and gave his version of what happened:

> I saw Dick [Cavanaugh] coming across the street, coming across from the south side of the street to the north side. He went into Little Jake's when I got to the railroad track. I saw Snyder going after him. I went right on over and they went into the back room, they were in the back room when I got over there. The words I heard Dick say was, "Snyder, I think you have abused me this morning. No man that is a man would beat a man over the head with a pistol that way." Snyder said, "If you don't like it you help yourself." Snyder said, "Any time you want anything out of me, if you don't think I sued you right, I am ready at any time." Dick said, "I don't want any trouble out of this thing, let it drop." He stepped out of the back room into the front room that is, to the barroom. Dick said, "Come on Snyder, come on and take a drink. Let us part in good friends." The bar-keeper drawed a glass of beer and set a bottle of whiskey on the counter, [and] says, "Dick, here is your drink." Snyder said, "No, I will not drink with you." Snyder said as he was walking out, "I am your enemy from this time out." Snyder stepped from the door to the platform and commenced talking to [D. B.] Powers. I stepped out of the door myself and stood between the door and the window. I see Snyder make a jump and jerk his pistol out. Two shots was fired, I guess. There was a second or a second and a half difference btween [sic] [them]. After the shots, both of them clinched, Dick threw Snyder on the ground. I went up, grabbed the pistol out of Dick's hand, took the pistol away from Snyder out of his hand; took the two pistols in one hand and caught Dick by the shoulders and pulled him off Snyder. Whitney came running up. Snyder got up and said, "I am shot." Says Whitney, "You take charge of Dick" (to me). Whitney and Frank Osbourne taking Snyder by each arm crossed the railroad track. Snyder fell down. Whitney hollowed [sic] for a doctor, turns around to me and says, "Give me one of them pistols." Came right up to Newton's office, went into the office. Whitney deputized Jack New's barkeeper and handed him the pistol he had in his hand. I stayed there about fifteen or twenty minutes with him, and this man with Dick, [Enoch] Pendleton comes in he says, "Have you got Dick's pistol?" He says, "I want it, I will go and get you another one." He brought me back another pistol and I turned Dick's pistol over to him. One load fired out of the pistol.

I stayed there a few minutes longer, then I was relieved. That is all I know about it. I would know the pistol again if I saw it. The Army pistol in court is the one I took from Cavanaugh. I had Dick's pistol from the time I took it from him about three quarters of an hour. I looked at the pistol, one shot was fired out of the pistol. I could tell the pistol I took from Snyder. The Navy pistol produced in court is the pistol I took from Snyder. I examined the pistol I took from Snyder, there was one load out of it. There was one load out of each pistol. Know a good deal about Army pistols. One man could not fire as fast as them two shots was fired.

When called to give evidence on May 24, 1872, Snyder denied making threats against Cavanaugh and was also sure that Cavanaugh had fired twice despite the evidence of the one empty chamber. He admitted that he occasionally worked for Joe Lowe as a "fiddler." After the shooting, when he was left for dead, Snyder said he "was in bed for nine days nursed by his wife." Later, under cross-examination, Justice of the Peace Michael Newton confirmed that the army pistol produced in court was the one taken from Joe Lowe by Whitney and handed to him in his office. Newton went on:

I examined the pistol when it was handed to me. One charge was out. I looked at the chambers. It is in the same condition now as it was when handed to me. Loaded with four slugs and one round ball. I found remains of a cartridge back of my desk, ball and paper and powder. This was two or three hours after the defendant was brought in. Do not know the size of ball found. The usual quantity of powder was on the floor that is generally in cartridges.

When cross-examined, Newton said:

I was in the room when Lowe brought Cavanaugh into the room. I was there all the time that Lowe was there, until Whitney came in. I did not see Lowe load any pistol while in the office. I might possibly have went [sic] out of the room while Lowe was there. Lowe possibly might have loaded his pistol and me not have seen it.

Newton's testimony is curious, for no suggestion was made that Lowe actually reloaded Cavanaugh's pistol. If he had, it could only have been to discredit Snyder's claim that Cavanaugh had fired twice and Snyder not at all. But that allegation came later. We must also remember Lowe's claim that he had been asked by Pendleton for the pistol and had in fact handed it to Pendleton in exchange for another one. Therefore, if the weapon was tampered with, it was not Joe Lowe's doing.

Chauncey Whitney in his testimony informed the court that at the time of the shooting Joe Lowe ran a saloon cum dance house which included fiddling and dancing and was frequented by "all classes good and bad, men and women."

In his summing up on May 24 the judge reminded the jury of the salient points of the case, particularly the confused evidence concerning motive. The jury took little time to render a verdict — not guilty — and Cavanaugh was discharged.[33]

Whitney's reference to Joe Lowe's saloon activities, which was also an abiding interest of the city fathers, must have convinced Joe that too much legislation would ruin his business and curtail his profits. And besides, the growing "civilizing" influence of law and order and petty restrictions did not suit him at all. Perhaps the final straw came on July 28, ten days after the Cavanaugh-Snyder shootout, when P. I. Pendleton, county attorney, petitioned the county commissioners to make compulsory the closing of saloons, dramshops, and stores on certain days and at certain hours. The county commissioners considered his request and decreed that from July 29, 1871, all such establishments, including groceries and stores, within the county of Ellsworth be closed on Sundays and that the sale of all intoxicating liquors and merchandise be prohibited. The sheriff and his deputies were instructed to see that the order was strictly enforced and that violators would be dealt with by law.[34]

Such restrictions, and the threat of more to come, prompted Joe and Kate to close up their establishment within days. They decided to move to Newton, where the cattle trade was about to make itself felt, as would Rowdy Joe Lowe.

Notes

1. Wichita *Eagle*, October 25, 1925; Elaine C. Everly, Navy and Old Army Branch, Military Archives Division, National Archives, Washington, D.C., to Joseph G. Rosa, May 18, 1981; *Rocky Mountain News*, February 12–13, 1899.

2. George Jelinek, *The Ellsworth Story: 90 Years of Ellsworth County History* (pages unnumbered).
3. Robert C. Dykstra, *The Cattle Towns*, 32–35.
4. Leavenworth *Conservative*, July 6, 1867; Andreas, *History of Kansas*, 1275.
5. Junction City *Union*, July 13, 1867.
6. Leavenworth *Daily Conservative*, July 26 and August 23, 1867.
7. Junction City *Union*, July 27, 1867; Leavenworth *Daily Conservative*, August 6, 1867; Ellsworth County Commissioners Record Book A, Vol. 1, 1867 and 1868.
8. Ellsworth County Commissioners Record Book.
9. Leavenworth *Daily Conservative*, September 29, 1867.
10. Ibid., October 29, 1867.
11. Nyle H. Miller and Joseph W. Snell, *Why the West Was Wild*, 630; Leavenworth *Daily Conservative*, November 7, 1867.
12. Junction City *Weekly Union*, March 7, 1868; Leavenworth *Daily Commercial*, July 7, 1872.
13. Ibid., December 13, 1868; Ellsworth County Commissioners Record Book.
14. Microfilm copy, Manuscripts Department, Kansas State Historical Society (cited hereafter as KSHS).
15. Leavenworth *Daily Conservative*, August 21, 1867.
16. W. F. Thompson, "Peter Robidoux: A Real Kansas Pioneer," *Collections of the Kansas State Historical Society*, Vol. XVII (1926–28), 285–6.
17. Docket Book, Justice of the Peace, Ellsworth, Kansas.
18. State of Kansas vs. Joseph Brennan, Indictment for Murder, Justice of the Peace Records, Ellsworth County; Clerk of the District Court, Ellsworth County, Kansas, to Joseph G. Rosa, September 1987.
19. Justice of the Peace Records, Ellsworth County.
20. Ibid., Junction City *Weekly Union*, July 24, 1869; Colonel George A. Armes, *Ups and Downs of an Army Officer*, 301; Francis B. Heitman, *Historical Register and Dictionary of the United States Army, 1789–1903*, 880. It is reported that Jim Bush was the brother of William ("Billy") Bush, manager of a Denver showplace. Jim was later involved in a killing at Leadville and, against all odds, lived to old age, dying of a stroke at age seventy-eight in 1920 (Robert K. DeArment, *Knights of the Green Cloth*, 351).
21. Leavenworth *Times and Conservative*, August 4, 1869; Lawrence *Daily Tribune*, August 7, 1869; Topeka *Daily Commonwealth*, November 24, 1869; Joseph G. Rosa, "J. B. Hickok, Deputy U.S. Marshal," *Kansas History*, Vol. 2, No. 4 (Winter 1979), 243.
22. Ellsworth County Ordinances for Ellsworth, 1870.
23. Ibid.
24. Miller and Snell, *Why the West Was Wild*, 257–58.

25. Ellsworth County Commissioners Record Book, 115; Topeka *Daily Commonwealth,* April 25, 1871.
26. Mr. Dodge's recollections were among a number of old-timers' reminiscences included in *Biographical History of Barton County, Kansas,* published in 1912.
27. Junction City *Weekly Union,* December 10, 1870; Case No. 828, U.S. vs. Manley B. Gilman and James Stitt, Topeka District Court Records (1869); Leavenworth *Daily Times,* November 6, 1870.
28. Topeka *Daily Commonwealth,* August 4 and 7, 1870; June 9 and 14, 1871.
29. Ibid., June 14, 1871.
30. Secretary of War: Habeas Corpus, *Opinions of the Attorney General,* 451–56.
31. Topeka *State Record,* October 28, 1871.
32. Mark Corriston, National Archives, Kansas City, Mo., Branch, to Joseph G. Rosa, April 7, 1987. He kindly checked the district court docket books in the archives' possession.
33. U.S. vs. Richard Cavanaugh, Records of the District Court, Ellsworth County, Kansas.
34. Ellsworth County Commissioners' Record Book.

3

Newton
The Wickedest Town in Kansas

Joe and Kate found Newton to be a wide-open place and a haven for gamblers and other sports who had found Abilene or Ellsworth too hot to handle. The place owed its existence to the Wichita and Southwestern Railroad, which in the summer of 1870 had selected the site as a suitable place for a station or town, but it was not until July 17, 1871, that tracklayers reached there. Named after Newton, Massachusetts, the town was laid out on the Texas cattle trail some thirty miles north of Wichita. Generally called the Chisholm Trail because it followed the route of Indian trader Jesse Chisholm from Texas through the Nations and into Kansas, it ended officially at Wichita. Because Wichita lacked a rail link, Joseph G. McCoy, an Illinois cattle buyer, had persuaded the Texas drovers to push on to Abilene, a small stop on the tracks of the Union Pacific Railway Company, Eastern Division, then build west to Denver. This route became known as McCoy's Extension and the Abilene Trail. When Abilene banned the cattle trade early in 1872, McCoy, not a man to miss an opportunity, induced the cattlemen to divert their herds to Newton, where he had negotiated with the railroad to erect shipping pens.

A contemporary report noted that the pens were located about a mile and a half from the city and had been "erected by the railroad company into which cattle are driven that are to be shipped. These yards contain six 'shoots,' through which the cattle are driven into the cars. The area of these yards is 300 × 450 feet, and their capacity is four thousand head. . . . They were designed by and erected under the immediate supervision of Joseph G. McCoy mayor of Abilene." Later, McCoy alleged that a Topeka "cattleman" who had joined him in the venture conspired with a member of the railroad to oust him from the project. McCoy therefore derived some satisfaction when the expected cattle boom at Newton did not materialize because the region was settled very quickly. And by the time Newtonians were preparing themselves for a Texan invasion, the railroad had reached Wichita. Within months the cattle trade in Newton was practically dead, but not before the murder and mayhem associated with the trade had taken its toll in the burgeoning city.[1]

Ellsworth's early reputation for lawlessness was soon overtaken by that of Newton, which, if anything, was tougher. A few hardy souls reached the townsite as early as March 1871, when a frame building was moved there from Darlington Township by Stockwell & Walton for use as a blacksmith's shop. Others followed, and Peter Luhn's Pioneer Store and a bakery were welcome additions. On May 10, when Judge R. W. P. Muse first came through, he found some men still living in tents on the west bank of Sand Creek and others on the embryonic townsite. By late August or early September, however, an estimated twenty-seven saloons, eight gambling halls, and a flourishing brothel district known as "Hide Park," together with hotels, restaurants, grocery stores, and other essential establishments, were catering for the needs of twelve to fifteen hundred residents. And as was the case in Ellsworth, it was the unruly element that got the most attention.[2]

On July 16 a saloonkeeper named Johnson, formerly of Emporia, "shot a man whose name we have not heard, inflicting a dangerous wound. The shooting is said to have been accidental." On August 4 another Emporia resident, Dan Beckwith, "accidentally shot himself with a small revolver in the right arm, while showing some boys how to use the weapon. It is believed that the arm will have to be amputated. Another warning to be careful in the handling of firearms," declared the editor of the Emporia News. But these incidents were minor compared with a late-August affray in Perry Tuttle's dance hall that is remem-

Joseph Geiting McCoy, from a family portrait ca. 1867. His vision and enterprise led to the reestablishment of the Texas cattle trade following the Civil War. In 1867 he persuaded the Union Pacific Railway, Eastern Division, to put in a switch at Abilene, Kansas, and the Texans to head their herds north to the railroad via the Chisholm Trail. When Abilene banned the trade early in 1872, McCoy turned his attention to Newton. Courtesy the late Stewart P. Verckler.

bered today as the Newton General Massacre.[3]

On August 11, 1871, the citizens of Newton were scheduled to vote on a proposal to issue twenty thousand dollars' worth of county bonds to help build the Wichita & Southwestern

Newton: The Wickedest Town in Kansas   41

Newton, Kansas, photographed in the fall of 1872. Courtesy Kansas State Historical Society.

Railroad. A former night policeman for the railroad, Michael McCluskie (or McCluskey), was commissioned a special policeman for election day. It was his dispute with others that was to lead to bloodshed. He and another policeman hired for the election, a Texas gambler named William Wilson (also known as Billy Bailey), got into a row and their shouts soon led to shots. Wilson died the next morning. This infuriated the Texans, and to avoid further bloodshed, McCluskie left town. On the nineteenth, however, McCluskie returned and celebrated Saturday night at Perry Tuttle's dance hall. Word spread that McCluskie was back, and the Texans congregated at Tuttle's place. A graphic account of what happened next was published by the Emporia *News* on August 25:

> On Sunday morning last [the twentieth], a row occurred at Newton which resulted in the murder of two men and the wounding of nine others, three of whom have since died from wounds received in the affray. This affair occurred in one of those sinks of iniquity near the town called a dance house. A former resident of this town, who was at Newton, gives us the following particulars of the affair. It seems that this murderous affair was the result of several less fatal shooting scrapes which have been happening at Newton for some weeks. It must be borne in mind that the state of society in that town is now at its worst. The town is largely inhabited by prostitutes, gamblers and

whisky sellers. Pistol shooting is the common amusement. All the frequenters of the saloons, gambling dens, and houses of ill-fame are armed at all times, mostly with pistols.

About two weeks ago a Captain [A. R.] French from Texas [formerly of the Texas Central Railroad and currently employed by the Kansas City Railroad], had Geo. Delany, alias William McCluskie, a St. Louis hard case, arrested on a charge of garroting. He was tried before Esquire [Cy] Bowman and they failed to prove anything against him. On the day of the election on railroad bonds, McCluskie and a man named Bailey both of whom were on the special police, got into a difficulty about the matter of the arrest and about women. Bailey got drunk. The difficulty commenced at one of the dance houses just out of the town, and after coming to the village, Bailey was shot and killed by McCluskie.

French and other Texans, among whom was one named Bill Anderson, then swore that they would put an end to McCluskie's life, and break up his crowd. Several small difficulties occurred between the parties and their friends. At one o'clock last Sabbath morning, when all but one of the dance houses were closed, and most of their frequenters had left, the murderers proceeded to carry out their desperate threats. One of these disreputable places remained open. McCluskie was one of the loiterers. It proved to be his last hour on earth. If he had known this, he would doubtless preferred to have spent it elsewhere. Several of the bloodthirsty Texans entered the place, accompanied by a few lookers on who had found out the intentions of the murderers. One or two innocent men were shot in the affray, who were present only to see. Directly Anderson entered and immediately the bloody work commenced. With murder in his eye and his foul mouth filled with oaths and epithets he stepped up to McCluskie and shot him. The ball entered McCluskie's neck. He sprang to his feet and shot Anderson, and then fell to the ground. The shooting then became general. McCluskie was shot in three places and died in a couple of hours. John Martin, a herd boss, was shot through the jugular vein and died. Bill Anderson, an owner of Texas cattle, was shot through the thigh. John Anderson, his brother, was shot through the right arm and lungs. Garrett was shot through the lungs and has since died. Patrick Lee, a railroad employee, was shot through the loins and has since died. He was in no way a party to the difficulty. Hickey was shot in three places and, we believe, has since died. Wilkinson was shot through the jaw and nose. Bartless was shot through the left shoulder. On Sunday, two other white men and a negro were shot, but our informant did not learn their names. Neither of them were killed.

A coroner's jury was called on Sunday morning and after an investigation which lasted from eight o'clock a. m. to twelve thirty p. m., they found Bill Anderson guilty of manslaughter, and they having proved that he fired the first shot. They adjourned and soon after received notice that if they did not leave at once, their bodies would be found in the morning ornamenting neighboring telegraph poles. On Monday morning, three of them came away on the early train, and the other three went to Wichita. Anderson and his men had such control over the crowd, that the officers were afraid to arrest them. The Texans were talking Sunday night of burning the town and running out the prostitutes and gamblers. Several of them have left and as we have heard of no such action on their part, we conclude that they have abandoned the matter. This was one of the bloodiest affrays that ever occurred in our state and we hope that measures will be taken to prevent its reoccurence.

It is a part of Newton legend that a youngster named Riley, a consumptive befriended by McCluskie, appeared in the midst of the melee and avenged his idol's death by killing several of the Texans before disappearing. Anderson was served with a warrant by Deputy U.S. Marshal Harry Neville, but no further action was taken. Anderson's father came up from Texas and arranged for his return home. A bizarre sequel to the shootout is alleged to have occurred at Medicine Lodge, Kansas, on July 4, 1873, when Anderson fought a duel to the death with Mike McCluskie's brother Arthur. Opening up with six-shooters, the pair finally ended the gory encounter with knives after crawling the final yards that separated them.[4]

The Newton General Massacre received wide publicity, partly because of the graphic accounts written by "Allegro," whose identity remained a mystery until 1873, when it was reported that his name was F. J. Harrington.[5]

Rowdy Joe and Kate reached Newton some weeks before the August shooting and were in business when it occurred. It is probably only a matter of luck that the participants chose Perry Tuttle's dance house instead of Joe's and Kate's or some other establishment to wreak their vengeance upon McCluskie. Doubtless Joe was one of the many who pondered the repercussions following the shootout. "How this will end," fumed one editor, "is a problem that must yet be solved. It seems to be a great mistake that a town can only be incorporated and get organization in the three first months of the year, as something seems to be quite necessary in Newton — a good efficient police force and a set of officers that mean business and will take some measures to make it safe for people to walk the streets. It is worse than 'Tim Finnegan's wake.'"[6]

Perry Tuttle, whose establishment had been at the center of the fracas, was accustomed to Texas-style violence. A veteran of the Eleventh Kansas Volunteer Cavalry, Perry, who stood six feet one inch in his socks, was himself regarded as a tough customer. After the Civil War he spent some time at Topeka, where he became well known in horse-racing circles and as an ardent dog lover. The thrice-married Tuttle spent only that one season in Newton before returning to Topeka, later going to Texas (where he again met Joe Lowe), and ending his days at Creston, Iowa, in 1899.[7]

When Tuttle reached Newton some months after the first buildings were erected, he opened one of its first saloons. On July 4, celebrating Texans visited his dance house and "compelled the demi-reps to stretch themselves at full length on the prairie. Perry escaped through the back door. The place was riddled with bullets." Several days later Perry became one of the few men who survived being shot at by John Wesley Hardin, although he was probably never aware of his narrow escape. On July 5, William Cohron, a Texas cowboy working for Colonel Homer Wheeler, was murdered near Abilene by Juan Bideno, a Mexican. Hardin and three others set off in pursuit, and Bideno was cornered in a restaurant at Sumner City, where Hardin shot him between the eyes as he sat drinking coffee. On their way back to Abilene, Wes and his companions stopped off at Newton for a rest and to take in the town "in good style." He recalled that the policemen "tried to hold us down, but they all resigned — I reckon. We certainly shut up that town." The following appeared in the Topeka press:

> A report was prevalent in town this morning [July 10] that the Texans at Newton had attached the "branch" established at that place by

ladies of easy views from this city, had filled the house full of revolver shots and forced the enterprising manager, Hon. P. C. Tuttle, formerly of this city, to flee to the mountains.[8]

The police force that Hardin mentions was nonexistent at that time, and Perry had hardly patched up the bullet holes when, on July 20, another Texan undertook to "ride his horse into Perry Tuttle's dance house at Newton. He got in but the horse soon made his appearance with the rider following behind on foot. The ranger presented himself at the door the second time when Perry slung a bunch of fives against his smeller and he desisted from further trespasses. The dance went on." On November 24, however, a macabre but humorous incident occurred at Perry's place when a "revolver fell upon the floor in a row and was fired by the concussion, and the unfortunate man stood in the way. Though seriously injured, he will probably recover."[9]

It was reported on August 24 that after the shooting of Bailey, Mike McCluskie was appointed to the Newton police force. This statement must be questioned. However, after the shootout, a special election was held within the township to select a police force. According to Allegro, an informal meeting of the principal citizens of Newton was held on August 25. Tom Carson and Carlos B. King were nominated for "sheriffs," which probably meant deputies or constables. A later report described King as a "deputy sheriff" and Carson as an "acting constable." On the 27th it was also reported that steps were being taken to form a city government. All those actually living in Newton would be permitted to vote.[10]

The appointment of Tom Carson did not sit well with the Texans. On August 24, the Abilene *Chronicle* had noted:

On Monday evening last [the twenty-first] threats were made, by many desperadoes, that in case Tom Carson, late a policeman in Abilene, was placed upon the police force, that they would kill him. He was, however, appointed a police officer, and that evening patroled his alloted beat as unmolested as if he were in Abilene, no disturbance whatsoever occuring.

The Texans at Newton made the same objections to Carson that they had expressed when he served in a similar capacity at Abilene: they disliked his overbearing manner and his habit of striking offenders. Neither had he been popular amongst his fellow policemen. First appointed in a temporary capacity on June 23, he had been upgraded to regular but soon ran afoul of policeman James H. McDonald and later the marshal, Wild Bill Hickok.[11]

When James H. McDonald and James Gainsford were dismissed from the Abilene police force on September 2, 1871, "by reason that their services are no longer needed," McDonald went to Newton, where he was appointed city marshal. Here he proved himself an able officer and on one occasion pursued John Williams and a man named Wallace to Humboldt, Kansas, where he arrested them. Williams was charged with horse stealing and Wallace with stealing "four hundred dollars in cash, and a fine watch from Newtonians." It was also noted that "McDonald appears to be a wide awake, efficient marshal." His career in Newton was short lived, however, and he moved on to Kansas City.[12]

Rowdy Joe and Kate were running a profitable business by September. Their dance hall was well patronized. It was also the scene of yet another act of violence. On Saturday, September 23, police officer Carlos King, making his rounds, looked in on Joe's place and saw that a man named Thomas Edwards was wearing a pistol, contrary to local ordinances. King stepped up to him and demanded his pistol. Edwards refused, but the sudden appearance of Tom Carson, pistol leveled, and the command "Throw up your hands" convinced him otherwise, so he handed the revolver over. Carson holstered his own pistol and retreated from the saloon. Later, Edwards came up to King as he stood outside the saloon and shot him through the heart at close range. One report stated that he also "accidentally" shot a bystander through the thigh, and another claimed that "David Lisle, a grocery keeper in Newton," was "mortally wounded." He "was not dead this Monday morning [the twenty-fifth], but no hopes are entertained of his recovery." Despite a concerted hunt by Newton citizens, Edwards escaped justice.[13]

Many of the townsfolk attended King's funeral, and most of

Newton: The Wickedest Town in Kansas 47

the business premises remained closed during the ceremony. King, a Civil War veteran, had enlisted in Company B, Sixteenth Michigan Infantry, in 1861 and, following reenlistments and promotions, ended the war as a captain in Company C of the Third Infantry in 1864, when he was wounded and discharged with a disability. In 1878 there was a minor scandal when it was learned that King's widow had returned to Michigan and had sworn under oath that her husband died of his war wounds. When it was learned that she and her attorney had defrauded the government to get her a pension, the two were arrested and charged with perjury.[14]

The police force in Newton had a hard task. The saloon business continued to boom and to attract the sort of undesirables that sent shivers up the spines of most town council members. Graphic accounts of these activities from "Allegro" reached an avid readership. On September 13 he mentioned some of the incidents that had made Newton "the wickedest city in Kansas" — a title that he was at pains to point out was not justified. The influx of Texas cowboys up the trail, along with their antics, which both attracted and repelled the curious, merely added to Newton's growing reputation as the "*par excellence* of a frontier town." Allegro noted that "business men have come here, too, but not of the order of your eastern shopkeeper, who insists on clear coffee and polished boots. 'Rough and ready' is the cherished motto of Newtonians." He then rendered a semihumorous description of a magistrate who was not easily surpassed when it came to running up fines, a lawyer who had never gained a case, a hotelkeeper who measured his guests by the complaints they made about bedbugs, and a policeman "who tries to keep the peace by offers to fight the crowds, and a reporter [Allegro?] who could not sleep when his first article appeared in print." He referred to "dancehouses" but made no specific reference to Rowdy Joe. It was the gambling elite who gained his close attention:

> There is a mania for gambling in Newton. In the heart of every man who has been here long enough to dig down a little to the sub-strata of life, nestles the germ of this passion. In some it has bloomed into a full blown flower. These latter are mostly professionals, who sit on the per-

cent side of the table. Most of them are well known all over the extreme west. Listen to their chat as they sit together after dinner or supper smoking their cigars and re-counting by-gone experiences, and you will discover that they are well traveled, earnest men — thinkers in a rough sort of way, and invariably readers of human nature.

As for the saloons, the Gold Room was considered to be the best:

Games elsewhere radiate from it, as it were, like spokes from a hub. In one sense, it is the pivot of the town, for its influence is greater than that of any other house . . . it is situated on main street about midway between the railroad depot and the post office, which are the respective termini of Newton. The stranger on entering it finds himself in a frame building about sixty feet in length by thirty in width roughly put together, with the roof freely ribbed with timbers, which slant downwards and outwards in the shape of the letter A. Daylight glimmers through cracks here and there . . . on the left of the entrance is a bar, extending back some twenty feet, and behind which is shoved a long row of barrels stored with all kinds of liquors and wines. Over these stands the mantle or show part of the bar, lined with clusters of decanters daintily arranged and polished until their shimmer is like that of diamonds. On the other side of the hall, and commencing immediately at the doorway, are the gaming tables . . . they are all covered with green baize, and are square, with little semi-circles cut out in one of the long sides, so that the dealer can have the board closer and have a better control of his "layout." . . . A the rear of the hall is a raised platform, made expressly for the "negro song and dance man," J. T. smith, an old eastern varieties artist, who, by some curious freak of fortune, wandered to Newton. He is out of his element, however, like all good talent that comes to this country.

Behind the building was the accommodation for waiters and the girls who worked for the saloon — but no suggestion was made that these were cribs used by prostitutes. Allegro also mentioned some of the well-known gamblers who were working in the Gold Room, among them John Gallagher, Dick Clark (later well known in Tombstone), Jim Moon, Pony Reid and Trick Brown. There was also one man, whom Allegro deemed it wise not to mention by name, who could deal monte "with the endurance of a machine."

Joe Lowe was acquainted with these men, in particular Jim Moon (whose real name was John E. Wilcoxon), with whom he is reported to have had an altercation at Denver in later years. Moon's reputation as a gambler-gunfighter was widely known. Shortly before Clay Wilson put four bullets into him at Denver on June 16, 1881, ending a checkered career, Jim was asked his opinion of shootouts and was reported to have said of his first killing: "It goes pretty hard with you for a while, but after the second or third you don't mind knocking over one of these gunfighters any more than you would a sheep. The man who pulls a gun on you when you have nothing in sight is a cur. All you need to do is walk right up to him, take it away and beat him over the head with it, so he won't try it again. Nearly all my men came for me. Of course, I went after some of them — had to."[15]

Gambling may well have been the most lucrative pastime, but prostitution was by far the most popular, which is not surprising in a population where men outnumbered women. Most of the dance halls boasted at least a half-dozen or more girls, some loosely described as "singers" and others as "hostesses" or "waitresses," but their principal aim in life was to entertain, preferably with sexual favors. "I have been in a good many towns," wrote a traveler, "but Newton is the fastest one I have ever seen. Here you may see young girls not over sixteen drinking whiskey, smoking cigars, cursing and swearing until one almost looses [sic] the respect they should have for the weaker sex, I heard one of their townsmen say that he didn't believe there were a dozen virtuous women in town."[16]

The inmates of these places were every bit as tough as their customers. Some of the "ladies" concealed weapons (ranging from knives to derringers) in the most intimate of places, and they were not afraid to use them. Fights between women over the favors of a man were common. Unrequited love also had tragic consequences. In a report from Newton dated September 3, 1871, it was stated that Annie Glinn, a girl from St. Louis, who had worked for a time as a waitress before becoming a professional courtesan in "one of the numerous bagnios of Hide Park," fell in love with one of her customers. When he spurned her, in desperation she tried to poison herself, and when that failed, she obtained a large-caliber revolver, "cocked it, placed the muzzle against her stomach and pulled the trigger." Her dying request was to see the man who had driven her to such a drastic act. "He came and her eyes never left him from the moment he entered until the film of death shut out the sight of the outer world." [17]

The partnership between Joe Lowe and Kate was by no means platonic, but they apparently never let it interfere with business and concentrated on running what was a highly profitable venture. Others in similar partnerships, however, seemed to be constantly at odds.

William Dow, known in Wichita as "Rattlesnake Bill," got into a fight with Lottie Foster, a demirep well known at Newton, and "he beat her badly and put a cap on one of her peepers. Lottie, disliking the manliness which characterized her interview with Dow, procured a revolver and as he was passing along the street, fired five shots, the fifth taking effect in his hip, inflicting a severe wound." Dow managed to hobble as far as the railroad depot before he collapsed. He was carried to his home, where it was found that the ball had glanced off the bone and "buried itself out of the reach of the doctor's probe." Later, it was reported that "no legal steps will probably be taken by Dow on account of his general unpopularity." As for Lottie, she passed through Topeka several days later and announced that she had "abandoned her wicked life and was on her way to the Cincinnati Home for Friendless Women." [18]

Male-female fights were only a small part of the disruption in most of the saloons and dance houses. The origin and outcome of gunfights also appealed to Allegro. Writing in December 1871, he said:

We still have occasional disturbances among the rougher element of our society, such a thing, however, as a square standup fist fight is unknown. One must always have the drop on an antagonist or nothing more than an exercise of the vocal muscles ensues. The code of chivalry seems to be to fight only a smaller man who is unprepared and unsuspecting. Shoot him in the back, bite his ear or nose off as a memento, and your reputation as a fighting man is made. This and nothing more is what the so-called dangerous characters have to boast of and this is why such men as Wild Bill who fight with the weapons best adapted to the circumstances almost invariably carry the day, even in the face of immense odds. Newton is not a very dangerous place. A fair show and a stout heart carry a child through safely.

Allegro then devoted some space to entertainments to be found in frontier habitats. At a time when wagon shows and circuses were plentiful, touring companies of actors and musicians were a rarity, and many communities went to great lengths to secure such entertainment. Touching upon the fact that musical entertainment was provided mostly by single musicians or perhaps a trio (a far cry from the full orchestras of Hollywood westerns), he noted:

Along in the summer all of the dance houses and nearly all of the saloons employed music and for a time, there was a keen rivalry as to which could furnish the best talent. As high as seven dollars a day was paid musicians who were accomplished on several instruments. The dance houses had small orchestras which were employed only at night. The saloons had music both day and night. At present, dull times have driven most of the musicians to other fields of labor, so that the best only of them are left. First and foremost is Edward Silsbee, a violinist who uses an instrument of his own make. Mr. Silsbee is well known all over the frontier and is one of the oldtimers, and for the beauty of his touch and rare execution. William Armstrong, an old English brass band player, who has served the world over, is also an old frontiersman, and an excellent musician. Sam Overlin, commonly called Professor, was one of the early California settlers, at one time director of one of the theatrical orchestras in San Francisco. Mort and Harrison Berry, and George Perry furnish the musical part of the entertainment offered nightly at the town dance house of Josephine De Merritt. Each of them has seen every phase of Western life, Harrison Berry having figured in nearly all of the battles and skirmishes in which the Kansas and Colorado troops were engaged in. Ed Jones, William Cronk, and Jake Ritter complete the list. It is amusing, and instructive at the same time, to drop in on a group of these musicians as they recall bygone days and experiences. Berry, Ed Jones and Silsbee grew up with the Western railroads and have a vast fund of anecdotes, thrilling oftentimes as it drifts into sketches of old Indian fights and hand to hand encounters with wild beasts.[19]

As did other places, Joe Lowe's establishment made a profit, and true to form, Joe was averse to paying taxes. Fred Schattner claimed in 1913 that he managed to wear down Joe's opposition at a time when the "Newton saloons would not pay their Quarterly Licenses of $25 per Quarter, and never could Walk Walker, sheriff, collect a cent and [he] was run out of town, with his deputies in 1872 [Walker had served as sheriff of Sedgwick County in 1870, before Newton, which was in Harvey County, was founded]." The county commissioners asked Schattner to collect the taxes (he was county clerk at the time), and county scrip was selling at 60 percent discount:

> I told them I could collect it all, but amicably without Sheriff or Constable, and no revolvers or guns in sight. Some saloons were 4 or 5 quarters overdue. They deputized me to collect it "carte blanche," in my own way. After getting my bulk of licenses together I took the stage to Newton, and as Joe Lowe, who was nicknamed "Rowdy Joe" was 4 quarters behind, was the biggest rowdy and cut throat there so generally admitted as such, I bounsed [sic] him first in his Lion's Den a Hurdy-Gurdy of the blackest dye. I stopped the dance and called everybody up to drink on the County Clerk, after they got through I told Rowdy that the deplorable condition of the County made it necessary for me to come. "What's my bill, Fred?" he said. I threw him 4 quarterly licenses and he shoved me *one* hundred Dollars on the Bar — and "By God when a white man comes here to Newton, I & we all can treat him white" and he introduced me afresh to the rabble & I wished to "set them up again" — but he said, "No by God it's on me this time, and more I am going with you to collect over the whole damn town & see that every S. O. B. pays his license to a white man, that's you." Rowdy and me visited every saloon (first calling all up to drink) then Rowdy would explain — and in every instance came the cash on all the licenses I had, there were 2 places he halted me saying, "I wouldn't go in there that dam[n] fool ain't got enough money to pay for 1 jug of whisky in advance, let him go." I answered all right Joe, just as you say. In all I collected every license we demanded except the 2 places mentioned & it was about $3000.00, less treating money, that the treats amounted to considerable was sure, for when I threw down a $10 bill, I wouldn't stop for change & if I had, in most places, they never would have offered me back any. The old records of the County treas[ure]r will show my return of am[oun]t.

Schattner's unsupported claim makes a good yarn. He and his brother, Charles, were at one time proprietors of the Wichita Saloon, the Custom House, and later perhaps the Bon Ton. Schattner later lived in St. Louis and was recalled as being quite an artist.[20]

Joe and Kate continued to keep things lively in Newton, especially their personal relationship, which was sometimes stormy. Joe's bouts with the bottle led him into trouble with the law when he and Kate had a row. Joe would lose his temper and strike her and get himself arrested. Kate then would ask the court for a continuance and pay the costs. In effect, Kate saved Joe's neck on several occasions, and in spite of their volatile relationship, we think that in his way, Joe was very fond of Kate.[21]

An incident that points up friction between the pair, occurred on February 18, 1872. According to a report received at Topeka from Newton:

> On Sunday evening there was a dance at Rowdy Joe's house, at which there were several strangers. During the festivities, one of the strangers made overtures to Rowdy Kate which she resented. The stranger complained to Joe of his treatment, and Joe slapped Kate for the alleged insult. Seizing the opportune moment, a man by the name of A. M. Sweet, formerly of Topeka, "made up" to Kate, got her drunk and took her to the house of Fanny Gray, formerly of Leavenworth.
>
> On Monday, Rowdy Joe heard that Sweet had threatened to kill him, and went to Fanny's house to see about the matter. As soon as he presented himself, Sweet pulled his revolver; but before he fired, Joe fired two shots, both taking effect in Sweet's body, from the effects of which he died in three hours.[22]

Sweet was described as the owner of a Newton saloon known as the "Through Ticket," and many felt he got his just deserts. After the shooting, claims that Joe "skedaddled and has not been heard of since" were soon scotched. The *Commonwealth* noted that "Rowdy Joe immediately went to the sheriff and gave himself up." It was later reported that Joe had a preliminary examination before a justice of the peace on the twenty-first and was acquitted on his plea of self-defense. Rowdy Kate, meantime, took a trip to Leavenworth, but her separation from Joe was only temporary, for she was soon back at Newton, where their business continued to boom.[23]

The killing of Sweet and other violent episodes convinced the city fathers that a renewed attempt at law and order was imperative. In December 1871 it was reported that Wild Bill Hickok, who had enhanced his reputation at Abilene, was to become marshal of Newton at two hundred dollars a month, but he did not take the job. Early in February 1872, Newton was incorporated as a third-class city and on the twenty-eighth Harvey County was organized with Newton as the county seat, after which every effort was to be made to enforce the law. An added complication was the fact that although many citizens, some on the city council, wished to get rid of the cattle trade, the spur line to Wichita was still incomplete, so Newton resigned itself to remaining a cattle town for some time to come. James H. Anderson was elected the city's first mayor, and on April 1, 1872, William L. Brooks was appointed city marshal. As an assistant he had Charles Baumann, a German immigrant who is shown in city records as "Charles Bowman" and was recalled as a quiet-spoken individual. Brooks, however, had a bad reputation. He was well known on the frontier as a two-gun man and was said to model himself after Wild Bill, but he lacked the looks and the colorful reputation of the latter. Nevertheless, his reputation for violence was not based upon hearsay, and his appointment was prompted by his reputation rather than noted law-enforcement abilities.[24]

Billy Brooks (or Bully Brooks, as some called him behind his back) was renowned for his skill with a six-horse or six-mule team when he worked as a stagecoach driver between Newton and Wichita. When he forsook the whip for law enforcement, he armed himself with a rifle and a pair of Colt navy revolvers. Between them, Brooks and Baumann kept the peace, but Baumann had an altercation that was to have a lasting effect. Dan ("Cherokee Dan") Hicks, a half-blood Indian got drunk and shot up a saloon. When Baumann ordered him to stop, Hicks shot him in the leg, inflicting a severe wound that left him with a permanent limp. Hicks was later killed in a fight with saloon owner Harry Lovett. Perhaps because of his wound, Baumann was dismissed

Billy Brooks served as a policeman in Newton and later at Dodge City, earning himself a reputation as a tough character. Courtesy Kansas State Historical Society.

from his position as assistant marshal on May 29, leaving Brooks on his own.[25]

On the night of June 9 a number of Texans invaded a dance house in Newton and things got out of hand. The proprietor, Edward T. Beard, generally called "Red" on account of his reddish hair (and whose exploits will concern us shortly), was himself no slouch with a six-shooter, but he could not handle the crowd on his own, so he sent for Brooks.

When Billy Brooks walked into the saloon, things quieted down and he was able to escort the unruly cowboys off the premises. At the town limits, however, one of them suddenly cut loose with his pistol and wounded Brooks in the shoulder. Billy immediately gave chase. In a running fight, during which he was wounded twice more, Brooks pursued the Texans for ten miles before he gave up and returned to have his wounds dressed. The next day he swore out warrants for two of the Texans, who turned out to be James Hunt and Joseph Miller. Red Beard swore out a similar warrant for Hunt, and Red was in turn subpoenaed to appear before the Justice of the Peace George Halliday to give evidence in connection with Brooks's complaint. The county attorney asked for a change of venue, charging that the state could not get a fair hearing before Halliday and alleging that there was bias and prejudice between Halliday and Brooks. The motion was denied. Hunt later pleaded not guilty to the charges, but after an examination of the state's witnesses, he was bound over to district court and jailed at Emporia. Brooks, meantime, had resigned on June 17 and was paid $110 for one month and four days' services. Beard also applied for a fee as a special policeman for his part in the fracas with the Texans in his saloon, but his claim was refused. When Brooks left, Charles Baumann became marshal and remained in this capacity until September 4, 1872. As for Brooks, after a short stint as marshal of Dodge City, he became involved with a gang of horse thieves and was lynched in August 1874.[26]

An undated clipping, circa the 1920s, recounts a claim by James Armour, who arrived in Sedgwick County in 1871, that "Rowdy Joe left Newton with a hundred other gamblers, confidence men, and dancehall proprietors when the residents rose in arms against them. They left after the killing of a deputy marshal by the name of Holliday, who was also a Free Mason. The Masons of the city met and decided that the wild and crooked element should leave. The shotgun brigade which they organized was so formidable that none of the gunmen or gamblers wanted to shoot it out. They emigrated to Wichita and on the West side of the Arkansas River at Douglas Avenue built up another settlement."

George Halliday's death had nothing to do with Joe Lowe or any of the resident gamblers and saloon owners. On the morning of November 7, 1872, George Halliday was in the Gold Room, where he had been drinking, and was intoxicated. Michael J. Fitzpatrick, keeper of the Age, a "notorious gambling and whisky saloon," and described as "one of the most noted murderous and wicked men in the country, especially when under the influence of that which has caused more untimely deaths than any other thing — liquor," entered the place at about 10 A.M. He had been drunk on and off for about two weeks and during the previous night had prowled the town, pistol in hand, hunting individuals who he claimed had given him offense. Halliday and Fitzpatrick were friends, but on this morning they exchanged words, Fitzpatrick suddenly pulling his pistol. He struck Halliday on the head with it and then thrust the muzzle against Halliday's chest and fired. Halliday died almost instantly. Fitzpatrick then walked calmly into the street, defying anyone to stop him. City Marshal Jack Johnson called on him to surrender, but Fitzpatrick threatened Johnson with his pistol. Johnson then borrowed a Henry rifle and shot Fitzpatrick dead.

Halliday's death, whilst lamentable, it was noted in the press, was also responsible for one of the city's best days, for by reacting to such violence the population had shown that it would no longer give "shelter to men who live by murdering and robbing good people, but shall win that reputation near and far that shall be to it an honor and not a disgrace."[27]

Halliday's death actually occurred some months after Joe Lowe left Newton, and we suspect that the following indictment found in Harvey County records may have had something to do with Joe's decision to leave:

State of Kansas
Harvey County   SS   In the District Court of the 9"
                                  Judicial District of the State
                                  of Kansas at the July Term thereof
                                  1872 holden in said Harvey County

The State of Kansas ⎫
Against   ⎬ Indictment
Joseph Lowe   ⎭

    The Grand jurors for the State of Kansas in and of the County of Harvey, duly impaneled and sworn and charged to inquire of offences committed within said county, in the name and by the authority of the State of Kansas upon their solemn oaths do find and present that Joseph Lowe at the county of Harvey and State of Kansas on the 15" day of August A.D. 1871 and other days and times between that day and the day of the finding of this Bill of Indictment at the County of Harvey aforesaid unlawfully did set up, keep and maintain a certain Common Bawdy house and Brothel and in the said house for the Sucre and gain of him the said Joseph Lowe certain persons as well men as women of Evil name and fame, and of dishonest conversation, then and on the said other days and times, there unlawfully and willingly, did cause and procure to frequent and come together: And the said men and women in the said house of him the said Joseph Lowe at unlawful times, there to be and remain drinking, tippling, dancing, whoring and misbehaving themselves, unlawfully and willfully did permit, and yet do permit and that to the corruption of good morals and the common nuisance of all the citizens of the State residing in the neighborhood.
    Contrary to the form of the statute in such case made and provided and against the peace and dignity of the State of Kansas.

C. S. Bowman
County Attorney.[28]

    No record of further action has been found, but it was noted in the Topeka *Commonwealth* of June 6, 1872, that Joe was "moving his dance house from Newton to the island near Wichita."
    Joe's move was well timed, for within a year the *Kansan* was to announce gleefully (on May 29, 1873) that the "sale of the Hide Park property last week furnished a splendid opportunity for the truly virtuous to visit that place upon which they have so often gazed but would not venture near. The property was sold quite cheap, and nothing but a piece of hardware is left to mark

the spot where one year ago was a den of brothels. Let persons who tell of Newton's early years make a note of this."

Whatever the reason for his departure, Joe Lowe's name was soon to come before the public once more, and in a manner that ensured his lasting fame.

Notes

1. Topeka *Daily Commonwealth*, March 28, May 30, and August 15, 1871; Joseph G. McCoy, *Historical Sketches of the Cattle Trade of the West and Southwest*, 292, 423.
2. Andreas, *History of Kansas*, 772; Wayne Gard, *The Chisholm Trail*, 157.
3. July 21 and August 11, 1871.
4. For a detailed account of this affair, see Colin W. Rickards, "Vengeance, Kansas 1870's Style," English Westerners Society *Brand Book*, Vol. IV, No. 1 (October 1961), 2-9.
5. Wichita *Weekly Beacon*, December 24, 1873. The editor also noted that Harrington had turned up in Washington, where he had passed himself off as a representative of the Topeka *Commonwealth* in an attempt to obtain money from a congressman. It was made clear that he was "utterly unworthy of confidence or countenance" and that should he show his face again in Kansas he would face a jury.
6. Topeka *Daily Commonwealth*, August 22, 1871.
7. Perry C. Tuttle Pension File, National Archives, Washington, D.C. Ms. Charlene Hudson of the Creston Public Library told Joseph G. Rosa in March 1987 that Tuttle was buried in a soldier's plot with a Grand Army of the Republic marker and that the date of his death was shown as October 26, 1898, and not 1899 as recorded in his pension file.
8. John Wesley Hardin, *The Life of John Wesley Hardin*, 50; Topeka *State Record*, July 12, 1871; Topeka *Daily Commonwealth*, July 12, 1871.
9. Topeka *Daily Commonwealth*, July 25 and November 26, 1871.
10. Topeka *Daily Commonwealth*, August 27, 1871.
11. Topeka *Daily Commonwealth*, August 27 and September 28, 1871; Rosa, *They Called Him Wild Bill*, 199.
12. Rosa, *They Called Him Wild Bill*, 199.
13. Topeka *Daily Commonwealth*, September 27, 1871; Topeka *State Record*, September 27, 1871.
14. Dodge City *Ford County Globe*, June 4, 1878.
15. Topeka *Daily Commonwealth*, September 17, 1871; Denver *Daily News*, October 23, 1898.
16. Wichita *Tribune*, August 24, 1871.
17. Kansas City *Times*, September 6, 1871.

18. Topeka *Daily Commonwealth*, September 21 and 23, 1871.
19. Ibid., December 6, 1871.
20. Fred Schattner to Leon Fouquet, January 21, 1913.
21. Wichita *Eagle*, February 15, 1899.
22. Topeka *Daily Commonwealth*, February 21, 1872.
23. Ibid., February 25, 1872; Ellsworth *Reporter*, February 20, 1872.
24. Gary L. Roberts, "From Tin Star to Hanging Tree: The Short Career and Violent Times of Billy Brooks," *The Prairie Scout*, Vol. III, 13.
25. Floyd Benjamin Streeter, *Prairie Trails & Cowtowns*, 139–41.
26. Roberts, "From Tin Star to Hanging Tree," 14–16; Streeter, *Prairie Trails*, 139–41; Mrs. Linda A. Smur, Harvey County Historical Society, to Joseph G. Rosa, September 1987.
27. Newton *Kansan*, November 7, 1872. The following May, Jack Johnson and his wife fled Newton to escape creditors, owing the city fifteen dollars in collected license fees that were not handed in. Stopped at Atchison, the Johnsons were released on authority from Newton and disappeared (ibid., May 1, 1873).
28. Records of the District Court, Harvey County, Kansas.

4

Wild and Woolly Wichita

Wichita, when Rowdy Joe and Kate reached there in June 1872, had barely celebrated the arrival of the railroad, yet already the place was gearing itself up for the cattle trade. To some it was a means of economic survival, to others a glimpse of hell.

Named after the Wichita Indians, who had inhabited the area from 1864 until 1867, Wichita was situated some eighty-five miles south of Abilene at the point where the Arkansas and Little Arkansas rivers met. Few whites had visited the place before the Civil War; it was Indian trader Jesse Chisholm who put it on the map. Chisholm, a half blood, had arrived at about the same time as the Wichitas and was later adopted into their tribe. Although Jesse was illiterate, it was claimed that he could speak fourteen Indian languages, and he was also adept at sign language. His talents were quickly recognized by James R. Mead, who had established a store at the place. Mead financed Jesse, who then sold his goods to Indian agencies, other traders, and military posts as far south as Texas. The route he followed became known as the Chisholm Trail. By the late 1860s, Wichita was thriving but lacked one important asset: a railroad.[1]

Wichita was incorporated in July 1870 and elevated to city status in April 1871. In June 1870, William ("Hurricane Bill") Martin, a noted Texas bad man, was shot there when caught stealing cattle. Although "two balls took effect, wounding him very seriously," he survived. By 1874 he and his gang were well known in the city and that year they were rounded up by irate citizens and fined six hundred dollars, but not before Martin's heroics had induced a young man, Sumner Beach, to write asking him if he could join Martin's gang. Martin's later exploits in Texas provided material for newspapers for some time.[2]

In August 1870 a correspondent wrote from Wichita: "How this town does grow. Three months ago there were twenty-eight houses, all told; now there are about one hundred. There are some good two-storey houses. The foundation is laid for a large brick hotel. Every house that can afford a woman has to keep boarders." But later came a rival that many in Wichita wished would disappear. This was Delano, laid out in February 1871 and originally named Elgin. Once a post office was established, however, it was renamed Delano. Situated on the southwest side of the Arkansas River opposite Wichita, it grew rapidly. There was a good road link with Fort Sill, Indian Territory, which was ideal for government wagon trains, stagecoaches, and emigrants. "Taking all things into consideration there is no town in the south west that offers better inducements for those wishing to go into every kind of business in Delano," it was claimed. Although Wichita eventually received the railroad and the prosperity that went with it, it was Delano, now a suburb of Wichita, that housed the much-vilified but lucrative dance hall and gambling trade, and it was here that most of Wichita's wickedness was perpetrated.[3]

For a time it was feared that Delano's reputation would affect settlement. On June 7, 1872, the editor of the *Eagle* noted that "Wichita desires law and order, with their consequent peace and security, and not bloodshed and a name that will cause a thrill of horror whenever mentioned and which will effectually deter the most desirable class of people from coming among us. Right speedily will the latter follow if the former are not maintained." A visiting newspaperman who stopped by later in the month wrote that perhaps Delano's immorality was "not of such a terrible nature after all." He added:

The city [Wichita] is governed by an excellent body of officers, due strictness and enforcement being paid to law. We saw nothing there to induce us to encourage the report for crime and wickedness which has already gone forth. "Over the river" may be called the red-hot place of

Wichita, where everything originates and culminates to give a hard name to this youthful city. Some are agitating the addition of West Wichita to the city; but we believe that in doing so the city proper will be injured more than benefited; because authority will be required to cover too much ground, and in leaving it out the city has now some point for a vent to everything bordering upon crime. If West Wichita should become a part of the city there would be just as much freedom to transcend the decencies of civilization in one portion of the city as any, but leaving it out, all such parties will go over the bridge to be buried. With the present condition of things we ask no better protection than Wichita now offers.[4]

Delano's position outside city limits had advantages and disadvantages — a fact of life appreciated by Joe Lowe and his rivals. In effect, they became their own peace officers. When a drunken customer decided to break up Joe's place, he took it upon himself to restore the peace:

A fracas occurred at the dance house of Joseph Lowe, in West Wichita on Last Friday evening [July 19], in which a man by the name of Joseph Walters, who was at the time drunk, was badly bruised and cut about the face and head, by a revolver in the hands of the keeper of the house. Dr. [W. T.] Hendrickson dressed the man's wounds. From what we can learn Walters invited the attack by very disorderly conduct. At this writing the wounded man lies in a very critical condition.[5]

Despite Lowe's tendency toward violence, an early resident defended Joe and declared that he

was a rowdy but not vicious. He was short and heavy set. He and Rowdy Kate were immaculate in their dress. It was in the days when women wore the Grecian Bend style. Kate was a small woman, no more than 115 or 120 pounds. She was a fit partner of her husband, and they got along splendidly. To give you an idea of Rowdy Joe, if he knew you and you were standing on the sidewalk facing the street, he would run at you with all his force, and strike you in the small of your back with both hands. Of course, with his great bulk, he would almost break his victim's back. He would then run up the street laughing. You might call him all the names imaginable, he would only laugh. He was a rowdy and that was the kind of rowdy he was. Rowdy Kate took care of the dance business in a business way and was as straight as they make them. At least that was her reputation. But when she dressed up for an afternoon stroll down Main street or Douglas Avenue, take it from us, she was a dream of feminine fashion, and easy to the eyes. Along with it, she was a very handsome woman and took good care of herself, too.[6]

Nevertheless, Joe's reputation as a hard man and a tough customer in a fight was well known by the time Allegro reached the place in September. He noted that "there has not been a single murder or serious fracas . . . within the limits proper of the city of Wichita since its foundation." This, he thought, was odd, considering the close proximity of Newton, where twenty men had been slain within a few months, and Caldwell, some fifty miles away, where "any number of bloody troubles had occurred." Even Wellington, thirty miles away, had witnessed scenes of violence. He attributed this remarkable state of affairs to the diligence of the police force; but when he came to describing "West Wichita" — by now most of the populace was referring to Delano as such — things were a little different. He noted that the place was about half a mile from the corporate limits of Wichita, from which it was separated by the broad Arkansas River and connected by a heavy wooden bridge. "A diminutive forest faces the traveler as he leaves the bridge, in the center of which and to [its] right stands the dance-house of 'Rowdy Joe,' otherwise known as Joe Lowe."[7]

When a brawl was reported at Delano on September 22, it was immediately assumed that it took place in Joe Lowe's dance hall, but it actually occurred in a saloon kept by Charlie Jennison, described as a "heavy, thickset man with great brawny muscles, and a dogged, determined look, that at a glance would indicate danger to the most unsophisticated of physiognomists." That evening Jennison entered his saloon about nine o'clock, the worse for drink, and got into an argument with a man named Davis. The pair then left the saloon and moments later shots rang out. Davis shot Jennison through the neck, just missing the jugular vein, while Charlie's ball lodged in Davis's bowels. As Davis collapsed, he determined to "die game" and managed to get off one last shot, which wounded Jennison in the arm. Davis died minutes later. It was later disclosed that the fight started when Jennison made some disparaging remarks about Davis's wife. His death "brought great grief to his friends with whom he was highly popular." A coroner's jury summoned by Dr. H. Owens heard the evidence of Dr. P. A. Medlin, who stated that a ball had entered a little below the umbilicus. Davis, a Virginian, was about twenty-four years old.[8]

Despite Delano's reputation for violence and its disregard for law and order, there was a justice of the peace. M. Aley fulfilled this function in 1872, and an examination of his records has revealed that in May of that year, Jennison acted as a constable of his court. In 1871, Jennison and a man named Walker had operated a hotel and a saloon in Delano. By 1872, however, Jennison was believed to be in sole charge. On March 8, 1875, he was killed in a saloon at Del Norte, Colorado.[9]

Despite the violence that followed the cattle trade, it was nonetheless galling for the citizens of Wichita to watch the herds pass by en route to Abilene during the summer of 1871 because Wichita lacked a rail link. And when the railroad reached Newton and it, too, benefited from the trade, Wichitans grew frustrated by the delay. To make matters worse, their chief rival, Park City (the two towns were involved in a bitter county-seat war in 1870; Wichita won), tried to persuade the Texans to divert the cattle trail from Wichita to establish a special Park City cutoff. They were encouraged by the Kansas Pacific Railway (formerly the UPED), which tentatively sought to build a line through Park City in an effort to cripple the Atchison, Topeka and Santa Fe trade at Newton. In reprisal, the Wichitans kept Park Citians out of their new "Wichita and South Western Rail Road Company," a subsidiary of the Santa Fe. After more wrangling and disputes, the Santa Fe finally pushed a branch line into Wichita in May 1872.[10]

The Texans, who had been driven out of Abilene, were aware of the impending demise of Newton as a cattle town, so they welcomed the arrival of the railroad at Wichita. The place soon rivaled Ellsworth. Indeed, some 70,600 head of cattle were shipped out that year, almost double Ellsworth's total, and 20,000 more than had been driven from Abilene during its last season. That year an estimated 600,000 to 700,000 head of cattle had entered Kansas, some being shipped out by rail and the remainder driven overland to other points. Wichita's days as a frustrated onlooker were over; from now on it would get its share of the lucrative cattle trade. A Topeka visitor noted: "The business is now so well established here that stupendous efforts will be required to draw it away."[11]

The cattle business at Wichita thrived in spite of intense rivalry from Ellsworth. By July 1873 it was reported that shipments from Ellsworth were increasing, and some months later it was claimed that Ellsworth was preparing to ship three hundred thousand head. Wichita was not impressed. What Ellsworth proposes, Wichita disposes, remarked an editor, who noted that the largest shipment of Texas cattle ever made in Kansas was sent from Wichita "when one hundred and twenty-one carloads of cattle, requiring four separate trains averaging twenty to the car, left the vicinity of the stock yards at different hours on Sunday for Chicago." He added (doubtless for Ellsworth's benefit) that there "are over one hundred thousand head of cattle still upon our ranges." Wichita believed that it, not Ellsworth, was "number one" on the drive.[12]

Meanwhile, the comings and goings of Wichita residents continued to reach a wide audience. Citing the *Beacon*, the Leavenworth *Daily Commercial* declared on October 22:

> Wichita is a source of open-eyed wonder to strangers coming there from the East. The tawny-skinned Mexican, the heavy-spurred Texan, the buckskin-clad frontiersman, the Indian half-breed and shabby genteel, are all represented daily on the principal thoroughfares, adding a novelty from their curious dress, to the aspect of busy trade.

Rowdy Joe Lowe's activities also aroused interest. A revealing description of him was published in October, and one wonders whether its author (possibly S. S. Prouty, general manager of the Topeka *Daily Commonwealth*) was as well informed about Joe Lowe as he thought:

A description of Wichita would be incomplete without a notice of the notorious dance house on the west side of the river, kept by that singular personage

ROWDY JOE,

or Joseph Lowe, his real name. Joe has been a frontiersman for many years, and has experienced about as much roughness as any other man. His dance house is patronized mainly by cattle herders, though all classes visit it; the respectable mostly from curiosity. I understand that the receipts over his bar average[d] over one hundred dollars per night for months. The receipts are for drinks. No tax is levied for dancing, but it is expected that the males will purchase drinks for themselves and female partners at the conclusion of each dance. Joe is his own policeman, and maintains the best order. No one is disposed to pick a quarrel with him, or infringe upon the rules of his house. A dancing party at this place is unique, as well as interesting. The Texan, with mammoth spurs on his boots, which are all exposed, and a broad brimmed sombrero on his head, is seen dancing by the side of a well-dressed, gentlemanly-appearing stranger from some eastern city; both having painted and jeweled courtezans for partners. In the corner of the hall are seen gamblers playing at their favorite game of poker. Jests and conversations suitable to the place and oc[ca]sion are heard. I would not recommend the establishment as one adapted for the schooling of the rising generation, but to those of mature years, who should become acquainted with all phases of society, Rowdy Joe's is a good place to get familiarized with one peculiar phase. While I would not recommend Rowdy Joe as a model for Sunday school scholars, yet I am constrained to say that there are many men passing in society as gentlemen whose hearts are black in comparison with his.[13]

Further proof of Joe's benevolent ways was offered by L. C. Fouquet, who recalled being thrown from his mule in a race when the animal stumbled, threw him over its head, and then rolled upon him:

When I came back to life, I found myself in the kind care of women attending me. Rowdy Joe and other wild guys were looking at me with most loving sympathetic faces, but oh I realized with horror as to what kind of house I was in. I was absolutely surprised at such unexpected kindness during the rest of that day and night. But I was glad when a dear neighbor, Jim Menafee, came over with his covered wagon to take me to his home for care.

I was in bed about two weeks, when I called on my sweetheart who turned me down, as my opponent had told her without any explanation, at what kind of place I had stayed overnight.[14]

Another testimony to Joe Lowe's integrity, if not his morality, noted that "the hardest case in town now is Rowdy Joe, whom all unite in representing as a man who despite his associations is of a most peaceful disposition and values his spoken word in a commercial transaction more highly than many more reputable men do their spoken oaths. There is of course the usual frontier license in Wichita, but the law and order party have always been in the majority and there has seldom been any exhibition of a ruffianly license and when they appeared, they were summarily checked."[15]

By May 1873, Joe Lowe was accepted as a local character. On the twenty-second the Wichita *Eagle* reported that "on returning from the races last Saturday, Joseph Lowe's — familiarly known as Rowdy Joe — horse fell, throwing Mr. L. under him. He was picked up insensible and carried into the house of Ida May and a doctor sent for. At this writing (Monday) we have not heard further, but several who saw the incident thought him badly hurt." Joe made a quick recovery, however, and was soon back in business.

The subject of law and order in most frontier settlements was a vexing question, and Wichita was no exception. Ordinances banning firearms and other dangerous weapons within the city limits followed the general trend, but this item in Wichita's city records, dated May 10, 1871, suggests that the city nevertheless expected its police force to be frugal with ammunition and to make every shot count:

> Resolved — that the City Clerk issue an order upon the Treasurer of each Special Policeman provided for by Resolution adopted at Special Meeting held Saturday May 6th 1871 to the amount of six dollars ($6.00) for each Policeman.
>
> Moved and Carried that the following bills be allowed and that orders be drawn for amounts
>
> City of Wichita to Geo. Schlichter Wichita   D
>   6 rounds Cartridges .36   75¢

May 8th	6	"	"	.44	75¢
	1 Box Caps				20
					1.70
May 9th		Powder, Shot & Cartridges			$1.35

On June 28, 1871, the following Motion from Mr. Schattner was adopted and its wording painted on two pine boards measuring 3 feet by four feet. It read:

NOTICE

All persons are hereby forbidden the carrying of firearms or other dangerous weapons within the city limits of Wichita under penalty of fine and imprisonment.

By Order of the Mayor
M. Meagher
City Marshal

Michael Meagher was Wichita's first marshal and was appointed on April 13, 1871. He held the position for five years with only one break (1874–75).

Firearms continued to preoccupy the authorities. In 1872 the tollkeepers who operated the privately owned Chisholm Trail bridge were sworn in as special policemen and ordered to exchange all weapons for a metal token, to "receive such salary as may be paid to them by the bridge company." The scheme was not a success, and by 1873 notices appeared ordering visitors to "LEAVE YOUR REVOLVERS AT POLICE HEADQUARTERS, AND GET A CHECK."[16]

State laws which forbade former Confederates from carrying weapons of any sort were blatantly ignored – indeed, they were unenforceable – and communities relied upon local policing to preserve the peace. To meet the cost, local taxation, backed by ordinances curtailing the activities of saloonkeepers and dance-hall operators, proved lucrative. The marshal's reports for September and December 1872 show a total of $490 collected in fines from gambling houses and houses of prostitution. A similar return for the month of January 1873, rendered by Marshal Meagher on February 5, realized $145. These fines did not, of course, include Delano.[17]

Not everyone accepted the city council's actions without question. Isaac Thayer, a survivor of the Battle of Beecher Island, who was elected sheriff of Ellis County in November 1868 and disappeared for no apparent reason some months later, had settled in Wichita and was involved in gambling. In January 1873 he addressed this message to the council:

> To the Honerable [sic] members of the Council of the City of Wichita. Your petitioner I. Thayer states that in the year 1872 he was running a room for gambling purposes and paying for the privilege therefore into the City Treasury of Wichita City the sum of fifty dollars per month. Your petitioner further states that having paid said sum of money to said city he was allowed to run his the said Gambling room that during this time the Marshal of said city demanded the further sum of twenty five dollars which sum was paid the said marshal. Your petitioner states that it was stipulated & agreed upon that it was to cost your petitioner no more than fifty dollars for running said gambling rooms that the said city of Wichita was not Entitled to the further sum of twenty five dollars which your petititioner paid to said city of Wichita, wherefore your petitioner prays that said twenty five dollars be remitted to him, or be applied on his saloon license for the month of February, 1873.
>
> I. Thayer[18]

Despite such protests, Wichita continued to benefit from the immoral earnings of the saloons and dance halls. In effect, they proved lucrative to both the proprietors and to the city. Prostitution in particular was a great attraction. W. E. Stanley, the county attorney of Sedgwick County in the rip-roaring days of the cattle trade (he served as governor from 1899 to 1903), made this observation in 1877 after the cattle trade had gone but not its evils:

> Houses of prostitution are advertising themselves, by open doors on some of the most public streets of our city, prostitutes in half nude forms take their morning airings under the eyes of our most respectable citizens and flaunt the indicia of their "trade" in all public places and gatherings without hindrance from the authorities . . . the time has come when these places of vice must be at least regulated if not entirely suppressed . . . as they are "city institutions" and as the city has received large financial benefits? [sic] from this source . . . they should be regulated through the city courts and by the city officials.[19]

Wichita, however, was not slow in skimming the cream from the ill-gotten earnings of brothels and other houses of ill fame. Prostitutes were fined $8 per month plus $2 court costs. Brothel operators were fined $18 plus $2 costs, but if they sold whiskey, there was also a flat-rate $25-per-month license fee. Should they have the misfortune to experience shootouts, bar fights, or other "disorderly conduct," the court took pleasure in extracting additional sums. During August 1873, for instance, Wichita's prostitutes parted with $390, which was considered average for the season. Liquor licenses amounted to $625, making total revenue of $1,796.26. By comparison, the cost of policing for the month was $450.60. The city boasted fifteen saloons and admitted to four brothels and fourteen girls, which by the end of the cattle season in November had dwindled to two brothels and six girls.[20]

Owners of gambling halls relied largely on their take from whatever operating fees they imposed on the gamblers, and they further boosted their income from liquor sales. Dance halls, however, were much more profitable, especially the two principal establishments in Delano, both outside Wichita's city limits and therefore beyond the reach of local licensing laws. Joe Lowe and his chief competitor, Edward T. ("Red") Beard, earned money from three sources: bar sales, fees charged to dance with one of the "hostesses," and perhaps a percentage if the dancing partners retired to one of the cribs at the rear to continue their gyrations. Under existing Kansas statutes, such establishments outside city limits had to apply for licenses from the county commissioners. These cost between one hundred and five hundred dollars annually, whereas rates charged within city limits and under the control of local councils were considerably lower.[21] We have found no evidence that either Lowe or Beard was in debt to the county, perhaps because their fortunes changed dramatically one night in November 1873 when the bitter rivalry that had been growing between them for months finally erupted in violence and Rowdy Joe and Red faced each other for the last time.

Notes

1. H. Craig Miner, *Wichita: The Early Years, 1865–1880*, 4.
2. Emporia *News*, June 3, 1870; Joseph G. Rosa, *The Gunfighter: Man or Myth?* 48, 106.
3. Emporia *News*, August 26, 1870; March 24, 1871.
4. Wichita *City Eagle*, June 28, 1872 (citing the Emporia *Ledger*).
5. Wichita *Eagle*, July 26, 1872.
6. Ibid., undated clipping ca. 1931.
7. Kansas City *Times*, September 26, 1872.
8. Ibid., Topeka *Daily Commonwealth*, September 24, 1872; Wichita *Weekly Eagle*, September 24, 1872.
9. Records of the City of Wichita, 1872; Wichita *Beacon*, March 24, 1875; Wichita *Eagle*, March 25, 1875.
10. Dykstra, *The Cattle Towns*, 50–55.
11. Ibid., 55.
12. Wichita *Weekly Eagle*, July 2 and September 24, 1873.
13. Topeka *Daily Commonwealth*, October 15, 1872.
14. "Stories of Wichita," scrapbook of news clippings from unidentified sources, Wichita Public Library.
15. Wichita *Weekly Eagle*, January 16, 1873.
16. Proceedings of the Governing Body, City of Wichita, Journal A, 69 and 187.
17. *Kansas Statutes*, 1868, 378. This law remained in force the whole of the cattle town era; Records of the City of Wichita; see also Miner, *Wichita*, 115.
18. Records of the City of Wichita.
19. Cited by Miller and Snell in *Why the West Was Wild*, 15.
20. Ibid.; Dykstra, *The Cattle Towns*, 104; Wichita *Eagle*, April 3, 1873.
21. Dykstra, *The Cattle Towns*, 126.

5

Red Beard

Joe Lowe established his dance house at Delano some time ahead of Edward T. ("Red") Beard. The pair had been aware of each other since they ran similar establishments at Newton in 1871, but they became rivals only when they found themselves near neighbors at Delano. Red (as we shall now call him) had fled to Newton when he and others were driven out of Abilene by City Marshal Wild Bill Hickok acting on the orders of the city council. In July 1871, Hickok was instructed to "stop dance houses and the vending of whiskeys, brandies, etc., in McCoy's addition" (a disparaging reference to the brothel area, which was actually on land owned by a man named Fisher and not Mayor McCoy). By September, however, it was decided to impose fines for prostitution, and this move, soon to be followed by a ban on the cattle trade, led to a general exodus, prompting the editor of the *Chronicle* to report on the fourteenth:

We are happy to announce . . . that within the last fortnight wholesome and magnificent changes have been wrought in the moral *status* of Abilene. For the last ten or twelve days almost every train eastward bound has carried away and relieved this community of vast numbers of sinful humanity. Prostitutes, "pimps," gamblers, "cappers," and others of like ilk, finding their several nefarious avocations no longer remunerative or appreciated in this neighborhood, are embracing their earliest possible convenience, by hook (mostly by hook) and crook, to obtain the necessary where withall with which to procure passage to Newton, Kansas City, or St. Louis, where in all probability most of them will end their miserable lives in dens of shame — unless the better angel in their nature leads them to forsake the paths of sin.

Soon after his arrival at Wichita, Red established a dance house next door to Joe's place in Delano.

Edward Thomas Beard was the son of the Thomas Beard, who founded Beardstown, Illinois, in 1819. A grandson of Amos Beard, a Revolutionary War sailor, Thomas married Sarah Bell in 1826. A daughter, Caroline, was born on July 1, 1827, Edward on October 19, 1829, and another daughter, Stella, on February 25, 1832. The couple divorced in 1834, and in 1837 Thomas married Mrs. Nancy C. Dickerman, widow of Willard A. Dickerman from New York. This union was blessed with more children.[1]

Edward Beard, according to James Kelly, editor of the Winfield *Courier,* had been a "jolly rollicking young man, without a single bad trait in his make up." However, when he got his hands on some of his father's fortune, he foolishly invested it in crackpot schemes, particularly in South America. An initial success prompted further speculation and he lost his entire capital, forcing him to return home penniless. Still ambitious, he tried other ventures but again met with failure. His marriage to a young woman from the same county seemed happy enough, and the union was blessed with two daughters and a son; but Edward's restless nature again had him on the move, and by the early 1860s he had deserted his family and headed west. He soon established a reputation as a "bad man" in parts of California, Oregon, and Arizona Territory.[2]

In appearance Beard was about six feet tall, with an enormous bulk. His shock of red hair and a reddish mustache quickly earned him the nickname "Red," by which he was best known. J. H. Andrews, a contemporary, described him as

slovenly in dress and personal habits, slothful and lazy in his walk. You would know Big Red if you should meet him on the street, for he never came over to the city from Delano without his double-barreled shotgun and that gun had the biggest caliber I ever looked into, yet he was a fascinating character to me, more so than Rowdy Joe, for I have followed Big Red, time and again to look at the big hunk of beef. And when he went into a saloon and took a seat with the big gun between his knees, I stood alongside of him to gaze and hear him talk. He was an unusual character and sure fascinated me. He often caught me looking at him as I stood against the wall and many times our eyes met. I have since wondered what he thought when he looked at me and why I was hanging around. But he did not speak.[3]

On July 29, 1873, Red and a local printer had a row in front of Allen's grocery store on Main Street. It was claimed that Red started the fracas. "A derringer was held against his commissary department and snapped, but it failed to do its duty and Red still lives. Both parties were arrested and fined this morning. People will learn, after a while, that printers are a self-protecting class, confound our brave hearts." What may be relative to this incident is to be found in the record of fines imposed by the city of Wichita in August 1873. Case No. 755 notes that "T. J. [sic] Beard was fined $3 which was collected on August 28 by City Marshal Meagher who 'reports two dollars case No. 755 paid by Confinement & labor.' Case No. 755 A. Jackson [the printer?] was fined $2."[4]

The trouble between Rowdy Joe and Red Beard arose, it was alleged, because of Red's dislike of Joe's frontier reputation and success in the saloon business, which Red deeply resented. Some claimed that with Joe out of the way, Red would be undisputed "king" of Delano. Perhaps, but the townsfolk thought it would be only a matter of time before the rivals came to blows or exchanged shots.

Where Joe ran his dance house in partnership with Rowdy Kate, Red relied upon Josephine DeMerritt and Walter and Carrie Beebe to manage his place. Beebe was his bartender, and Beebe's wife, Carrie, acted as a hostess. Miss DeMerritt was Red's mistress, and she, too, had a share in the place.

The rival establishments were similar in appearance. They were about twenty-eight feet wide by fifty feet long, had a minimum of foundation, and were constructed mainly of twelve-inch boards. Unpainted, they were basically functional, with no porches or other refinements. Like most such establishments, the "facilities" were crude and placed conveniently at the rear. Apart from the bar, there was space for some kind of musical entertainment. Lighted by kerosene lamps that hung from the ceiling, the effect was sparse. At the rear were the rooms occupied by the owners and employees and perhaps a crib or two for customers who wanted more than a drink or a dance. The two dance halls carried on business in a relatively peaceful manner until early June 1873, when there occurred an incident that led to problems for Red; these were not lost on Rowdy Joe.

In a general deployment of troops in anticipation of Indian troubles, Companies A and C of the Sixth U.S. Cavalry under the command of Captain Daniel Madden, Captain Clarence E. Nasmith, Lieutenant Homer F. Winchester, and Second Lieutenant John A. Rucker arrived at Wichita on May 11 and went into camp on the west bank of the Arkansas River not far from the dance houses of Red Beard and Joe Lowe. The troops promptly adopted the two establishments for recreation purposes.

On the night of June 2–3, one of the cavalry troopers quarreled with Emma Stanley, a dancer in Red's place. It was claimed the dispute was over five dollars. The trooper was drunk and pulled his pistol, shooting the unfortunate Miss Stanley in the thigh. Red Beard and Beebe promptly opened fire from behind the bar. In a fusillade of shots, a Private Dolely was shot in the throat and another trooper named Boyle suffered a splintered shinbone. That there was no loss of life can be accounted for only by the agility of those present. Bystanders later reported that the doors and windows were jammed or smashed by erupting cowboys, soldiers, and inmates. A member of the orchestra took refuge under his bass violin – recalled by a witness as resembling a huge turtle with a man's arms and legs protruding from beneath.

The troopers beat a retreat, swearing vengeance, but the sudden appearance in camp of breathless troops and the news that some of them had been shot was too much for Captain Madden. He broke camp and moved his troops ten miles north of the city. Boyle, the bugler from Company A, was sent to Fort Riley for treatment of his leg; Red's (or Beebe's) six-shooter ball was removed from Dolely's throat and he survived. Meanwhile, back at Delano, Red and Beebe took stock of what had happened and began repairing the damage.

In the camp north of Wichita, the troopers planned their revenge on Red and Beebe, disregarding the fact that it was a trooper who had started the trouble in the first place. After taps, about twenty men sneaked out of camp and made their way to Wichita. Posting a guard at the residence of the county sheriff (John Meagher), the troopers marched in formation across the bridge and surrounded Red's dance house. On signal, they fired a fusillade of shots into the hall but purposely aimed high, for the troops had no wish to wreak vengeance on anybody but Red and Beebe. When neither appeared, the troopers rolled barrels of kerosene against the walls of the house and ignited them. With that, the soldiers reformed ranks and marched back across the bridge and out of town. On June 5 the *Eagle* described the reaction in Wichita:

> The soldiers have carried out their threat. This morning about 2 o'clock we were aroused from sleep by the rapid discharge of firearms across the river. Hurrying on our clothes we ran down to the bridge, by which time the lurid flames were bursting from "Red's" dance house, accompanied by a yell from a squad of some thirty soldiers, whom we met on the bridge, marching by fours. They appeared to be perfectly possessed, and after the order to "shoulder arms," asked us "how is that for high?" pointing to the burning building. Being the first upon the ground, we found a man lying some fifty yards in front of the burning building, who gave his name as Chas. Leshart, wounded through the body. We saw no one else that was hurt, but we heard that one of the girls was wounded, and that the girl wounded in the melee on Monday night had received a fresh shot. In a few minutes hundreds of citizens were upon the ground, and by prompt action and considerable exertion the house of Joseph Lowe was saved. The soldiers went off up Water street. We have no room for comments, but upon the whole the affairs of Monday and last night are no credit to our neighbor town.

By morning, when the flames had died down and cool heads had surveyed the damage, it was found that Red's place was a mere shell; for the time being at least, he was out of business. Ten miles away, just as the troops were preparing to break camp after receiving orders to proceed to Fort Hays, Sheriff John Meagher rode in with warrants for the arrest of the arsonists. Captain Madden told the sheriff he must be mistaken, for none of his men had left camp. To prove it he summoned his sergeant, who swore that all his men had answered roll call at taps the night before and at reveille that morning. The more the sheriff insisted, the more the captain resisted, until finally he ordered his men to mount up and resumed his march to Fort Hays. Angered and humiliated, Meagher returned to Wichita empty handed.

The incident was reported widely and there were complaints to the military. The Wichita *Weekly Eagle* noted on June 9 that Lieutenant Winchester had been ordered by the department commander to gather all available evidence relative to the shooting and burning for a full report. An examination of the records of the Department of the Missouri failed to reveal an official report on the incident. Lieutenant Winchester did submit a report, dated June 6, from the camp near Wichita, but this concerned the murder of a cattleman at Pond Creek by Osage Indians. The National Archives has concluded that the report on the shootout has been lost or perhaps misfiled.[5]

Red engaged McClury & Company to rebuild his dance hall, and by early August he was back in business. Beebe resumed his old position behind the bar, at each end of which, on the back bar, now resided sawed-off shotguns loaded with blue whistlers — three lead balls per barrel. This time, the partners reckoned, they would be prepared for anything.[6]

The showdown between Joe Lowe and Red Beard came on the night of October 27 and the event is still regarded as one of the wildest during Wichita's wild and woolly days. Old-timers have recalled much of what happened that night, and many attempts have been made to chronicle the actions of both Red and Joe, but the full story, if the still extant records of the subsequent trial can be believed, has never been told.

The mutual dislike of both parties is very evident when one examines the volume of material, both factual and fictional, that survives. Indeed, it does seem that Red was jealous of Joe's reputation and for his ownership of the "swiftest place in Kansas," which was known the length and breadth of the Chisholm Trail, and no cowboy could say that he had "seen the elephant" until he had paid Joe's place a visit. This, then, was what was gnawing at Red, and on the fateful night he was deep in his cups. As the evening wore on, his drinking increased and his temper worsened. He went to his room and came back with a shotgun and a pistol. He laid the shotgun on the end of the bar, near the door, and took another drink. He then picked up his guns and walked out into the night. Walter Beebe, who had been tending bar all evening, stated that he did not see him for about an hour and a half and when he returned:

He came into the house & he had his pistol in his hand. The first thing he done he shot at the white door knob on the hall door. There was another man there at the time by the name of Tom Pope. He drew his pistol & was going to shoot at the door knob too, & Mr. Beard put his pistol at his head & told him to put up his pistol or he would shoot him. There was dancing after the shot occurred & Mr. Beard danced himself. I suppose they danced probably an hour & Mr. Beard was out & in the house two or three times & I sent this Billie Anderson & Ohmert to watch him. I was afraid he was so drunk that he would get into some trouble & and they would prevent it. The last time he came into the house he had been out of the house then I suppose 5 or 10 minutes.

Then when he came in he went up to the east window of the dance hall. He stood there probably 5 minutes looking through the window & I saw him raise his pistol up which he had in his hand all the time & he raised it up & took aim just so (with both hands a hold of the pistol) aiming right out of the east window & before I could say anything at all he fired. I went out from behind the bar & went to the window to see what he had shot at or where the ball had went to — I saw that the ball had went through the window & through Mr. Low's window too, I then returned behind the bar & I was talking to Billie Anderson about Mr. Beards shooting & I made some remark that I expected that he had shot at Mr. Low & then I saw Mr. Low come in at the front door & he made a remark he asked who had shot at him. I heard Mr. Beard say something that I (Beard) done it, that was the substance of the remarks he made in answer to the remark that Mr. Low made. At the same time Mr. Beard raised his pistol & shot it off & Mr. Low shot his gun off at the same time. I could hardly distinguish the two different reports. At this time Mr. Beard was standing between the East end of the music stand & the east window & Mr. Low was standing in front of the front door about 2 feet in the room & Mr. Billie Anderson was standing at the north end of the bar & I was standing behind the bar near the north end watching the parties, and at the time these shots were fired I saw two men run going out at the east door. They were Texas men. Mr. Low's gun was pointed more at the direction of these men going out at the east door. He had his gun with the stock at his hips & the muzzle elevated. The shot would not have hit these men.

Mr. Beard was then going toward the south door.

At the time these shots were fired there was [E. A.] Ohmert in the room, Billie Anderson was there. I think Miss Kate Low was there, think she came in with Low. There was 4, 5 or 6 Texas men there I do not know the names of them.

Billie Anderson was shot. He was standing right at the end of the bar when he was shot. I did not know he was shot until I saw the blood dripping off the bar. I passed out behind him & did not notice that he was shot at the time. I did not distinguish more than than two shots at that time. There was no other shot fired after Mr. Low got to the east door. After we let Mr. Beard up he stood at the hall door & shot the girl, before he shot the girl I asked him if he was shot & he said he was not shot — was not hurt at all. Up to the time he stood in the door & left the house he was not hurt at all. He had his pistol in his right hand all the time from the time he came into the house until he left the house. I saw Mr. Beard the next morning & did not see him any more that night. I did not see Mr. Low after the shooting until the next Wednesday.

When I saw Beard again after the shooting he was shot in the right arm & had one shot in the hip.

It is a part of tradition — or folklore — that Red and Joe met in the middle of the street for a classic shootout, but in reality their encounter was a sniping exercise, each biding his time for a clear shot at the other. Joe was particularly incensed because Red's shot had creased his neck, inflicting a painful but not serious wound — later he must have felt thankful that Red had not been sober! Billie Anderson was the real victim; standing in Joe's line of fire, he had received a ball across the bridge of his nose that robbed him of both his eyesight and his sense of smell. Beebe's description continues:

Mrs. Low started out the side door at that time & Mr. Beard started & run out at the front door, but before he left Mr. Beard snapped his pistol twice at Mr. Lowe & Low snapped his shot gun at him, Mr. Beard, and the cap snapped [failed to explode], then Mr. Beard had been out of the house I suppose probably a minute & I saw him look in at the west window at the south end of the house, then he came in at the front door. He asked for his shot gun as soon as he came in. I told him he had left it over in Lowes. He made some remark that he did not & went to look for it in his room & he could not find it. Then he came out & stood at the hall door of the dance room, then he came out in the dance room & looked around there. He had his pistol in his hand all the time & he saw this Joe DeMerritt in the room & he accused her of putting up a job on him. She said she had not & he asked her where the shot gun was. I believe she told him he had left it over in town. I think that is what she told him. He caught hold of her & threw her down on the floor & was going to shoot her I think, he had his pistol cocked right at her, then myself, Ohmert and this Texas man caught hold of him & held him until Miss Joe got away. Then we let him up & he got up & he went to the middle hall door. He stood there probably a minute or so. He raised his pistol & shot it off back in the hall. I heard a woman scream & he, Beard, run out at the front door & I went back to see who he had shot.

The testimony of others indicated that Red Beard had mistaken another dance-hall girl, Annie Franklin, who was crossing the dimly lit hall, for Josephine DeMerritt, the momentary object of his rage. When he fired down the hall, he shot Annie in the stomach.

Beebe also described the physical layout of the area. The two dance halls were about 50 feet apart, on the west bank of the Arkansas River, north of the bridge about 350 feet. Lowe's place was on the east, nearest the riverbank.

Another witness, Charles Smith, sometimes better known as "One-armed Charlie," who was living at Beard's place at the time of the shooting, corroborated the incident of Beard shooting at a door knob and claimed that Red ordered him to go over to Joe Lowe's place to see who was there. He reported back that Red had a better crowd than Joe did. Red pondered for some moments then stepped to the window and raised his pistol. Smith and Ohmert promptly pulled him away. Red then walked outside and Ohmert brought him back again. Josephine DeMerritt suggested that they go to bed. She sat by the stove and Red walked over to her and asked if she had ever seen blood. She said she had. He then walked to the music stand and from there to the window. It was then Smith claimed that Red, pistol in hand, stepped back from the window and said:

"Now all you sons of bitches keep away from me for I am liable to give it to any of you." Then he throwed his pistol down & with both hands ahold of it fired through the window. He stepped back to the window, looked through it & said, "I have done it." Then he came walking down towards the stove in the south end of the dance hall. I do not remember of hearing him say anything, I think it must have been 5 minutes or so after this shot that Joe came in. He asked for the man that shot at him. Beard says, "Here I am you son of a bitch," that time both fired and Miss Joe says to Joe Low "don't kill him, he is drunk." Joe points to his neck & says, "Look there, see what he has done to me." Joe punched him with his gun & Beard grabbed hold of it with his left hand. He was snapping his pistol with his right hand. Joe jerked the gun away from him. Kate took hold of Joe & shoved him out of the side door. Beard jammed the pistol against her breast & snapped it. Then I think Joe went out the side door & then Beard went out the front door.[7]

That should have been enough action to satisfy the most gore-thirsty shootist, but Red's and Joe's exit from the dance house was only an intermission. Red had made it pretty plain that he had tried to kill Joe and his further attempts when Joe turned up (and his fortunately abortive attempt to shoot Kate) was the sort of provocation that would drive Joe Lowe to the limit. Joe rushed to his own dance hall and reloaded his shotgun. Rowdy Kate bathed and bandaged his bleeding neck, doubtless attempting to dissuade him from his course, but he stepped out once more into the night. Red, meantime, was making his own way across the Douglas Avenue bridge, oblivious to anyone. It was then that someone fired both barrels of a shotgun and stepped back into the shadow of a pen erected for holding cattle at the west end of the bridge. At the sound of the reverberating roar of the shotgun, people ran out of Red's dance hall and found him on the bridge, one arm shattered and a ball lodged in the after portion of his hip. It was obvious that this had been no stand-up fight, but, rather, an ambush. Some people might claim that it was tit for tat, but Joe's friends, townsfolk and Texans alike, urged him to give himself up, which he did.

At this point, another legend bites the dust. Wyatt Earp, made ubiquitous by his zealous and unreliable biographer, is reported to have been deputized by Sheriff Meagher to arrest Joe, which

The famous Douglas Avenue bridge that linked Wichita and Delano, separated by the Arkansas River. Red Beard was shot on the west end of the bridge. Courtesy Kansas State Historical Society.

he did without difficulty. Unfortunately for Mr. Earp, local records do not place him in the city in any official capacity until 1875, but he was known to be in the city as early as 1874. Also, John Meagher had resigned as county sheriff some time before. His twin brother, Michael, however, was city marshal. It was Mike Meagher who arranged Joe Lowe's surrender. Under oath he stated:

> I reside in the city of Wichita Kan — am City Marshall [sic] of City of Wichita. Am acquainted with Joseph Low [sic], was acquainted [with] E. T. Beard in his lifetime.
> I heard of the circumstances of Red[']s being shot. I saw Mr. Low on the night that Beard was shot. I saw him at the corner of the Progressive [Billiard] Hall standing outside the door. He told me there had been some shooting [a]cross the river & he wanted to give himself up to witnesses & I told him I could not take care of him that he had better go & see Bill Smith [sheriff of Sedgwick County]. I went with him & found Bill & he Low gave himself up to Bill Smith. He said he did not know but what he had shot Red, that he did not know whether he had or not.

Low looked to me as though had been shot. He was bleeding at the neck. He, Low, said that Red had shot through the window.

An examination of the testimony of Sheriff William Smith and Deputy Sheriff Charles B. Jones shows it was identical to that of Marshal Meagher. None of them mentioned the presence of Wyatt Earp, and we doubt that at that time they had ever heard of him.[8]

Joe Lowe was freed on two thousand dollars' bail to await trial and carried on his dance-house business. Red, meanwhile, had been removed to his home, where he lingered in great agony for two weeks before expiring at three o'clock on the morning of Tuesday, November 11. An autopsy was performed by Dr. Owens, the coroner, and an inquest at the Eagle Hotel was attended by seven doctors and a coroner's jury. The Wichita *Eagle* reported on the thirteenth:

> The examination disclosed that his right arm at the elbow had been shattered fearfully and was in a state of decay. The wound in the hip was also in the same state. In the latter wound a bullet was found imbedded in the bone. Traces of pus were discovered, we believe, about the wound in the lungs. The examination was thorough, but we withdrew before the entire process was gone through with. At the hotel were several frail women, who had been inmates of his house who seemed much affected. We noticed also Rowdy Joe, who is charged with shooting Red, who wore a solemn countenance. The post mortem examination, technically and properly stated, revealed the fact of death by infiltration of pus in the blood, the result of gunshot wounds.

The *Eagle* editor went on to state that Beard had been well educated and had had Christian training. His family knew nothing of his western life. As was common at the time, the editor claimed that Red had prophesied that he would not live out the summer and had said only a short time before his death that "he followed the disreputable business only in the hopes of getting a start in the world again, but if he got over his wounds, he would never go inside a dancehouse again. Beard left some property and money in the hands of parties here for the use and benefit of his children, in the shape of a regular bequest."

It was later revealed that although Red and his wife, Deborah, had been divorced, she arrived in Wichita to take charge of his affairs. Described as "very much a lady, intelligent and refined," she came to "look after her children's property." Once that was achieved she would return to her home and children. Mrs. Beard, however, decided to settle in Wichita and soon after going back east she returned with her three daughters. An examination of the records of Sedgwick County Probate Court have revealed that Red's estate was not worth that much. The lot and his house were appraised at three hundred dollars, total about twelve hundred. Bills for nursing, the doctor, and assorted claims relative to the dance hall took care of most of the money. But there was another problem to be faced by his former wife: ownership of the dance hall itself.[9]

A correspondent for the Kansas City *Times* wrote from Wichita on November 2:

The dancehalls are still running. Jo DeMerritt, Red's mistress, is in charge of his house. There seems to be no diminution in the attendance in the consequence of this fearful affray. The county authorities have taken no action to suppress these vile haunts of the depraved and the vicious and any night, similar scenes may be enacted more horrible than anything that has yet occurred. How long they will permit these hellholes to exist, in violation to the demands of all law-abiding citizens, who realize the stigma and disgrace that will attach to their county by permitting their existence, to say naught of the crimes that are perpetrating nightly in these dancehouses, is a question that the people would like to have their county attorney and other officers to solve.

The writer noted that "Anderson who was shot by Rowdy Joe Tuesday night is the man who killed a blacksmith in West Wichita last summer. It was claimed to be accidental as they were scuffling at the time. He is a tough customer and has but few friends." A local report stated that Anderson was "in a fair way to recovery. It is astonishing how near a man can get to death's door and be shoved back into the full tide of life. His history as far as we already know it, would furnish sufficient groundwork for a ten cent novel." As for the unfortunate Annie Franklin, in what is thought to be a reference to her, it was noted: "The girl Mollie, who everybody thought must die, will, in all probability, yet live to dance again."[10]

Joe Lowe's trial began on December 9 with Judge W. Campbell on the bench. The *Eagle* of December 11 reported:

The court room filled with curious and interested people. In securing a jury the usual number of preemptory challenges were exhausted by the defense, but an unobjectionable jury was empannelled within an hour or two. H. C. Sluss for the state, [B. H.] Fisher, [S. M.] Tucker and [J. Smith] Deveny for the defense. Much interest has been evinced by court, jury and bar in the evidence given by the witnesses for the state, who, at this writing, Wednesday morning, we give in their testimony, and the prosecuting attorney will, in a few moments, rest his case. We understand that a large number of witnesses will be examined for the defense, and when the case will be given to the jury it is impossible to say, although a verdict may be reached before tomorrow morning. To give an opinion, or even to hazard a guess, as to what the verdict will be, would be impossible, of course, in this conection, but should one be rendered before going to press to-night we shall append it to this article.

Walter Beebe's testimony and that of Charlie Smith have been noted, and most of the witnesses at the trial made similar statements. Said Josephine DeMerritt, who was called as a witness for the state and who had testified previously before Justice of the Peace E. B. Jewett that she had been present when Beard's first shot was fired through Joe's window:

I was acquainted with E T Beard in his lifetime, I was at his house on the night of the 27th of October. I am acquainted with Joseph Low I saw Mr Low that night the first I saw him Mr Low he came in at the front door of Beards house He had a shot gun. He came in & wanted to know who it was that shot him Red was walking from my room out into the dance room & Miss Kate came in right after Joe or at the same time a step or two behind him After Joe asked this question he fired the gun He fired it [at something?] at the side door I was so excited I could not tell as to [who] fired the gun he saw Red coming & he turned the gun & the shot went up through the roof of the house. The other shot hit Billie Anderson

As near as I could judge & since both barrels of the gun were fired at this time Joe at the time he fired the gun made some such remark as take it you sons of bitches. Red walked down the dance hall towards Joe and snapped his pistol at Joe It did not go off, then Miss Kate interfered and pushed Joe out of the side door.

Red was not shot by either discharges of the gun at that time Mr Low did not come back into the house any more Red then went out of the front door & went around the side of the house and looked through the window then he came in and asked me to hunt for the shot gun I told him that the shot gun was not there that he had left it up in Town.

It is notable that Miss DeMerritt makes no mention of Red's threatening her with a pistol or the shooting of the unfortunate Miss Franklin. Miss DeMerritt, however, soon had problems of her own. She claimed that in September Beard had deeded his property to her in the event of his death. Later it was discovered that the original deed had been lost and that she had forged a new one. Josephine was sentenced to ten years in the state penitentiary. In 1876, however, Judge Fisher took steps to have her pardoned on grounds that she might have been legally guilty but not morally. In thanking the judge and others who had helped and in expressing her gratitude to Governor Osborn, she said her "soul has been saved and my life too." She then planned to go "south to her kindred as soon as her health will permit."[11]

Joe Lowe's defense counsel claimed that although he admitted shooting Red on the night of the fight, he subsequently confessed that he was too drunk to be sure. And here the court was faced with what to many was an embarrassing situation: few of the witnesses were prepared to prejudice Joe's chances. In fact, the defense lawyers put up such a brilliant character study that Joe himself must have wondered who was in the dock. S. M. Tucker reviewed the legal aspects; Smith Deveny appealed to the jury by reciting all of Joe's redeeming traits (unfortunately, these were not recorded), with a few asides on how villainous Red Beard had been, and by the time H. C. Sluss got up, he was positively embarrassed. Most of the state's witnesses had proved to be sympathetic toward Joe Lowe, and his pointed remarks concerning the depraved existence of most of the witnesses and their reluctance to recognize the majesty of the law fell upon deaf ears. At the conclusion of his speech, however, there was a round of applause from "the better class of citizens of the able and conscientious manner in which the attorney for the people had discharged his duty."[12]

A further problem was the reaction among certain so-called taxpayers, who were probably saloon or dance-hall keepers. On November 26 the *Weekly Beacon* published a letter, signed by "Many Tax-Payers," deploring the three thousand to four thousand dollars which would be expended on such a trial. While wishing that the law be maintained at whatever cost, having investigated the shooting, and having reached the conclusion that there was no possibility of a conviction, "it is acknowledged almost universally that Lowe is not guilty of the crime as charged in the affray of October 27th last." Evidently, some of the embittered taxpayers found their way onto the jury, for the unanimous verdict was predictable: not guilty.

Joe had little time to celebrate, however, for there was still the matter of William Anderson. What happened next was described vividly by "Mark" in the Kansas City *Times* of December 18. After reporting the verdict of the Beard trial, he wrote:

> The defendant, Lowe, was also held on another charge of assault with intent to kill William Anderson at the same time, and place of the charge of shooting E. T. Beard, the trial of which was set for today, Monday. Anderson has commenced suit against Lowe for damages, in the sum of ten thousand dollars. Since the court convened on the eighth instant, Rowdy Joe had been placed in the charge of a trusty guard, who was constantly with him. Last Saturday evening about nine o'clock, the guard conducted him from the sheriff's office in the courthouse, where they slept, to his reisdence, recently rented and situated two blocks distant. Soon after entering the house, Rowdy Joe mysteriously disappeared and has not been found. Walter Beebe and his paramour, with Rowdy Kate, Joe's woman, were in the house. It soon transpired that Walter Beebe had taken from the stable Rowdy Joe's fleet horse, early in the evening, and had him near the house.
>
> John Nugent, the guard, Walter Beebe, Carrie Beebe, and Rowdy Kate are under arrest, charged with aiding and asisting the escape of Lowe. They are held under bonds of $100 each till their examination which has been continued till Thursday next. Much excitement exists and many contradictory accounts are given of the affair, but one phase of the matter is certain, that Joe has left the precints of Wichita. We will give more particulars as they transpire.

A reward of one hundred dollars was offered by Sheriff William Smith, and on the eighteenth the *Eagle* published Smith's description of the wanted man:

He is about 28 years old, 5 feet 9 inches tall, heavy set, dark complexion, black hair, and heavy black moustache, gruff manners, — formerly proprietor of a dance house. Had a scar on right side of neck from a pistol ball. Had on, when last seen, black pants, brown frock coat, and a brown overcoat, trimmed with fur; rode a bay horse with a California saddle.

Joe's first stop was Osage Mission (now called St. Paul) in Neosho County, where the editor of the *Mission Transcript,* unaware of Joe's wanted status, remarked on December 19: "Rowdy Joe the famous Wichitan is in town and not much rowdy about him after all." Once the editor became aware of the fact, however, he promptly advised the editor of the *Eagle* that had his paper arrived a day sooner "Rowdy Joe would have been taken. He has been here for several days, but left here yesterday morning for Texas. The horse is still in the stable. He watched the papers regularly in my office." [13]

Wichita, however, was less concerned about apprehending Joe than it was in celebrating his departure. On January 8, 1874, the *Eagle* expounded:

Wichita is fast getting rid of that element which has proved such a curse to her prosperity, thanks to the county attorney and the improved sentiment of the place which is backing him up. Rowdy Joe made a telling shot that night. It shot "Red" into eternity; himself out of the country; Anderson through the head; Beebe, Red's bar tender, into the penitentiary [for assisting Joe to escape]; Jo[sephin]e DeMerritt, Red's mistress, into the penitentiary; Rowdy Kate to parts unknown; and Smith, Ohmet and another into jail for perjury. "The mills of the gods grind slowly but they grind exceedingly small." Patten was sentenced for a year [no further reference to this individual has been found], Beebe for three years, and Josephine DeMerritt for ten years.

Local records disclose that Joe's dance hall changed hands several times; Joe registered the property on November 27, 1873, and paid $175 to West Wichita Town Company. He then sold the property on December 12, 1873, for $335 to W. W. Bailey and

Lewis Heath. Lowe signed his X, which was witnessed by S. M. Tucker and John Nugent on that date in the office of M. W. Levy, notary public. By February 1874 the partners had sold the property to M. R. Moser, who promptly tore it down and "moved it to his lots on Main Street and is rebuilding it. When completed it will be used as a wagon shop."[14] It is probable that Moser did not carry out his plan, for it was reported in July 1874 that "Carrie Beebe intends opening up Rowdy Joe's old dance house on the west side of the river. Let the movement be nipped in the bud. We want no more dance house troubles."[15]

Walter Beebe, thought by many to have taken Joe's place in the penitentiary, was released within a year when he was pardoned. The Kansas Supreme Court ruled that Lowe had not been in custody when Beebe assisted in his escape, for the county attorney had neglected to serve Lowe with a warrant concerning Anderson. Beebe returned to Wichita, where he was arrested a few days later for hog theft; the case was settled out of court and he joined his wife in West Wichita.[16]

The Beebes did not make much profit from the old dance hall; by 1875 it left much to be desired. The *Eagle* reported on August 12 that the current occupants had "concluded that there is more money and less wear and tear of shoes and nerves in agriculture and the old house which has been the scene of many a dark crime and many a startling denouement will now be hauled out to some rural retreat, where nature cheers with her smile and every element conspires to bliss." By November 11, the paper noted: "The old Rowdy Joe dance house is offered for sale cheap." The place was still standing, however, and in the Beebes' hands as late as September 1876, when, on the night of the twenty-fourth, Walter was killed there. The Wichita *Weekly Eagle* of September 28 tells the story:

Walter Beebe was shot and killed at his dancehouse over the river on Sunday evening by a Texas man. Some misunderstanding arose between them which compromised their dignity as chivalrous gentlemen, which had to be settled, so Mr. Texas man came over to the city, to get a pistol, returned and bravely marched up to a knothole in the side of the building, using it for a porthole and shot Beebe, killing him instantly. This same Beebe was sent from this county to the penitentiary about two years ago, but was released on some technicality in the proceedings, after having satid [sic] about one year. Surely the way of the transgressor is hard. How long are we to be cursed with these houses of ill fame and our city to be compelled to suffer such humiliation?

No other contemporary information concerning Beebe has come to light so far, but the Newton *Kansan* of October 5, 1876, said the "Texas man" was named Ward. It was claimed that Beebe slapped Ward, who vowed he would have his revenge. There was a bizarre postscript to the shooting on August 18, 1881, when the editor of the *Eagle* recalled that Billy the Kid had spent some of his boyhood in Wichita and added: "We are reminded, and we expect that it is true, that the shot that killed Walter Bebee [sic] in his saloon out on the west end of the bridge was fired by 'Billy the Kid.'"[17]

Walter Beebe's death was almost the last link with the Joe Lowe–Red Beard era. William Anderson, blinded by Lowe's carelessly aimed shot, gained nothing from his terrible loss. His ten-thousand-dollar lawsuit against Lowe came to court on May 25, 1874, by which time Joe was long gone. The court was told that Lowe had been summoned to appear but had disappeared. A jury was impaneled, and after listening to Anderson and his counsel and following instructions from the judge, it rendered its verdict: "We the jury in the above entitled cause do find for the plaintiff and assess his damages at ten thousand dollars." Curiously, that same month the police judge had fined the absent Joe Lowe two dollars and costs for an undisclosed misdemeanor beside which was written the cryptic comment "not paid."[18]

Safe in the knowledge that Joe Lowe was long gone, Mayor Hope, according to the *Eagle* of August 26, 1875, claimed that he had once "marched down to the river's edge and told Rowdy Joe and his crew to get away with his unfit enterprise or he would pitch it into the river."

Notes

1. Publication No. 23, Illinois State Historical Library, 1917.
2. Wichita *Weekly Eagle,* November 23, 1873; the reference to a son by the editor of the Winfield *Courier* was erroneous. Waldo E. Koop established that Red and his wife had three daughters: Clara, Inez, and Illian.

3. Undated clipping from *Wichita Eagle,* ca. 1931.
4. Records of the City of Wichita, Police Judge Returns, 1873; Wichita *Weekly Beacon,* July 30, 1873.
5. Elmer O. Parker, assistant director, Old Military Records Division, National Archives, Washington, D.C., to Joseph G. Rosa, December 18, 1969.
6. Case No. 91, Estate of E. T. Beard, Records of the Sedgwick County, Kansas, Probate Court.
7. State of Kansas vs. Joseph Lowe, preliminary statements taken before E. B. Jewett, J.P., November and December, 1873; State of Kansas vs. Joseph Lowe, Case No. 690, Indictment for Second Degree Murder, Sedgwick County District Court. On December 9, 1873, Joe Lowe appeared before the bar of the court and formally pleaded not guilty "of the charge contained in the information," and it was ordered by the court that he stand trial by jury the following day (State of Kansas vs. Joseph Lowe, No. 210, Journal B, 10, Sedgwick County District Court Records).
8. Stuart N. Lake, *Wyatt Earp, Frontier Marshal,* 102-3.
9. Wichita *Weekly Eagle,* November 11, 1873; Mrs. Deborah Beard, according to the *Eagle* of April 27, 1906, died at the home of her daughter, Mrs. Clara A. Garrett, the previous day. She was later buried beside her husband in the Highland Cemetery.
10. Kansas City *Times,* November 5, 1873; Wichita *Weekly Beacon,* November 5, 1873.
11. Wichita *Weekly Eagle,* December 14, 1876, and January 4 and 18, 1877.
12. Wichita *Eagle,* December 18, 1873.
13. Wichita *Weekly Eagle,* December 25, 1873.
14. Ibid., February 12, 1874; Deed Record Books, Office of the Registrar of Deeds, Sedgwick County, Kansas.
15. Wichita *Weekly Eagle,* July 30, 1874.
16. Wichita *Eagle,* December 17, 1874.
17. Waldo E. Koop, *Billy the Kid: The Trail of a Kansas Legend.* It was Mr. Koop who discovered that Henry McCarty had spent part of his boyhood at Wichita (1870-71) before his family moved to New Mexico.
18. Records of the Sedgwick County District Court, Case No. 693; Records of the Police Judge, No. 48, May, 1874.

6

Gone to Texas

Rowdy Joe's escape from Wichita made the headlines for weeks. From Osage Mission he set course for St. Louis, Missouri. There the antics of the Police Department gave cause for concern, for it was reported in Wichita that the chief of police and his detectives had not been on friendly terms for some time. Various reasons were given, "but the matter was kept very quiet, save for those whose daily duty brings them in contact with the police department." It was Joe Lowe who brought the matter to a head when attempts were made to arrest him.[1]

The story of Joe's arrest is best told by the St. Louis *Republican* of January 8, 1874. Its "graphic telegraphic" account is the most concise extant:

FACTS
THE CASE OF JOSEPH LOWE, ALIAS A. A. BECKER. ALIAS ROWDY JOE
The Action of the Chief of Police in Full
On the evening of the 2nd of January, 1874, at 8:35 o'clock, the following message was received and opened by Patrolman Donnelley, viz:
LEAVENWORTH, Kansas, January 2, 8:20 P.M.
Arrest and hold A. A. Becker, for breaking jail; about five feet, ten inches tall, thirty years old, square shoulders, heavy built, very full face; black moustache, eyes, and hair; fresh scar across back of neck. He is to meet Kate Lowe tomorrow morning on arrival of one of the trains from Kansas City. Kate left here at 3 p.m. Kate is slender built, light brown hair, waterproof suit lined with red; has with her one large bulldog in expresscar; also one small yellow lap slut. She will probably arrive by Missouri Pacific. A. A. Becker is an assumed name. Is stopping at the Laclede House, corner of fifth. Answer at Fort Scott.
(Signed) C. H. Hallett,
Deputy U.S. Marshal

Detectives Harrigan and Duckworth arrested Lowe on the 3rd Inst., between 1 and 2 o'clock p.m. and found on him $8,295 currency. The following telegram was immediately sent viz:

St. Louis, January 3, 1874.
To C. H. Hallett, Deputy U.S. Marshal, Fort Scott, Kan.
Joseph Lowe, alias A. A. Becker, is in custody. What is to be done?

(Signed) James McDonough
Chief of Police

After an elapse of 26 hours and no reply from Hallett, the following messages were sent, viz:

St. Louis, January 4, 1874
To C. H. Hallett, Deputy U.S. Marshal, Fort Scott, Kan.
Joseph Lowe, alias A. A. Becker is in custody. Answer quick what you wish done.

(Signed) James McDonough
Chief of Police

(The same message was sent to Hallett at Leavenworth, Kansas.)
After waiting 2 1/2 hours to hear from Hallett on the last two enquiring messages, a new party comes to the front with the following message, viz:

Leavenworth, Kansas
January 4, 1874, 8:14 p.m.
To Chief of Police, St. Louis:
Have you arrested Joseph Lowe, alias A. A. Becker? Answer immediately.

(Signed) W. Smith, Sheriff
Leavenworth, Kansas

The following reply was forwarded:

St. Louis, January 5, 1874.
To William Smith, Sheriff, Leavenworth, Kansas.
Joseph Lowe, alias A. A. Becker is arrested; what is to be done with him? Answer.

(Signed) James McDonough
Chief of Police

Having distinctly informed Sheriff Smith by the last telegram that Lowe was in custody; a delay of several hours occurred, when the following dispatch was sent:

Leavenworth, Kansas, January 5, 1874.
9:48 A.M.
To the Chief of Police of St. Louis:
Is Lowe still in your custody? Answer quick. If so, will be down next on train.

(Signed) W. Smith, Sheriff

The intervention of Deputy U.S. Marshal C. H. Hallett probably was prompted by the fact that it was a function of the U.S. marshal to deliver court processes and show a return that they had been served. Hallett must have been alerted when Rowdy Joe crossed the Kansas line, thereby providing an opportunity for federal involvement.

While Sheriff Smith was in a dither at Leavenworth, Joe was arrested at the Laclede Hotel by "Detective Duckworth, one of the shrewdest men on the force," who had had him under surveillance for some time. "Duck," as he was known to his colleagues, was aware of Joe Lowe's reputation and suspected that Joe's appearance in the city was not for the public good, so the arrival of Hallett's original telegram prompted swift action. The Wichita *Eagle* of January 15, citing the St. Louis *Democrat,* now takes up the story:

> When Lowe was arrested, the snug sum of $8,295.00 was found on him. He passed under the assumed name of A. A. Becker and was having a good time with the boys. Yesterday morning [January 4?], Mr. R. S. McDonald and Kate Lowe, the prisoner's wife, called on Chief McDonough and had a conference, which resulted in the Chief sending a note to Mr. A. W. Mead, the attorney for the board, asking whether the money found in Lowe's possession could be turned over to his wife. Mr. Mead answered that if he was not arrested on a charge which involved the money, such as larceny it could be turned over on an order from Lowe. The next step was to secure Lowe's release before the arrival of the Sheriff, and McDonald proceeded at once to the Court of Criminal Correction and took advantage of the "great writ of habeas corpus."
>
> In the petition it was claimed "that Lowe is now unlawfully and illegally restrained of his liberty by one Capt. James McDonough, Chief of Police, that no warrant or criminal process had been issued against him, that he was not guilty of the violation of any law of the state, that he was arrested by order of said McDonough illegally, and was in the custody and control of said McDonough, and is held by said McDonough in confinement against his will and consent, that there are no papers or process against him and that his imprisonment is unlawful and unjust."
>
> Judge Colvin ordered the writ issued and it was immediately delivered to the Chief who made the following note thereon: Executed the within writ by delivering the within mentioned Joseph Lowe to the St.

Louis Court of Criminal Correction this 5th day of Jan. 1874. James McDonough, Chief of Police.

Lowe was then taken before Judge Colvin by Detectives Duckworth and Tracy. The Judge asked Duckworth if that was all the return there was to be made and was answered that there were some telegrams. The Chief, however, was willing to have the man released, but the detective wanted him held until the Sheriff arrived. Judge Colvin said he could recognize only the Chief and asked Duckworth to go and ascertain if that was all the return to be made. Duckworth soon returned with a note to the Judge, saying that the only authority he had for holding the man was the above telegrams which he forwarded to the Judge for his enlightenment. Judge Colvin was in a quandary after reading them, and in a very hasty manner told the detective that he might have kept the writ back 24 hours if he wanted to and knew the sheriff was coming after his prisoner. "Duck" replied that he did not answer the writ. Mr. McDonald moved that the prisoner be discharged, which was accordingly done, and Lowe with several friends, rapidly disappeared from the court, entered a carriage and drove swiftly away.

There were many comments on the case made and several parties were so rash as to hint that someone in authority received a portion of the small change that Mrs. Lowe received – a most preposterous idea? Lowe is said to have escaped from jail, where he was confined on a charge of murder.[2]

Chief McDonough's actions were influenced not by greed but by official procedure. Indeed, the *Republican* of January 6, 1874, went so far as to reproduce the chief's note to A. W. Mead requesting his permission to turn the money over to whomsoever Lowe dictated and Mead's confirmation that if there were no charges involving the money, there was no reason to hold it. Joe in turn requested that the chief hand the money to M. Goldsoll; he and R. S. McDonald then witnessed the transaction. To strengthen his case, Chief McDonough had put before the court the facts as he knew them, concluding with the following:

The above is the true and full history of the transactions in the case of Lowe. My action in the premises was based upon an exact precedent which I will now recite:

Judge Stewart, when occupying the position which Judge Colvin now holds, sent the marshal with a FORTHWITH writ on me to bring before him Tom Allen, whom I had under arrest. I declined to respond, and was arrested by the marshal and brought before the court for contempt. I pleaded that I had 24 hours to make the return. The judge informed me that such was not the case, that under this writ I was bound to answer IMMEDIATELY, and gave me a very severe reprimand. The writ for Lowe has the word FORTHWITH written (not printed) in the body. I felt certain that I was bound to obey the writ, and did so. I felt equally certain that Lowe would be remanded on the evidence of the dispatches which were placed in the hands of Judge Colvin. The court, however, seemed not to place much importance on the dispatches and discharged the prisoner. I felt that all through the case I was acting properly, and have since seen no reason to change my opinion.

Former Sheriff Smith (he had lost the November election to Pleasant H. Massey, and the Lowe episode was his last official act) returned to Wichita from Leavenworth an embittered man. He recounted his telegraphic efforts to have Joe detained but canceled his trip once he learned of the writ of habeas corpus. His conclusion was that "somebody in St. Louis was bought up."[3]

Joe and Kate probably left St. Louis together but separated later. For reasons still undisclosed, he returned briefly to Ellsworth, where he stayed three times at the Grand Central Hotel. On June 28 and October 29, 1874, he registered as being from Cheyenne, and on July 5 he gave his previous address as Omaha. All entries were in the hand of the hotel clerk, and his brief appearance in the city went unrecorded by the press.[4] By September, however, both he and Kate were in Texas.

Writing from Marshall, Texas, on October 1, 1874, a correspondent for the Wichita *Beacon* who had left Wichita a few weeks before to avail himself of a pleasant train trip via the Missouri, Kansas and Texas line from Emporia, Kansas, to Denison, Texas, remarked: "Denison is purely a frontier town and one need only to walk up one street to be convinced of the fact. . . . Farmers coming in with cotton, and the usual number of loafers and gamblers standing on the corner, among whom might be seen 'Rowdy Joe' of West Wichita fame."[5]

Denison was founded in 1872 and was named after George Denison, vice-president of the Katy. The town company was organized on September 20 and lots went on sale the twenty-third. On Christmas Day, the Katy ran its first train through Denison.

The one hundred passengers included a number of "distinguished guests," among them Satanta and Big Tree, powerful Kiowa war chiefs en route to prison at Huntsville. The presence of the Indians, although they were in chains and posed no no danger to their fellow passengers, caused some concern, for Satanta often boasted that he had killed more white men than any other Indian.

Denison was laid out on northern lines — a broad main street dominated by the railroad — whereas most of its southern neighbors were built around a central plaza. Main Street was eighty feet wide and ran east and west, the remaining streets conforming to the points of the compass.

Within a year of its founding, Denison was a typical frontier boomtown. The town company, anxious that gambling, prostitution, and all other forms of dissipation be kept away from Main Street, confined them to the next block on Skiddy. The illusion thus created was one of peace and tranquility — provided one stayed on Main Street — but elsewhere the tough establishments and their equally hard-boiled inhabitants soon earned Denison a reputation as one of the toughest towns on the border.

Naturally, the saloon business, gambling, and prostitution boomed. By early April 1874 it was reported that "five saloons have been opened this week, the San Francisco on Skiddy street, the Grotto, just opposite, the Gold Room on Main street, and the Beehive. The latter name however has given place to the more fashionable title of Long Branch." Soon afterward it was noted that "the Sazerac and Grotto, two popular institutions on Skiddy street, have consolidated."[6]

Once the entertainment business was in full swing, the town council set about imposing the taxes authorized by Denison's charter. The previously mentioned Skiddy Street (named after the fastidious Francis Skiddy, a Katy director and president of the Land Grant Railway Trust Company; it is now Chestnut Street) had a wicked reputation in the early days. It consisted of a collection of tents, shacks, and cotton-cloth and board houses frequented by a motley crew of railroad workers, cutthroat gamblers, pimps, prostitutes, and bawdyhouse operators who ranked with anything that Abilene, Wichita or Dodge City could come up with. It was on Skiddy Street that Rowdy Joe finally surfaced after his disappearance from Missouri.⁷

Joe Lowe is remembered in Denison as a man who loved to brawl – a characteristic noted by others. To Joe, a gun was the ultimate deterrent, whereas, it was recalled, if he could get to grips with his fists he was much happier. He was noted for a tendency to beat troublemakers with his sledgehammer fists and, if he could, land a disabling kick to the lower extremities. It is reported that on one occasion at the Crystal Palace he got into difficulty with some sporting types. The sheriff intervened, drawing his Colt navy pistol and leveling it at Joe. Rowdy Joe promptly showed the palms of his hands, spat on them, rubbed them together, raised his hands shoulder high, and kicked the gun out of the sheriff's hand. But as his boot struck the pistol, the sheriff jerked the trigger and a bystander, Billy Campbell, was shot through the neck. Rowdy Joe's reputation as a "bad man to fool with" was now established in Texas.⁸

The Wichita press had barely announced Rowdy Joe's whereabouts in Texas when it reported his death in the Black Hills of Dakota Territory. Under the banner headline ROWDY JOE MURDERED it declared:

Mayor Hope received a letter from J. W. Brockett, now of Yankton, containing the information that Rowdy Joe, alias Joseph Lowe, so well known at Wichita, was with the party which was en route for the Black Hills and which was attacked by Indians and a portion of its number killed. The notorious Rowdy Joe fell first, mortally wounded. We last week published an account of the attack, but the dispatches had his name John Lowe instead of Joe. Thus this violent man met a violent death. Several of his victims are taking their last long sleep beneath the prairie sod of this border. Anderson, another is here in Wichita, totally blind: Walter Beebe, who helped Lowe to escape the officers of the law at this place, is in the penitentiary, and Josephine DeMerritt keeps Beebe company. What a list of crimes Joe has gone to answer for.⁹

As it turned out, the Black Hills papers had the story right the first time: it was one John W. Lowe who was killed. We suspect that confusion arose from the fact that there was a J. W. Lowe in Wichita in the early days. According to the report of the police judge for October 1872, one J. W. Lowe paid a fine of four dollars, plus two dollars' costs, for an unspecified charge. The misidentification of Joe for John was J. W. Brockett's fault. He was a former hardware dealer who had gone to the Black Hills, and he claimed to have identified the body. We are left with the thought, was this wishful thinking on somebody's part?

Many years after he moved to Denison in 1874, Major A. B. Ostrander recalled that he had remained there until 1879. Ostrander was the former telegraph superintendent of the St. Louis, Lawrence and Western Railroad, a short-line outfit running from Pleasant Hill, Missouri, via Lawrence, Kansas, to Carbondale, Kansas, where it connected with the Santa Fe. When the line went into liquidation, Ostrander was out of a job and applied for a position with Western Union. The St. Louis office promptly sent him to Denison to take over the night job. Ostrander had spent time in Wichita during the summer of 1873, and one of the sights he had taken in was Delano. He recalled a shootout between two dance-hall proprietors and one had taken over the other's business, including "his woman," and now the place was "run by 'Red Joe & Rowdy Kate.'" Despite this slightly garbled version of events at Delano, the major did provide an interesting sighting of Joe and Kate, even though he was confused by names. At Denison's Sazerac he received a surprise:

As I stepped up to the bar, at its end stood a man immaculately dressed, with a big diamond blazing on his shirt front, smoking a cigar. His face looked familiar, but I couldn't place him. Over in a corner was a faro game going on. Walking over there, I saw the dealer; a woman in full evening dress and blazing with diamonds. The minute I saw her face I recognized Red Joe and Rowdy Kate, formerly of Wichita. Never heard what become of either of them afterward.[10]

Joe and Kate tired of Denison by December 1874 and focused their attention on yet another railroad boomtown: Luling. Founded in July of that year, Luling was the terminus of the Houston, Harrisburg and San Antonio. According to one report, it "is the newest and probably the fastest town at present in the state. The Exchange says there are twenty legitimate business houses in the place and forty saloons. Times are lively there and the trade in cotton, wool, and hides and cattle is brisk."[11]

Luling also attracted an unlikely visitor. Within months after it was established the House of Bishops instructed its recently appointed bishop for the Diocese of Western Texas, thirty-four-year-old Robert Elliott, to visit his new parish. Late in December he found himself at Luling when his journey to Seguin was halted because the San Marcos River had flooded and his train could proceed no further. The new bishop decided that his overnight stop should be productive, so, with the help of the train's conductor, who gave him permission to hold a service in one of the passenger coaches, and the cooperation of Luling's livery-stable owner, who spread the word, a service was arranged for that evening. Bishop Elliott reported to his superiors:

There is no church building of any description . . . though it has a population say of about eight hundred to a thousand. As it is a good specimen of towns of this sort . . . you discover people from all parts of the United States and from nearly all the leading races of the world. Nor are the good and bad thrown together casually as in older communities, but the contact is close and almost imperative. Those who struggle in the midst of such hastily gathered populations are compelled to live in dangerous and daily proximity to temptations, which elsewhere are not so incessantly and shamelessly advertised.

The evening service was well attended and included a good cross section of the population. As the congregation bowed its collective head in prayer to the Almighty, an "abomination calling itself the 'Celebrated French Can-Can,' was in noisy operation at the 'Headquarters Saloon,' within a stone's throw of our chapel on wheels. I think it was a good omen that my first Service was in a railway car. There is an earnestness of progress in which God grant may be fulfilled." The bishop set off the next morning on horseback for Seguin.[12]

Rowdy Joe and others (among them an individual recalled simply as "Monte Joe") were soon rubbing shoulders with some of Texas's most notorious figures. Conversation tended to dwell on the latest killings in the ongoing Taylor-Sutton feud or the exploits of noted gunfighters. It is also reported that John Wesley Hardin spent some of his time hurrahing the place when the mood possessed him. Indeed, lawlessness became so rife that the following petition was sent to the state legislature in January 1875:

> Bad men, by their vicious acts are daily and hourly rendering unsafe the lives and property of peaceable citizens. The continual rattle of firearms upon our streets every night reminds us of a real war. We are without officers and are powerless to protect ourselves except by main force . . . the present Mayor of this city is in the Caldwell County jail, and there is no presiding officer before whom offenders may be brought and punished. We beg that you will declare the office vacant and put us in a condition to elect some one else to fill the position.[13]

The mayor's difficulty followed a dispute between himself and the Board of Aldermen which led to his incarceration and later his release early in 1875. In defense of the place, however, a visitor had this to say regarding Luling's morals and its prospects:

> Seeing a disposition on the part of some of the self-righteous of the land to berate Luling, and to cry aloud and to spare not, about the vice and immorality of the city, I thought I would speak a word in its behalf to those who would back up Luling. . . . I do not mean to exculpate Luling from all fault or guilt. To say that there are no cess-pools of iniquity here, would be to utter an untruth; but, on the other hand, to say that it is a modern Sodom and that there are no good people in it, would be to utter an untruth. It is true, Luling, like all railroad towns of any size or note, has many gambling dens.

Recalling the fate of the mayor, the visitor continued:

> During his absence, bad men who cluster around the terminus of the railroads, taking advantage of the powerless condition of the municipal authorities of this place, have by their unlawful acts injured it. They have discharged firearms in the streets and into houses at late hours of the night. There being no Mayor before whom to bring offenders, the policemen were powerless. The citizens, however, have taken the matter in hand now, and we hope for law and order in the future. The Legislature, also, has passed a general bill which will in future relieve us of any trouble.[14]

The records of the district court of Caldwell County reveal that Joe Lowe was one of those people whom city authorities were anxious to put out of business. On January 9, 1875, Joe was charged with permitting a gaming bank to be exhibited in a house under his control, and on the eleventh a similar charge was brought for "permitting Joel Collins to exhibit a certain gaming bank in a house under his control." Through his attorney Joe pleaded guilty on January 15 and waived his right to trial by jury. The court then assessed his punishment at a fine of ten dollars plus costs. Joel Collins, a noted gambler and petty criminal, was fined twenty-five dollars. Evidently, there was some fear that Rowdy Joe might not pay his fine and it was ordered that he be placed in the custody of the sheriff until it was paid.[15]

A fictionalized biography of Ben Thompson makes the claim that Ben and his brother Billy cleaned Joe out on a visit to Luling, where Joe ran what is described as "the toughest dancehall in America." The chronology is poor because it infers that Joe appeared in Luling on a "fast trip" along with "all the sporting world" before moving on to Newton and Wichita, when in fact Newton and Wichita were behind Joe by the time he reached Luling.[16]

Another romantic but perhaps factually based reference to Joe Lowe at Luling comes from Colonel Lewis Ginger, a circus owner who claimed to have hired Wild Bill Hickok for a brief appearance with his troupe at Sherman in 1870. Of his sojourn in Texas, Ginger wrote:

> I became acquainted with numbers of men who were well known to the people of Texas in those early days. Among them was one who stands out in my memory of those days as a typical Westerner. Joe Lowe, "Rowdy Joe," as he was known, though why he should have received the cognomen, I never knew, for he was a quiet, very peaceable individual, but one of those who had the reputation of being quick on the draw. And that was a very useful accomplishment in those days of long ago.
>
> I first met Joe at Luling when that place was the terminal of the Galveston, Houston and San Antonio Railway. When those terminal towns sprang up over night, Joe Lowe was the pioneer to establish the first dancehall and saloon. Luling was one of the "bad" towns. In a short time it became built up with saloons, dance houses, gambling halls, hotels and livery stables. A stage line ran from Luling to San Antonio, a six horse Concord coach. Joe's large dance hall was south of the railway, which ran through the center of the town. It was presided over by Joe and his wife, Kate, known as "Rowdy Kate" a fine limbed powerful

woman, who was the only one who could handle the cowboys when they got too much of the cordials served over Joe's bar.

When one or more got too loud and were flourishing their six-shooters, Kate would try to pacify them, and if she did not succeed she threw them bodily out through the front door, and they did not come back again. I got real friendly with both Joe and Kate and liked them very much.

Colonel Ginger then related how, during a stagecoach trip, a huge rattlesnake spooked the lead horses and Joe got out and shot its head off. The reptile was said to be eight feet long "and as large around the body as the leg of a good sized man. The rattlers were twenty in number and about five inches long and as thick as my two fingers."[17]

Joe's activities continued to interest the authorities and on September 9, 1875, he was charged with "permitting a game with cards to be played in a house under his control." An examination of the available records reveals that the case was adjourned until February 8, 1876, when Joel Collins and H. W. Bennett stood bail for Joe for two hundred dollars. When the case came to trial on April 2, Joe and his two bondsmen failed to appear. On April 15 there was still no sign of the trio, so the court ordered that the two securities appear at the next term of court to explain their nonappearance, and a warrant was issued for Joe Lowe's arrest. Joel Collins's disappearance can be explained by the fact that he had become mixed up with Sam Bass and joined Bass on a cattle-driving enterprise to the Black Hills. There, for a brief period, the pair ran a freight outfit. Later, on September 18, 1877, Bass, Collins, and others held up a train at Big Springs, Nebraska, and got away with more than sixty thousand dollars. They split the money and separated. A week later, Collins and another of the robbers, Bill Heffridge, were gunned down and twenty-five thousand dollars was recovered. Bass was killed in a shootout with Texas Rangers at Round Rock on July 21, 1878.[18]

San Antonio, scene of some of the state's most turbulent history, was Joe Lowe's next stop. In 1718 a settlement was started there as a way station between northern Mexico and Los Adaes (near present-day Robeline, Louisiana), which was then capital of the province. San Antonio became the provincial capital in 1773. Following Mexican independence from Spain in 1821, San Antonio became the official residence of the lieutenant governor for the combined state of Coahuila y Texas. Consequently, when the white Texans (or "Texians," as some preferred to call themselves) revolted against the Mexicans in 1835, San Antonio became a focal point. It was captured from the Mexicans, who attempted to regain it early in 1836. This led to the heroic stand of native white Texans and outsiders, notably Davy Crockett and James Bowie (of knife fame), who both perished at Mission San Antonio de Valero (immortalized and revered as the Alamo) when the place was besieged by Mexican dictator Antonio López de Santa Anna, who was himself defeated shortly afterward by General Sam Houston.[19]

By the mid-1870s, San Antonio, long a military center (Fort Sam Houston was established there in 1879), had enjoyed a long association with the cattle trade. Since the 1830s cattle had been shipped from there to points east and west or had passed through San Antonio on the Chisholm Trail headed for Kansas and other states. Despite its growth, however, the place retained its frontier image, for it was a place where Texas herds gathered before the long drive north over the Chisholm and other cattle trails. San Antonio's entertainment facilities attracted cattlemen and cowboys alike; they quickly found "diversion in the many saloons and gambling halls."[20]

Discovery of the Luling court cases involving Joe Lowe and Joel Collins suggests that Joe divided his time between Luling and San Antonio, for it is reported that in March 1875 he, Kate, and other former Wichitans had settled there. In May the editor of a Wichita paper clipped from the San Antonio *Daily Herald* an item which he thought might interest the "numerous friends of 'Rowdy Joe Lowe's'": "Mr. Joseph Lowe was found guilty of assaulting Kate Lowe yesterday afternoon and fined $100. A motion for a new trial was over-ruled, and notice of appeal given. The alleged cause for the offense was inconstancy."[21]

Joe's appearance in Texas prompted an enterprising individual to write to Kansas authorities and ask whether there was a reward for information on Joe's whereabouts. Writing from San

Antonio on April 16, 1875, to the Secretary of State, W. A. Crafts, who described himself as "Secret Detective Agt," asked:

Sir:
I am informed that one "Jo[e] Lowe" alias "Rowdy Jo[e]" is an outlaw from your State and that a reward has been offered for his apprehension by the Governor thereof.

If such is the fact, or if you have any information of a reward for his apprehension in your section of country please forward a requisition upon the Governor of this State, together with an accurate description of the man and an account of the crime committed and the reward offered.

There is no evidence of a reply, and it is unlikely that such a request would have merited one without some authoritative backing. Apart from the initial one hundred dollars offered for Joe's capture by Sheriff Bill Smith when Joe fled Wichita, we have found no evidence of any other rewards being offered for Joe's capture. But there was no shortage of bounty hunters and others eager to apprehend alleged evildoers for a reward.[22]

According to an account published in the 1930s, Joe and Kate ran a combined variety show cum saloon and gambling house on the north side of San Antonio's Main Plaza at the corner of Soledad Street. It was claimed that they formed a partnership with Joel Collins, which, in view of Joe's known association with Collins, may be true. The same writer alleges that Joe Lowe joined Collins in his career of banditry and was himself "killed by an officer in an attempt to arrest him." This, of course, is nonsense.[23]

By the time Joe's court appearance at Luling fell due, he had established himself at Fort Worth. The thriving community was born when the army established a military post in 1849 and named it after General William J. Worth. The fort was abandoned in 1853, but its name was retained by the settlement. Incorporated in 1873, Fort Worth enjoyed a booming economy, thanks to the cattle trade. The city was on the Chisholm Trail and was blessed with a lively business supplying cattlemen with provisions for the long drive north. On July 19, 1876, the tracks of the Texas and Pacific arrived, and with the railroad came stock pens (in anticipation of an increasing share of the cattle business) and more people, many of them farmers who considered wheat as important as cattle. The place also attracted the saloon set in large numbers.[24]

Joe and Kate had hardly settled in Fort Worth when their long-running partnership finally came to an end. By August, Kate had her own place, as is attested by this September report:

> An "infernal cuss" who does not deserve the name of a man, but who, we hear, bears the human form, cut up a nymph du pave at Rowdy Kate's dancehouse night before last [September 27]. He was pursued by the officers of the law, but his legs which proved longer than the sidetrack of the Texas and Pacific landed him in Dallas at one p.m. He's home now.[25]

The ending of Joe's and Kate's relationship may well have been prompted by his announcement that he was about to get married. Little is known about the lady in question, Mary or Mollie Field, but a search of the marriage records of Tarrant County, Texas, for the period 1876–85 has revealed that on July 31, 1876, a license was issued to J. T. Lowe and Mollie Field and that the couple were married by C. W. Berry on August 2, 1876. At first glance, the second initial would seem to preclude the groom's being Rowdy Joe Lowe; however, Joe's father's name was Thomas, so it is possible that Joe's full name was Joseph Thomas Lowe. No matter, for by the late 1880s the marriage had ended. In 1899, Mary (or Mollie) was living at 1320 1/2 Lorimer Street in Denver, "just across the bridge from the city jail." She informed the press:

> I was married to Joe Lowe in Fort Worth, Tex., in 1877. He was running a variety theater there. In 1879 we removed to Leadville, where he conducted the Central theater and afterwards the Woods opera house. . . . No, I am not his first wife, there were five before me. His first wife he married in Ellsworth, Kan. She was known as "Rowdy Kate" and he was "Rowdy Joe." I knew one other of his wives, Frankie Almond, but she only lived with him about six months. . . . We did not have any children. The divorce was obtained by Mr. Lowe."[26]

Mary's recollections concerning date and events were a little hazy. It was she and not Joe who filed for divorce. In her 1887

This photograph of Rowdy Joe Lowe has been reproduced many times, and only one unretouched version has come to light. It appeared in an unnamed Texas newspaper about fifteen years ago and was among a number of early photographs that had recently come to light. The version published in the paper was three-quarter length and depicted Joe sporting a watch chain. The original plate is believed to have been made in Fort Worth in 1876 or 1877. Courtesy Joseph G. Rosa Collection.

petition she stated that the couple had been married at Fort Worth on February 1, 1879, and that they had cohabited as husband and wife in the state of Colorado since April 11, 1879.[27]

Rowdy Kate, meantime, had moved on from Fort Worth, but her movements from then on are rarely documented. On May 18, 1877, the Jacksboro *Frontier Echo* noted that the Weatherford *Exponent* "is in a towering rage because Kate Lowe, alias Rowdy Kate, conducts a den of infamy within the business portion of the 'most moral town in northwest Texas.'" A search of court records has revealed that in March 1877 Kate was charged with keeping an immoral house, a resort for "the purpose of public prostitution, and as a common resort for prostitutes and vagabonds." Charged on March 30 with committing the offense on the twenty-fourth, Kate was acquitted; but on April 20 she was charged with a similar offense and fined. Through her attorneys, Watts, Lanham & Roach and Hood & McCall, she took her case to the Court of Appeal at Austin. The appellate court considered the possibility that Kate might well have kept "an orderly, peaceable, and quiet house during the month of March, and yet in the month of April may have opened it up and kept it for the purposes of public prostitution, and by the 20th of this latter month it might have become a common resort for prostitutes and vagabonds." Alleged errors in procedure were considered, but it was ruled that the "evidence abundantly supports the verdict and the judgement rendered, and the judgement is, therefore, affirmed."[28]

In September 1880, Kate was again charged with keeping a disorderly house and employed the same attorneys to defend her. The case was reported in the Weatherford *Exponent* on September 21:

County Court.

This court met last Monday for criminal business, and adjourned on Thursday. The State vs. Kate Lowe for "keeping a disorderly house" was the principal case tried. The county attorney had unguardedly given the lady the alias of "Rowdy Kate," in the Indictment, which seemed very offensive to her. On this trial, which consumed a whole day, defendant being ably and ingeniously defended by Mr. [S. W. T.] Lanham, convinced the jury that her "virtue like Ceasar's [sic] wife was not to be questioned," or at least assailed by the county attorney; the result of which was a verdict of acquittal by the jury and the "fair but frail" defendant left the court room with "flying colors," apparently much to the chagrin and disappointment of the county attorney. Then the rumor became prevalent on the streets that Kate Lowe had engaged able counsel and intended, with the verdict and judgement of acquittal in her hands, to bring an action against the county attorney and his principal witness for damages in the sum of ten thousand dollars for malicious prosecution. But lo! and behold! before this resolution could be put into execution, the county attorney evidently fearing that there might be some truth as well as legal pith and substance in the rumor, on the next day, again draws a fresh indictment against the "fair and frail" creature, issues his capias, and again places her "in durance vile." In vain did her ingenious counsel, though reinforced by another Richmond in the person of Mr. McCall, argue a former acquittal to the judge and jury in bar of this prosecution. They insisted this was persecution instead of prosecution, but, unfortunately for Riotous Katherine neither judge nor jury seemed to so regard it. In vain too did the county attorney like Shylock of old demand before the jury the full penalty of the law's bond. The jury evidently hesitated long as to their verdict, but finally came into court with a verdict of guilty with the lowest possible penalty attached, thereby showing their belief that if the "fair but frail" one was guilty, she lacked a great deal of being guilty to the full or even half the extent of the law. But the defendant not being satisfied with what may seem to be a compromise verdict, has, we learn, through her counsel taken the necessary steps to appeal her case to the Court of Appeal at Austin, in order that perfect and absolute justice may be done between her and the State of Texas and county attorney. *Fiat Justitia.*

― ― ―

Squelch It.

In County court this week, Kate Lowe, familiarly known as "Rowdy Kate" was on trial in two separate cases, charged with keeping a house of ill-fame. The shrewdness of her attorney procured for her an acquittal of the first charge, but in the second, she was convicted and mulcted in the sum of $100 and costs. An appeal was taken we believe to the higher courts as is usually done in such cases, and generally with no other motive than that of gaining time in which to pursue their nefarious and immoral traffic. We presume there is not an individual in this city who will deny that the general character and reputation of Kate's establishment is a bad one, and that the keeping of such a house is, to say the least, unlawful. Still it is allowed to stand in the very heart of town, in defiance of law, and a reproach to public decency. It is a mystery to us how the people of Weatherford, a people who for culture and refinement, have not their superior in Texas — a moral and religious people — too have managed to tolerate this saturnalia of crime in their very midst, insulting law, order and decency with their midnight brawls and shouts of drunken revelry. This is a subject, with which we dislike to deal in public print, but nevertheless it is a desperate evil, and requires a desperate remedy.

People cry out that it is a necessary evil which must be tolerated, and we admit, to a certain extent that its complete suppression might prove detrimental to the public morals. But there is no reason why this hydra should be allowed to rear its head in the most public portion of town, to insult morality and the broad light of day with its disgraceful scenes. If it must exist, let it be removed out of the way, where its riots and debaucheries will not disturb quiet people.

Whether Kate carried out her threat to take her case to the appeal court is uncertain, but in view of her previous experience there, we doubt it. Evidently, she remained in Texas at least until the late 1880s (and perhaps longer), so she could not have been the "Rowdy Kate" recalled by Billy King of Tombstone, Arizona, who claimed that she and Joe Lowe had appeared there briefly in 1878 or 1879. Neither is it likely that she was the lady who is reported to have run a dance hall in Dodge City (an unsourced reference suggests that it was in fact the Green Room).[29]

In 1886, Kate was at Big Spring, where John McManus, a brakeman employed by the Texas and Pacific, raised a ruckus in her place and was shot twice for his trouble, once in the head and once in the arm.[30]

Josiah Wright Mooar, former buffalo hunter and noted early-day immigrant in Texas, where he became a successful rancher, said in his later years that he had known Rowdy Kate. On one occasion, he said, he was a member of a jury that refused to convict her on a charge of vagrancy because she showed consideration for others. At Fort Griffin she reportedly befriended a young girl and persuaded her to give up the dance-hall life for that of a schoolteacher. According to Mooar, Rowdy Kate "died in [San] Angelo, and it turned out she was a pretty well off woman and she also turned out to be a real church worker." That statement is not only romantic, it is unsubstantiated.[31]

After his marriage to Mollie Field, Joe went into the hotel business, at least temporarily, for by October 1876 it was announced that the "Centennial Hotel is undergoing a thorough change and will be opened next week by Mr. Joe Lowe, as a theater. The house is eighty feet deep, with a stage 22 1/2 by 18 feet. Harry DeVere has gone to St. Louis to engage a first class company." On the twenty-second it was reported that the theater had been playing to good houses since its opening. Encouraged by their success, its proprietors announced that they would add a new feature within a week: "two female negro delineators, which will certainly attract. The Centennial folks possess one good trait, they all read the *Democrat*."[32]

The Centennial Theater did attract a varied clientele. Joe's partner, Harry Devere, in his capacity as general booking agent, went out of his way to secure good acts, among them Fay Templeton and her troupe, and in November it was announced that "a legitimate play" would be produced which was expected to continue for some time.[33]

Behind Joe Lowe's apparent interest in culture there lurked another and (for him) much more pressing reason for calling his establishment a theater: there was a crackdown on the saloon business in November. Vice and lawlessness long had gone hand in hand, and by 1876 the populace feared that violence would get out of hand. Prostitution and gambling were rife, and at night thugs stalked the streets, preying upon citizens brave or foolish enough to venture away from the bright lights of the plaza. And behind the scenes was villainy. Ruthless and unscrupulous politicians and others viewed city government, which had become complacent, as a path to personal wealth. The result was a political tug-of-war. An ordinance forbidding businesses and places of amusement to open on Sunday was passed in November 1876, but it was repealed less than a month later. Similarly, a motion was placed before the city council on November 14 forbidding the sale of intoxicants in any place where shows were held. This was tabled with the motion that it would be enacted "unless Joe Lowe, owner of the Centennial Theater, started paying his taxes regularly."[34]

Some indication of the problems faced or posed by the city council is explained by this story from the Fort Worth *Daily Democrat* of November 25, 1876:

> DANCEHOUSES TO BE SUPPRESSED
>
> The proprietors of the dancehouses on Main Street, three in number, were before the mayor yesterday evening and found guilty of violating the ordinance in such cases made and provided and each contributed $10 and costs to the city treasury. The Marshal informs us that they shall not be reopened after Saturday night under any circumstances, and that hereafter he intends to visit the penalties of the law on the violators.

The council then levied property taxes, but these were subsequently declared illegal and the council was forced to refund the money. The violence continued, however.

The marshal of Fort Worth at that time was the celebrated Timothy Isaiah ("Longhaired Jim") Courtright, whose checkered career included service as a soldier, scout, lawman, mine guard, ranch foreman, and, according to some, racketeer. Courtright served as marshal of Fort Worth from 1876 until 1879, when he left the area. He later returned and set up the T.I.C. Commercial Agency, believed by some to be a front for his racketeering activities. On February 8, 1887, acting (so it was claimed) on behalf of businessmen who objected to their gambling rackets, Courtright confronted Jake Johnson and his partner Luke Short, owners of the White Elephant Saloon. It was claimed that Courtright wanted money and Johnson was prepared to pay, but Luke, who had a gunfighting reputation similar to that of Courtright, refused. Both men went for their pistols and Luke emerged the victor. Later it was discovered that Courtright's revolver had a broken cylinder bolt, which had jammed the cylinder. Luke was arrested but released on two thousand dollars' bond. The case never came to trial.[35]

Rowdy Joe's relationship with Courtright was friendly enough, but one of his erstwhile rivals fell out with the marshal in late December 1876. N. H. Wilson, former proprietor of the Senate Saloon, was shot in the left leg by Courtright when the latter accused him of carrying concealed weapons and demanded to search him. Wilson objected and backed into the street, followed by the marshal. Courtright drew his pistol; Wilson grabbed for it, at the same time drawing his own gun. Courtright promptly pulled the trigger and the ball hit Wilson in the leg four inches above the kneecap. A policeman named William Phares stepped in and disarmed the pair. It was later claimed that Courtright had been accompanied by another policeman named Tip and that they were both "under the influence." Wilson said Courtright attacked him because he had accused Courtright and the mayor, H. H. Day, of making collections for themselves from illegal establishments. A warrant was issued for Courtright and Tip.

Courtright claimed that he had been warned that Wilson was armed, although Wilson tried to deny it. It was further alleged that Wilson's pistol got caught in his coat pocket and that as Courtright tried to draw his pistol Wilson freed his own pistol and struck Courtright twice over the head, felling him. As Courtright rose, he fired at Wilson, and Tip caught hold of Wilson only after Courtright fired. Courtright was charged with assault to commit murder. The case was filed on March 20, 1877, but on August 19, 1878, it was disposed of with no further action.[36]

Rowdy Joe's Fort Worth exploits received little publicity until August 1878, when there was a killing in the Centennial Theater. Joe's bartender-manager, Billy Cregier, was shot by Al Houter, known locally as "Buffalo Bill" on account of his shoulder-length hair. First reports claimed that Houter and his partner, Henry Hester, had spent the evening at the theater and later joined some of the girls for dancing. It was when they walked up to the bar and ordered drinks for their female partners and then refused to pay for them that trouble started. When Cregier intervened, Houter drew his pistol and shot him three times. Houter and Hester promptly fled and a "vigilant search" was made to find them.

Billy Cregier's death shocked and angered many people, for he was generally liked. It was claimed that the murder had been premeditated and that the intended victim was not Cregier but Joe Lowe. This information came to light when an anonymous individual wrote the Fort Worth press claiming to have been present when Houter boasted that he had been laying for Joe Lowe for years because Joe had killed his brother in Kansas. But for the unwitting appearance of a former policeman as he stood in the doorway of the theater in the line of fire, Joe would have been killed ten days earlier. Joe's immediate reaction to that was to inform authorities that he wanted a "persuader" to protect himself and was advised that "the law permitted a man that privilege, provided it was for the protection of his own life and property."

Henry Hester was arrested and appeared in court on September 24, while the hunt continued for his partner. Witnesses testified that much of the aggression had come from Cregier himself and that Hester had been unarmed during the conflict. The consensus was that "Hester and Houter were both entirely justified in what they did, and that Cregier's blood is on his own head."

Following Hester's acquittal, Al Houter himself appeared, having surrendered, and said he had no quarrel with Joe Lowe. "As for a grudge with Joe Lowe in Kansas, I never saw Mr. Lowe in Kansas and have no ill feeling toward him," Al said. Asked why he was called Buffalo Bill, Houter said he had no idea. "I never knew before that I was called Buffalo Bill," he said. Houter said he had fled because, having killed a man amongst his friends, he feared witnesses might perjure themselves. Now, he said, he was confident of acquittal because the truth was known.

Joe Lowe must have breathed a long sigh of relief when he learned that he was not in danger from Houter, for Joe preferred to get a fight over and done with rather than creep about in the shadows to avoid assassination. Yet in spite of his preoccupation with potential extinction, Joe found time for a magnanimous gesture. On September 7 the Centennial staged a benefit night and Joe turned over the receipts, $51.40, to the cashier of City National Bank to be distributed to the poor as was thought fit.[37]

The *Democrat* reported on December 1 that "Joe Lowe wants to sell out the Centennial and go to Leadville, Colorado." This decision may well have been influenced by the following, which appeared in the same paper on the seventh:

The County Criminal court adjourned yesterday, following the disposition of the case of the State vs. Joe Lowe, charged with keeping a disorderly house, particulars of which will be found elsewhere.

THE LOWE CASE

THE REASON WHY HE "SLIPPED UP"

In the case of the State of Texas vs. Joe Lowe, which was tried in the County Court yesterday, the jury found a verdict of guilty and assessed a fine of $100. It was strenuously fought on both sides. The County Attorney deserved credit for the able manner in which he conducted the case, and Frank Ball, Esq., was in his best mood. The Judge, it was admitted on both sides, gave the defendant full latitude in his points, so that there was but one bill of exception by defendant as to admission of evidence and but one bill as to the charge. The result of the case is that the jury found the house to be a disorderly house within the meaning of the law. The charges of the court, on which the case hinged, were: First, that employees of the house, though they lived in the house, must be freed from the taint of bad reputation as to virtue. The defendant contending that they were not resorting there, but lived there, and hence the house could not come under the definition of a common resort for prostitutes. Second, for the defense, he ruled where parties under a bad reputation for virtue visited such places as the one in question, the Centennial Theater, that if they behaved themselves as decent people and committed no lewd acts, they were entitled to witness theatrical performances as other people. The County Attorney insisted that though they acted in every way decent, yet having a lewd reputation, they were under the denunciation of the statute.

In Old West parlance, the word *theater* seems to have had a number of meanings. As late as February 4, 1885, the El Paso *Lone Star* was calling theaters "leg operas." With Joe's departure in late December 1878 or early 1879, the Centennial changed hands several times — and also its name. A man named George Holland owned it sometime after Joe Lowe left, and in later years it was known as "My Theater," which seems a curious title for a place that in its time had witnessed so much of the good and bad sides of frontier life.[38]

When Joe Lowe and Mary finally said good-bye to Texas and set out for Colorado, they made one or two diversions because Joe wanted to meet old friends or settle some business. He left behind a reputation and, surprisingly, his nickname. From now on he wished to be known as Mr. Joe Lowe instead of Rowdy Joe Lowe.

Notes

1. Wichita *Eagle*, January 15, 1874.
2. Ibid.
3. Ibid., January 8, 1874.
4. Grand Central Hotel Register, microfilm copy, KSHS.
5. Wichita *Beacon*, October 14, 1874.
6. Denison *Daily News*, April 8 and 15, 1874.
7. Ibid., September 23, 1874.
8. V. V. Masterson, *The Katy Railroad and the Last Frontier*, 177, 185-87; V. V. Masterson to Waldo E. Koop, June 1, 1961.
9. Wichita *Eagle*, October 29, 1874.
10. Major A. B. Ostrander, "Old Days in Denison," *Frontier Times*, Vol. VII, No. 9 (June 1930), 399-401.
11. Denison *Daily News*, December 30, 1874.
12. "Letters from Bishop Elliott," published in *The Spirit of Missions*, Corpus Christi, Texas, January 26, 1875. These and other items relative to early-day Luling were supplied by F. W. Wilson, M.D., F.A.C.P., a lifelong resident of the city. His father established in the early days there an "Immigration House" where settlers could live until they could afford to buy land or homes of their own.
13. Secretary of State, Memorials and Petitions, File 19, No. 296, Letter C.
14. Galveston *Daily News*, March 9, 1875.
15. State of Texas vs. Joseph Lowe, Case Nos. 1250, 1276, and 1249; State of Texas vs. Joel Collins, Case No. 1266.
16. J. H. Plenn, *Texas Hellion: The True Story of Ben Thompson*, 102.
17. Marvin Hunter, Sr., "Reminiscences of Colonel Lewis Ginger," *Frontier Times*, Vol. XXX, No. 2 (April-June 1953), 224.
18. State of Texas vs. Joseph Lowe; Walter Prescott Webb, *A Century of Frontier Defense: The Texas Rangers*, 373.
19. Howard R. Lamar, ed., *The Reader's Encyclopedia of the American West*, 17-19; 1064-5.
20. Wayne Gard, *The Chisholm Trail*, 77-78.
21. Wichita *Beacon*, May 26, 1875.
22. Governor's Correspondence Files, "Crime and Criminals."
23. Frank H. Bushick, *Glamorous Days*, 110, 189, 247, 250.
24. Lamar, *The Reader's Encyclopedia*, 399.
25. Fort Worth *Daily Democrat*, September 29, 1876.
26. Denver *Rocky Mountain Daily News*, February 12, 1899.
27. Marriage Records (Vol. I, 1876-1885), 2, Tarrant County Court

Records, copy supplied by Mr. Jean D. Baker. We are also indebted to Charles and Doris Van Trees and Thomas Hughes, district clerk, Tarrant County, for additional information; Case No. 8621, Mary Lowe vs. Joseph Lowe, Petition for a Divorce, Denver District Court Records, copy supplied by Philip Panum. Ironically, on the day Joe Lowe was married, a fellow Illinoisan, Wild Bill Hickok, was assassinated by Jack McCall at Deadwood, Dakota Territory. McCall was later hanged.

28. Weatherford *Exponent,* May 12, 1877; Kate Lowe vs. State of Texas, 4, Ct. App. 34 (1878), 34–39, copy supplied by Richard Miller, attorney-at-law.

29. C. L. Sonnichsen, *Billy King's Tombstone,* 93–96; Stanley Vestal, *Dodge City: Queen of the Cowtowns,* 24–27.

30. Fort Worth *Gazette,* June 22, 1886.

31. San Angelo *Standard-Times,* August 23, 1964.

32. Fort Worth *Daily Democrat,* October 1 and 28, 1876.

33. Ibid., November 22 and December 26, 1876.

34. Oliver Knight, *Fort Worth, Outpost on the Trinity,* 112–14.

35. Ibid., 134–5.

36. State of Texas vs. James Courtright, Case No. 1476, Tarrant County Court, Criminal Case Index.

37. Fort Worth *Daily Democrat,* August 27 and 29; September 6, 10, 25 and 26; December 6, 1878.

38. Texas Writers' Project, *Fort Worth and Tarrant County,* 506.

7

Interlude at Leadville

Joe Lowe's move to Leadville certainly was not prompted by its location. Situated at 10,188 feet in the Colorado Rockies, the place later boasted that it was the "highest incorporated city in the United States." Its rarefied atmosphere was so thin, said an early visitor, "that you've got to fan it to a corner to get a square breath." Most people, however, were prepared to accept the environment for the simple reason that the place was said to be composed almost entirely of silver. It later became the silver capital of America.[1]

Silver was mined in the region as early as 1860, and by 1880 Leadville boasted a population of forty thousand. Several railroads competed to be first to run tracks into the place, but it was the Denver and Rio Grande that did so, in 1880. An estimated seven hundred million dollars' worth of gold, silver, and other minerals were produced in the span of a century, but the boom years were 1878 to 1881, when silver was the main product. Perhaps the most prominent of the many millionaires who populated the place in the early days was Horace Tabor, who had a controlling interest in most of the mines and other businesses. The town boomed, and by 1880 there were 5 banks, department stores, churches, even newspapers, schools, and, it was claimed, 1,200 saloons, 110 beer gardens, 118 gambling halls, and "35 seraglios."

Oscar Wilde is reported to have visited Leadville in 1879 and to have entertained the masses at the Tabor Opera House. In 1880, John B. Omohundro, the celebrated "Texas Jack," who had appeared for several years with Buffalo Bill Cody's theatrical

119

troupe before embarking on his own, arrived in the city. His health had bothered him for some time and he hoped the climate would help him; he also expressed interest in investing in the mines. Sadly, Jack was not to know that pneumonia, prevalent in the thin air and aggravated by the unsanitary conditions, could prove fatal. Late in May he developed a cold that swiftly turned to pneumonia; in spite of expert medical attention, he died on June 28. His funeral was one of the most spectacular events in Leadville's history. Led by a fifty-piece brass band, the Tabor Light Cavalry (part of the police force), and various dignitaries and friends of the deceased, Jack was interred in the new Evergreen Cemetery.[2]

Joe Lowe made his way to Leadville via Newton, Kansas, where it was reported in February 1879 that he had stopped off to visit "the boys" en route. City directories for the period reveal that Joe had several addresses in Leadville. He resided at 318 West Second Street for a time, then 219 West Third, and finally at 609 Pine Street. His occupation was listed as "miner."[3]

Among those who knew Joe at Leadville was W. W. Rupp, a former Wichita saloonkeeper who had known him for some years. When Rupp reached the place in March, he found Joe and other old friends, who, he recalled, "don't know when Sunday comes and there is not business enough or employment enough for one quarter of the men already there." Property values were high. Rupp observed that "houses for business that are not worth more than $1,000 rent for from $1,700 per month to $500 per week."[4]

Leadville's reputation for wealth and violence soon spread. Where only a few years earlier wanted criminals in Kansas and other places had "gone to Texas," Colorado in general and Leadville in particular now proved a great attraction. Even the legendary Bartholomew Masterson visited the mushrooming city. Masterson, who preferred to call himself William Barclay Masterson, but was generally known as Bat, had just completed his one term as sheriff of Ford County, Kansas. He left for Leadville on February 25, 1880, but by March 6 he was back in Dodge City, where he gave a glowing account of the burgeoning city and the fortunes to be made there. It is probable that during his brief sojourn he renewed his acquaintance with Joe Lowe. In later years Bat was to recall that he first met Joe Lowe in 1870 "when I was hunting buffalo on the Kansas plains. He was running a dancehall in Ellsworth, and the following summer moved to Newton, following the terminus of the Santa Fe as it changed from one town to another. . . . People may talk about his tough reputation, but I say that he was as square as any man."[5]

When he moved to Leadville, Joe Lowe did his best to rid himself of his nickname, and eventually it was only those who had known him in earlier years who recalled it. His appetite for violence preceded him, however, and he suffered the public scrutiny common to all men of reputation. He had hardly settled in before it was reported, on December 31, that he was involved with one A. E. Jones in what was loosely described as a "money demand." The outcome of that particular episode has not been established.[6]

The great influx of speculators and men anxious to work in the mines soon caused problems. Lawlessness was rife, and to combat it a number of militia units were formed. These included the Leadville Guards, the Carbonate Rifles, the Wolf Tone Guards, and the previously mentioned Tabor Light Cavalry. Day and night these groups patrolled the streets. Then in May 1880 came a miners' strike. The situation got so bad that Governor Frederick W. Pitkin declared martial law and appointed David J. Cook to enforce it.

Cook was a remarkable individual. He had been in Colorado since the late 1850s and had led an adventurous life as a farmhand, miner, saloonkeeper, supply-train runner, policeman, marshal, police chief, and detective before being appointed major general of the Colorado Militia. On June 14, 1880, the governor addressed the following letter to him:

> As you have full authority in Lake County to do everything necessary for the public safety, you will see that no acts of violence are committed on either side. Every class of citizens must be protected against unlawful acts. No committee or organization of either citizens or miners can be permitted to interfere with the personal safety of the leaders of the other side, nor with property of any nature. Power of the State, having been invoked for the protection of Leadville, that power must be

impartially exercised for the protection of all classes of citizens. The punishment of offenses belongs to the court. Leadville wants peace, the state wants peace, and you will be careful that the power of the state is used to secure peace.[7]

When reviewing the events which had made such a letter necessary, the editor of the *Herald* wrote on October 23: "Every man in Leadville on the 13th of June is tolerably familiar with the occurrences that lead to the declaration of martial law, and most men are agreed as to the necessity for stern measures for the suppression of incipient violence." When Cook arrived in Leadville, he found a very serious situation: mine owners, businessmen, and property owners were ranged against the miners, and a large number of lawless individuals were busily playing one side against the other in the hope of plunder once the conflict started.

General Cook promptly took over Horace Tabor's apartment at the opera house, which became his headquarters. Reliable men were dispatched to each faction to learn their views, particularly those of the "Committee of Public Safety" (shades of the French Revolution!). Cook soon realized that the local militia units were not to be trusted, either. He then recruited about three hundred men to whom he entrusted the task of checking suspicious gatherings and arresting anyone who defied the curfew order. Learning that there was a plot to hang miners' leaders at midnight one night, he sent for the leaders of the Tabor Tigers and advised them of it. To his relief, they shared his dislike of "stranglers" and went swiftly to work arresting those they considered the most troublesome. Two days later, Cook deemed it safe to allow the saloons to reopen.[8]

In later years David Cook had much to say about Joe Lowe. Joe, he said, had a hand in the miners' strike:

During the Leadville strike in 1880, Lowe was sergeant of the Old Tabor Tigers. The place was under martial law. One evening I learned that a vigilance committee was preparing to hang several members of the Miner's Union. Several of my detectives belonged to the Vigilance Committee and kept me posted as to their intentions. Lowe being sergeant of the company gave me confidence in the men, who were all of

Interlude at Leadville   123

his caliber. The committee was waiting for me to go to bed. The detectives informed me of the intentions of the committee. I called together several companies among them being the one to which Lowe belonged. When I informed Capt. Murphy of his duty, Lowe who was under his direction, said: "Show me something to strangle." That shows how Lowe did everything and he fought the same way. In Leadville he carried a gun. Everybody carried a gun then.[9]

Bernard M. Slack, who knew Joe at Leadville and contended that Joe did not carry a gun there, had this to say:

> The first I remember of Joe is about his life in Leadville. That was in 1879. He was a gambler about town, had no recognized vocation that anybody knew of and was regarded as a pretty tough customer. We all knew that he came to Colorado from Texas, where he had a record of killing three or four men, and where he ran dancehouses and saloons. He used to win regularly in Leadville, and lived rather high while there. . . . As far as I know Lowe never killed a man in Colorado. His reputation preceded him, and he continued to follow the calling of a gambler. A peculiar trait of his character was that he never carried a gun. He was really brave. Though he often talked wildly as men who are addicted to the use of liquor will, I never knew him to falter or to fail to support with his fist any statements which he may have made. He was mixed up with many dancehall and saloon brawls while in Leadville, but none of them resulted seriously.[10]

Mary Lowe claimed that while she and Joe lived at Leadville he was involved in the Grand Central Theater and later the Woods Opera – which conflicts with Joe's city-directory description of himself as a miner. However, there is evidence that connects him with the Grand Central, but it post dates an incident which occurred in October 1880: one thousand dollars disappeared, and Joe was present at the time. W. J. Glencross claimed that he was sitting in a box with Joe Lowe, John Wall, and a waitress named Dolly Lathrop when he discovered that he was a thousand dollars short. He claimed to have had eight five-hundred-dollar bills on him, but when he checked his roll two were missing. Billy Nuttal, another guest, had excused himself some minutes before and when he returned he had five hundred dollars; previously he had only three. Billy strenuously denied that he had taken the money, but Glencross was not convinced.

The police were called and Nuttal was taken to jail, where he was searched and it was discovered that not only had the five hundred dollars now disappeared, so had his original three dollars. Reluctantly, he was released. When a warrant was issued for his arrest, he had taken "leg bail" and could not be found. Glencross finally admitted that "he did not know whether the money had been taken from his pocket, or whether when he had it out the two bills fell on the floor and were picked up."[11]

Cynics may be excused for thinking that Joe Lowe was perhaps involved — after all, he had been charged on several occasions with offenses concerning money — but there is no evidence to suggest that he was. Joe probably had more important things on his mind.

In March 1881 Joe Lowe was involved in a saloon brawl that was not of his making, but the victim was later counted as one of Joe's notches:

TIMMS' TROUBLES
He starts out with the gang to celebrate
St. Patrick's Day but engages in a quarrel with
Jack Lewis in a saloon when Joe Lowe steps in to
take a hand, wounding Timms three times.

What commenced as a comedy yesterday when several gentlemen well known in this city started out with the intensions of showing everyone that Celtic blood flowed in their veins and that they were not of the kind to allow the 17th of March to go unnoticed. The party paraded the streets early in the morning and consisted of Joe Lowe, Jack Lewis, John Timms, Tommie Wade and one or two others. Each was armed with some new fangled and awful musical instrument with which they awoke the echoes and the tired slumbers of the city at the same time. They serenaded every newspaper office, theater, and any place of importance in the city, not forgetting to drink to the health of the patron saint whose memory they were celebrating at every place they stopped, excepting of course, the newspaper offices. As a natural result, they began to feel very much elated in the spirit and their hilarity attracted universal attention wherever they went.

After smashing the head of the bass drum, demolishing the long tin funnel which had been converted into a trumpet, and converting into toothpicks the washboard which had lent harmony to the general melody, the party entered the Clarendon barroom, and a quartet of the party began to serenade the bartender with "Never Take the Horseshoe From the Door," but the sweet strains were interrupted by an altercation between Lewis and Timms, the two men having differed in regard to some trifling matter. And just about that time, Officer Milner entered and asked that the noise be stopped. Timms stepped back, knowing that the officer was justified in making the demand for silence. Lewis, however, who was probably more under the influence of liquor, was not to be quieted and began an assault upon the policeman, who had quieted him by striking him in the head with a revolver, harsh measures being necessary in that case. Lewis was bruised considerably by the blow and the blood flowed from his head in a perfect stream.

The whole party was piloted down to the city jail by the officer, with the assistance of some others who had arrived on the scene. There they gave bonds for their appearance and secured their liberty, not in the best of spirits, however. From the city jail, the men went to Joe Billings' saloon, on Harrison avenue, where Timms and Lewis renewed the quarrel. Those two, with Joe Lowe, went into the club room in the rear, from where those in the first room heard criminations and recriminations, and finally after some minutes, Joe Lowe was heard to exclaim, "G — d — — n you, put down that knife," which he repeated several times, and they heard pistol shots and a heavy fall on the floor. Those persons in the first room rushed into the doorway and found Joe Lowe standing in the center of the room, with a smoking pistol in his hand, while on the floor was John Timms, bleeding profusely and groaning under the pain caused by his wounds.

He was picked up and taken to 141 West 8th street, when a surgeon was called and the wounds examined. It was found that the three shots had taken effect in the left arm. The first ball struck the arm just above the wrist, fracturing the bone and being cut out of the muscles near the base of the hand. The second ball which struck Mr. Timms passed through the upper portion of the arm and entered the left breast, striking a rib and glancing off. The third ball struck near the elbow, causing a painful wound. The wounded man was made as comfortable as possible, and under the care of good nurses, will probably recover without losing any portion of his arm.

Immediately after the shooting, Mr. Lowe was taken into custody by officers and lodged in the county jail, but as Mr. Timms and his friends refused to bring any charges against him, he was soon after liberated and taken home. The large amount of liquor he had taken serving to deprive him of his strength, and he wasn't very clear in his own mind as to what had occurred anyway.

To a reporter, Lowe said that during the quarrel, Timms had picked up a huge butcher knife, which he flourished around in a dangerous manner, and which he refused to lay down when commanded so to do, but instead, continued to advance. Then he, Lowe, lost control over himself, and leveling his pistol at him, fired with the result above given.

Mr. Timms was found at his rooms on 8th street, in a cheerful mood, not withstanding the pain he was suffering, and with the consent of the attending surgeon, he gave his story. He stated that during the procession in the morning, Lowe had carried the knife in lieu of a sword, and that when he picked up the knife in the saloon, it was only in fun, and when Lowe commanded him to put it down, he took no heed, supposing that the other man was merely in fun. He stated that he bore no animosity against Mr. Lowe, and in proof of that, had refused to prosecute him.

The pistol which was used in the fracas is a veritable infernal machine, being of the "whistler" pattern and shooting a ball larger than a rifle ball [evidently a form of "Bulldog" based upon the British Webley .45-caliber pocket revolver of that name, which was a popular import and had been copied by several American makers].

Lewis will wear a sore head for some time, the blow from the officer's revolver having been a heavy one.

Mr. Billings, in whose place the affair occurred, states that although he had been a liquor dealer, wholesale and retail for over seven years, he has never had any such experience before.[12]

It was later reported that "John Timms, who was so seriously shot by Joe Lowe Thursday morning, started for Denver last evening under the care of Harry Newland. Mr. Lowe will pay all expenses of Mr. Timms' sojourn in Denver."

During the time he spent at Leadville, Joe Lowe managed to avoid publicity, and it was almost a year after the Timms shooting before his name cropped up again in the press. The incident in question was, of all things, a footrace:

Court Thompson, a foot racer of Denver, who ran against Campbell of this city, now languishes behind the jail bars of Lake County. The race took place on Tuesday afternoon last, and created intense emotions among sporting circles and firemen. The firemen confided in "pointers" and bet their money on Thompson. His defeat was accomplished with little difficulty and the high rollers commenced to charge him with selling out. He did not tarry long, but left for Denver. Joe

Lowe, a well known sport and backer of Thompson, with three others went before justice Curron, and upon complaint, a warrant was issued for Thompson. He was captured in Buena Vista and brought here today and placed under $2,000 bond. The complaint charges him with obtaining money under false pretenses and fraud. $875 were found sewed up in Thompson's pants leg. The case comes up on Saturday. "Pointers" cannot be relied on in Leadville and the duped should not kick.[13]

It was alleged in 1883 that during his sojourn at Leadville Joe Lowe killed a man who had humiliated him. According to the story, the individual involved, "named Simmons, a sort of 'bouncer' for a dance hall," had ordered Lowe "out of the hall one night, and getting the drop on him, enforced his order by repeatedly kicking that part of the desperado's anatomy that he used in sitting down." Joe later returned and, assuring the bouncer that he did not want any trouble, asked him to have a drink. "The unsuspecting bouncer complied and said he would take whisky. When the bottle was set out and he took hold of it to pour out a drink Lowe saw his opportunity, and whipping out a revolver yelled to him to get down on his knees. Simmons dropped and began to beg for his life, while Lowe smashed in [words illegible on original] with the weapon. He afterward died of his injuries. Nothing was ever done with Lowe."[14] The truth or otherwise of this story has yet to be established, but we think it most unlikely that Joe Lowe killed anyone in Leadville, least of all in the manner described.

Mary Lowe's statement that Joe was involved with the Grand Central Theater makes no specific mention of dates. Despite the difference in Christian names and the addition of a rank, we suspect that the following, published in the Leadville *Daily Herald* of January 1, 1882, may be relevant:

The variety business has fallen off considerably during the past year and only two houses may be said to be on a permanent basis, the Globe and the Grand Central. The former has sprung up during the last year and at once gained popular favor by giving a good entertainment. The Grand Central has changed managers since last January the reins now being held by Colonel Charlie Lowe, who is giving a first class show and seems to be making money. There are enough theater goers in

Leadville to support two variety establishments, and as long as those two add new business and engage good people, there need to be no fear of a lack of patronage.

For Joe Lowe, however, Leadville was beginning to lose its appeal. The mine owners and miners were still at loggerheads, and capitalist investment in long-term projects was limited. So for Joe it was yet another case of the grass being greener the other side of the hill. Bernard M. Slack said Joe stayed in Leadville only to gamble "until he made enough money to set himself up in business out in South Denver. I don't remember just when that was. Between the time that he left Leadville and the time of his arrival in Denver he went to Deadwood and the Black Hills. I do not know what were his actions while there, but I suppose they were along the lines of his former life."[15] When Joe and Mary reached Denver early in 1882, although he did not know it, Joe was destined to remain there.

Notes

1. Hays City *Sentinel* March 3, 1879; Lamar, *The Reader's Encyclopedia*, 60.
2. Herschel C. Logan, *Buckskin and Satin*, 178, 186–87.
3. Sherrill Warford, Historical Research Cooperative, Leadville, Colorado, to Joseph G. Rosa, September 26, 1987.
4. Wichita *Eagle*, February 6 and March 6, 1879.
5. Dodge City *Times*, February 28 and March 13, 1880; *Rocky Mountain News*, February 13, 1899.
6. Leadville *Daily Democrat*, Janaury 1 and 4, 1880.
7. Leadville *Daily Herald*, October 23, 1880.
8. George F. Willison, *Here They Dug the Gold*, 243.
9. *Rocky Mountain Daily News*, February 13, 1899.
10. Ibid., February 12, 1899.
11. Leadville *Weekly Herald*, October 14, 1880.
12. Leadville *Daily Herald*, March 17 and 18, 1881.
13. Greeley *Tribune*, January 11, 1882.
14. Kansas City *Evening Star*, May 16, 1883.
15. *Rocky Mountain Daily News*, February 12, 1899.

8

Denver
A Sporting Life

By the time Joe Lowe made the place his home in the early 1880s, Denver had come a long way from the sprawling hamlet of 1858, when gold was discovered in the region. Named after James W. Denver, the seventh territorial governor of Kansas, "Denver City," as it was originally called, thrived and by the early 1860s was an established point on the transcontinental freight routes. In the early 1870s, it was also linked by rail to many of the principal western cities. An additional attraction was Denver's location in the Colorado Rockies about a mile above sea level, which lured many unfortunate "lungers" and others who thought the rarefied air would benefit their health.

General David J. Cook recalled that Joe Lowe was known in Denver well before he made it his home:

> The first I knew of Lowe was in 1865. At that time he was a scout under Buffalo Bill. He was carrying messages between the different posts on the frontier. In 1866 Cody came to Denver to hunt up a man who had stolen government mules in Junction City. Lowe came with him and Old Captain Green of this city was in the party. That possibly accounts for the story being spread that Lowe was a mule skinner. I was City Marshal at the time and in a few days became a good friend of Lowe. In those days he was recognized as a brave man and a badman. He lived with Rowdy Kate . . . He never was a quarrelsome man though in the early days of Denver, I have taken shooting irons off him many a time. When the old Whitehouse was opened in 1864 on what is now Larimer Street, we all gathered there. Lowe was present. Bert Holliday and Jim Connors were with us. Lowe had a grudge against one of the proprietors. He wanted to kill him, but I took his gun away. Lowe professed friendship for Burns after that, but called him aside in profession

of friendship and bit off the edge of his nose. Everybody present then formed an opinion that Lowe was a badman.[1]

We doubt that Joe Lowe or Rowdy Kate visited Denver during the early 1860s, and neither is there any substance to the story that Joe served as a scout for Buffalo Bill in 1865. In that year Lowe was still a private in the Union Army and had no frontier reputation whatsoever, and neither did William Frederick Cody, who was himself still in the army. There is no real evidence of Cody's services as an army scout before 1868, and his visit to Denver in search of mule thieves took place in 1869. At that time he was chief of scouts for the Fifth Cavalry. In company with William Hamilton Green (later well known in Denver), Jack Farley (a government scout who later became a policeman in Nebraska), and a man known as "Long Doc," Cody pursued two men as far as Denver, where they tried to sell animals stolen from Fort Lyon. Cody, in his capacity as a "government detective" authorized by the post quartermaster, arrested the thieves, William ("Bill") Bevins and a fellow named Williams. Williams later escaped, and when Bevins was handed over to civilian authorities, they turned him loose. He was arrested in the Black Hills for similar crimes and spent several years in the Nebraska State Penitentiary. The suggestion that Long Doc might have been Joe Lowe is not corroborated, and it will be recalled that in April 1869 (the month Cody's excursion to Denver occurred), Rowdy Joe was in trouble with the authorities at Ellsworth in connection with some stolen money. Our conclusion is that Cook mistook Lowe for someone else.[2]

General Cook remarked that soon after Joe settled in Denver they met one day on the street. Joe told him that he had given up "the gun business," saying, "Dave, I don't want to carry a gun, my habits are too bad." From that time on, Cook said, he never knew Joe to come to the city armed, but "he was a great practical joker and sometimes carried his fun too far. People became angered at him, but he was inoffensive. . . . Lowe was a good man to his family. He was reticent about his family affairs, but any woman with whom he lived, could find no cause for complaint of his treatment. Like all gamblers, Lowe believed in living with the woman who struck his fancy, regardless of any marriage ceremony.... Lowe was a loud talker, that was all there was to his bad behavior. He was not a bad man and in my life I never heard of a man whom he had injured, much less killed as the reputation given him by some people say."[3]

We suspect that the general was trying to be kind to his old friend's reputation, for Joe's marital record was not good; he was known to abuse his women, and he did carry a pistol at Denver when the mood possessed him. Nevertheless, having dropped his nickname, Joe did try to play down his image. Bernard M. Slack recalled the early Denver days: "His resort on South Broadway was always considered rather disreputable, and its history would have a tendency to substantiate that theory.... He engaged in many drunken rows at his place, but I cannot think of any in which he could have been said to be guilty of any crime."[4]

In May 1883, Joe's name was linked with a dispute that began in Kansas and had repercussions throughout the West. The root cause of the trouble began in 1880 when the state constitution was amended to alter drastically the drinking habits of Kansans. Predictably, many were unhappy when their favorite beverages were threatened. The situation was not helped when rival semipolitical factions were organized at Dodge City; these were composed of pro-liquor saloonkeepers and gamblers (known as "the Gang") and a group of "reformers" led by city council members backed by a few saloon owners — the latter presumably becoming involved because they wished to improve their public image. There were rumblings in several other cities, but it was Dodge, basking in glory as "Queen of the Cowtowns," that was threatened with civil disorder.

The Dodge City Gang included such notables as James H. ("Dog") Kelley, Bat Masterson, and W. H. Harris. The reformers also boasted some redoubtable characters, led by Alonzo B. Webster, Mayor Lawrence E. Deger (a former city marshal), and lawyer Mike Sutton. The reformers claimed that some members of the Gang had engaged in criminal pursuits, among them rigged games, confidence tricks, holdups, and even land frauds.

It was argued that these accusations, combined with Dodge's reputation as the "wickedest city on the plains," deterred settlement. When Webster was elected mayor in 1881, he stopped many of the rackets by imposing quasi-moral restrictions. Deger, elected mayor in April 1883, was described by some people as one of Webster's "creatures."

Luke Short, fresh from his appearance at Tombstone, Arizona Territory, where on February 20 he had shot and killed gambler-gunfighter Charlie Storms, went into partnership with W. H. Harris and purchased the Long Branch Saloon. By April they were in trouble. On the night of the twenty-eighth they defied a new ordinance against prostitution; the police raided the place and arrested their "singer" for soliciting. Luke was furious and claimed that it was a case of discrimination because the Long Branch was the only saloon raided. Later that same evening he exchanged harsh words and then shots with L. C. Hartman, a special policeman, but neither man was wounded. Luke was arrested but later released by a committee headed by Alonzo Webster. The committee then told Luke to get out of town and stay out — permanently. Luke was enraged and headed for Topeka, where he aired his grievance with the press and the governor. Worse, he spread the word to his gunfighter friends, who agreed to come to his assistance.

When the following appeared in the Denver press, it aroused much interest among members of the saloon set, who speculated on the outcome:

VERY SORRY FOR DODGE.
The Distinguished Party which
WILL STOP THERE
Doc Halliday [sic], Earp and a few kindred Colorado
spirits think they will return to Dodge City.

Kansas City, May 15. — The troubles at Dodge City, Kansas, are likely to assume a more serious form within a day or two, and unless there is prompt interference by the state authorities a tragedy is considered almost certain. Luke Short, one of the gamblers recently expelled from town, is preparing to return, accompanied by a party of friends, and says he proposes to stay. The party will rendezvous at Topeka and start from there tomorrow. It comprises eight men. The greater portion of them are said to be the most desperate characters in the West.

The members are Bat Masterson, "Rowdy Joe," Doc Halliday, Charles Bassett, Shotgun Collins, Jim Calhoun and Wyatt Earp. Each man has a record, and one or two of them have figured prominently in Dodge history. Most of them are from Colorado. They say they have a right to go to Dodge and stay there if they see fit, and if they carry out their purpose and are expelled by the Dodge authorities a fight is considered inevitable.[5]

In Kansas the news that Joe Lowe might appear in defense of Luke Short jogged many memories. A Kansas City, Missouri, newspaper reviewed the exploits of some of the characters who were expected to be featured in the "tragic climax in a very short time" and noted: "Every old timer here has heard of Joe Lowe, better known as 'Rowdy Joe.' He made A BLOODY RECORD for himself at Newton, Kansas, when he ran a dance house there and . . . is . . . a bad man in an encounter. He is a sure shot with a revolver and a life on the frontier has made him so proficient in the use of that pleasant weapon that he is a terror all over the West."

A day later the same paper noted that Joe "comes close to being a typical tough. He weighs about 200 pounds, is a Frenchman [sic] by birth and began his career as a hard man by 'freighting' over the plains. He used to have a mistress known as 'Rowdy Kate,' and the two ran a dance house at Newton, Kas." The writer then reviewed the events which led up to the Red Beard killing (without naming him) and alleged that Joe had also killed nine people with a "shot gun, with both barrels cut off to within about ten inches of the stock, and loaded with buck shot. . . . It is upon this incident that his reputation is mainly based. He is a quarrelsome man when under the influence of liquor, and the chances of his meeting a violent death are excellent."[6]

When the group eventually "invaded" Dodge and persuaded the city council to reconsider its action and reinstate Luke Short, it was not accompanied by Joe Lowe. We can only assume that either the newspapers included him to add weight to an already impressive list of hard cases or perhaps he had intended to go but had been prevented, for some reason, from doing so. In any event, a triumphant Luke and his friends posed for their picture, which within days was reproduced as a woodcut in the

Police Gazette and bore the caption that has immortalized it: "The Dodge City Peace Commission."⁷

Back in Denver, Joe Lowe displayed no warlike tendencies. Rather, he concentrated upon improving his establishment at Broadway Park, where in August he was injured in a riding accident (something to which he seems to have been prone). The *News* on the 20th noted that on the previous evening Joe had been seriously hurt "about the head" when his horse ran away and threw him "against a tree." He had recovered by the twenty-second, when he and Mrs. Lowe were reported to have appeared in court. They were charged with a "felonious assault" on one Patrick Cusick. When the evidence was presented before Justice Duffy, it transpired that Mr. Cusick had used some abusive and insulting language against Mrs. Lowe and had been "very properly punished." Reports of the action were confusing in that one of them suggested that Mrs. Lowe's "son Joe" had actually kicked Cusick out of the house, which appears to be a journalistic error.⁸

Joe Lowe's sporting activities continued to arouse interest, and he was particularly popular amongst the "sporting elite." He may have made every effort to keep out of the press and play down his past, but he still had his moments. In February 1884 he ran afoul of the police. It was reported on the twelfth that "Joe Lowe was arrested at about one thirty this morning for carrying concealed weapons. Lowe was at the Union Depot, and laboring under too much frost cure, became too demonstrative while in the ladies waiting room. Officer John Connors took possession of Lowe's gun and then placed him in the city jail. He will appear before Judge Mullahay this morning." The following day the newspaper added a little more detail:

> Joe Lowe, while bidding goodbye to some Leadville friends who were departing for Couer De Alene on Monday evening, got considerably full, and correspondingly boisterous. Officer John Connors remonstrated with him, when he became quite abusive, and upon the officer's attempt to arrest him, he made a motion to draw a revolver, observing which, the officer drew his and got the drop on him. He then surrendered and was taken to jail and the pistol taken from him. He was arraigned in the police court yesterday on the charge of carrying con-

cealed weapons, but obtained a continuance of the case until today giving up bond for $100.[9]

Somehow, by the time the story reached Wichita it was reported that Joe had been killed, and on February 21 the *Weekly Eagle* gleefully remarked: "Rowdy Joe, infamous in the early history of this city, was shot by a policeman in Denver the other day, since which time he fell into the rear of the long line of his victims and was marched down to his final home with his boots on."

As did their counterparts in other western habitats, the Denver authorities saw in the saloon and gambling businesses a means of economic survival and relied upon such establishments as a tax base. Denver's first charter in 1861 authorized the city fathers "to license, restrain, regulate, prohibit and suppress tippling-houses, dram-shops, gambling houses, bawdy-houses, and other disorderly houses." Gambling houses were the initial victims of annual license fees (ranging from $50 to $100), but by 1862 tavern owners were required to post a bond of $150 to $300 and pay an annual license fee ranging from $50 to $100, depending on whether they served beer and wine or sold hard liquor as well. By 1866 the cost of doing business had risen to $200 for selling spiritous liquors and $140 in liquor license fees.[10]

When Joe Lowe arrived, taxation was a real vexation, and at one point it was believed that he would quit. On August 1, 1887, the *Denver Times* published this revealing comment:

SOUTH DENVER LIQUOR.
"Pap" Wyman the only Dealer left in the Municipality.

One by one the liquor dealers in South Denver have yielded to the strokes of the authorities. Mr. York, who owned the saloon across from the exposition quit a few days ago, and the saloon keeper one block this side of the York Cottage, Mr. Lauster, did the same thing. This left only Joe Lowe and "Pap" Wyman.

Saturday morning Joe Lowe gave notice that he would quit his fight, as he was going to Leadville into a mining venture. He said that mining would pay him better than running a liquor place in South Denver under such fire as he had been getting. So that only "Pap" Wyman is left. "Pap" ought to be pretty good on a lone hand, but the big cards are against him.

This photograph of Joe Lowe and an unknown lady is in the possession of his grandson. The lady is unidentified, but we suspect that she may be his wife Mollie (or Mary) Field. Courtesy Kansas State Historical Society.

Joe's proposed mining venture at Leadville evidently did not prosper or perhaps it was just newspaper talk, for within six months he was still in Denver, where he found himself in divorce court. Mary (or Mollie) Lowe filed for divorce on July 1, 1887. Her grounds were cruelty, and in granting the divorce on October 20, 1887, the court ruled that Joe Lowe had "been guilty of the acts of cruelty charged in the plaintiff's complaint and that the allegations of said complaint are true." Mary was awarded costs, and the court set another appearance "upon the questions of alimony." It is possible that alimony (or the nonpayment of it) was behind the animosity between the couple in later years.[11]

Mollie described her successor as "my servant girl before we were divorced. She was a Swede girl we had working for us."

This was Lena Larson. Joe and Lena were married at Denver on February 11, 1888, and within weeks had moved from Broadway Park to Cottage Grove, which during the next ten years became widely known for its activities. Lena was described as a "tall, blond woman of Swedish descent and quite attractive." What was not mentioned by the press was the fact that the couple had probably been living together for some time, for it is now known that Joe Lowe had a son named Thomas Joseph. Joe's grandson has made available surviving material which records that Thomas J. Lowe died on January 19, 1890, aged "five years, six months and seven days," which makes his date of birth August 12, 1884. In 1889 their daughter Elizabeth was born, followed by Anna in 1895. Both girls were described as "bright and pretty" blondes with "beautiful flaxen hair and ruddy cheeks."[12]

Joe's Cottage Grove roadhouse was notorious. Nominally described as a "beer garden," the establishment was nonetheless widely regarded as a disorderly house; its "lewd, drunken regulars tarnished the image of South Denver," recalled one writer, and a contemporary description of the place noted that it was patronized by sports and women and that it was "located a short distance west of Broadway and north of Orchard Place. The dwelling stands in a shady spot. At one end, there is a large veranda. For ten years the place has been lively in the broadest sense of the term. The proprietor protected his patrons, and though at different times, trouble occurred at Cottage Grove, none of the details could ever be obtained from Lowe. He was boss of the ranch and the sports who gathered beneath this roof knew better than to ever attempt to run it over him."[13]

Joe Lowe spent much time away from his roadhouse, particularly at John Murphy's place on Larimer Street, where on one occasion it was reported that he took on too much liquor and had a row with the bartender. When Joe drew a long knife from his pocket, the bartender threw open a drawer, grabbed a revolver, and backed Joe out into the street. In 1892 it was claimed that Joe had a fight with Jack Kerwin (later marshal of Denver) which resulted in Kerwin's pulling his pistol on Joe (who was unarmed) and beating him about the head. Had no one inter-

No. 5795

MARRIAGE LICENSE.

STATE OF COLORADO, ARAPAHOE COUNTY.

Know all Men by this Certificate,

That any regularly ordained Minister of the Gospel, authorized by the rules and usages of the church or denomination of Christians, Hebrews or religious body of which he may be a member; or any Judge or Justice of the Peace to whom this may come, he not knowing of any lawful impediment thereto, is hereby authorized and empowered to solemnize the rites of matrimony between _Joe Lowe_, of Denver, in the County of Arapahoe, and State of Colorado, and _Lena Larson_ of Denver, in the County of Arapahoe, and State of Colorado, and to Certify the same to the said parties or either of them, under his hand and seal, in his ministerial or official capacity.

And thereupon he is hereby required to return his certificate in form following, as hereto annexed.

IN TESTIMONY WHEREOF, I have hereunto set my hand and affixed the seal of the said County, at Denver, this _Tenth_ day of _February_ A.D. 1888.

Jos. A. Shurtz
COUNTY CLERK.

Certificate of Marriage

I, _George W. Miller_, a _County Judge_, residing at Denver, in the County of Arapahoe, in the State of Colorado, do hereby certify that in accordance with the authority on me conferred by the above license, I did, on this _11th_ day of _Feby_ A.D. 1888, at Denver, in the County of Arapahoe, in the State of Colorado, solemnize the rites of matrimony between _Joe Lowe_ of Denver, in the County of Arapahoe, in the State of Colorado, and _Lena Larson_ of Denver, in the County of Arapahoe, in the State of Colorado, in the presence of _A. H. Gillett_ and _Wm. R. Perry_ _James Inman_

WITNESS my hand and seal at the County aforesaid, this _11th_ day of _Feby_ A.D. 1888.

IN PRESENCE OF
James Inman
Wm. R. Perry

Geo. W. Miller [SEAL]
County Judge.

This Certificate, duly executed, together with the License, must be returned by the Minister or Officer who shall have solemnized the marriage, to the office of the County Clerk who issued the same, within thirty days after the marriage; Twenty to Fifty Dollars fine for failure so to do.

The marriage license of Joe Lowe and Lena Larson. Courtesy Arapahoe

Lena Larson at the time of her marriage to Joe Lowe. The original is a tintype, which means that the image is in reverse. Courtesy Kansas State Historical Society.

Joe Lowe's son, Thomas, photographed with two bullterriers that look suspiciously like the animals used in the much-publicized dogfights that took place at Joe's Cottage Grove. Courtesy Kansas State Historical Society.

McGovern

RIVERSIDE CEMETERY,
—OF—
DENVER, COLORADO.

THE RIVERSIDE CEMETERY ASSOCIATION, hereby certifies that _Thomas Lowe_ of _Denver, Colo_ the owner of _NW¼_ Lot _35_ in Block _24_ on the plat of said Cemetery Grounds, in the County of Arapahoe, and State of Colorado, containing _80_ square feet, more or less, for which said _Thomas Lowe_ paid the sum of _Fifteen_ Dollars, and the said _Thomas Lowe_ and _his_ heirs and assigns are entitled to the use of said Lot, in FEE SIMPLE, for the purpose of Sepulture alone, subject to the By-Laws, Rules and Regulations of said Association, and to the provisions of the laws of the State of Colorado, now in force and hereafter to be passed, regulating titles in Cemeteries.

IN TESTIMONY WHEREOF, The said RIVERSIDE CEMETERY ASSOCIATION has caused these presents to be signed by the President thereof, and countersigned by the Secretary thereof, and the corporate seal to be hereunto affixed, this _10th_ day of _Feb._ A. D. 1880.

J. F. Brown PRESIDENT.
Charles D. Cobb SECRETARY.

Joe Lowe purchased a family plot in the Riverside Cemetery in the name of Thomas Lowe. Courtesy Kansas State Historical Society.

fered, witnesses said, he might well have been killed. Despite his reputation for heavy drinking and for violence, Joe Lowe was reckoned to have had his good traits, even by some of his enemies. "He was known as a dead game sport" and as a "man who would never tell a secret. He was liberal with his money and helped many a friend out of trouble. His failing was drink, and he was arrested a number of times for fighting and creating disturbances."[14]

So far as we are aware, Rowdy Joe Lowe did not stray far from Denver after he married Lena Larson, but a "J. Lowe" was indicted on a horse-stealing charge in Indian Territory in 1888. Writing from Pawhuska, I.T., on July 30, U.S. Commissioner J. E. Dodson informed the Honorable W. C. Perry, U.S. attorney at Topeka, Kansas, that he was forwarding the papers in a horse-stealing case, *U.S.* v. *J. Lowe.* Lowe was accused of stealing the animals from a man named H. Musgrave. Several witnesses were prepared to give evidence, and it was claimed that "you will have no trouble making a case against him, he told the Marshal that he 'would go up.'" The outcome of the case is not known. It was brought to our attention as a possible exploit of Joe Lowes, but we doubt that it was Rowdy Joe.[15]

In May 1897, Joe Lowe was again before the public when his place on South Broadway was the scene of the shootout over a ditch. What may have had a direct bearing on the incident can perhaps be traced back to a fracas that took place some weeks before. According to the press, in the spring of 1897, Joe Lowe took forcible possession of the S. S. Woodbury ranch on Cherry Creek, seven miles south of the city. Attorney W. W. Cooke, who formerly owned the property, removed a number of sheds on the land. Lowe, who gained possession through a deed of trust, caused the arrest of Cooke. Woodbury, the lessee, invited Cooke to dine with him. The lawyer drove to the place and at the door of the farmhouse, he met Lowe, who armed with a brace of revolvers, ordered him to throw up his hands. Cooke grabbed a stick and started for the new tenant. Sam McCall then appeared with a double barreled shotgun and chased Cooke off the premises. Lowe and McCall had previously run Woodbury out on the prairie. They were arrested on warrants issued at Castle Rock and fined on a charge of inciting a riot.[16]

On May 23, Jacob Kisthard and Daniel Kisthard were arrested for killing Samuel McCall and badly wounding John McKenna at a point near Joe Lowe's Cottage Grove resort, and there were suspicions in some circles that Joe Lowe was involved, even though he claimed that he never fired a shot. The shooting took place some four hundred yards from the roadhouse, which was occupied at the time by the usual Sunday afternoon crowd. Fortunately, when the shooting started, there were only about forty people left in the vicinity, many of them scattered around the grounds.

McCall and McKenna had been playing quoits when Joe Lowe sent Jack Phillips to settle his dispute with Jacob Kisthard over water rights. McCall and McKenna went with him. Shots were fired and McCall was killed. Kisthard and his son were arrested by detectives, and within hours Undersheriff Perry Clay had arrested Joe Lowe and his hired man, Jack Phillips, who were charged with involvement in the shooting.

Jacob Kisthard owned a ranch southwest of Joe Lowe's place, and water for the ranch was supplied from a stream known as Little Dry Creek. This creek also supplied a couple of other farms, which restricted Joe's water supply. Kisthard claimed that Joe Lowe had no right to any of the water yet had been taking it from a point where the ditch touched his property. When Kisthard approached a lawyer, he was advised to construct a flume to divert the stream from Joe Lowe's property. The work was completed on May 23, but before the new channel could be opened, Lowe sent Phillips to warn Kisthard not to turn off the water.

Back at Joe Lowe's place, observers saw several men standing around the new ditch, and about five shots were heard. Witnesses claimed that Kisthard shot McKenna and then the other man (identified only by dark clothing) opened fire on McCall, killing him. Phillips was not molested. One of Kisthard's sons, William, went to the police chief and said he had assisted in the construction of the flume until two o'clock, at which time he departed, leaving in his place at the ranch two of his wife's brothers, one of them fourteen-year-old William Smith. The boy fled to the house when the shooting started; he said Daniel

Kisthard shot one of the hired men because the man had attacked Jacob with a shovel and was about to attack him when Daniel shot him. At that moment, someone opened up with a Winchester rifle from the Lowe property. The boy was badly frightened, and his recollection of the fight was sketchy.

Joe Lowe said he was tending bar when the shooting started and did not see the men fall. He further declared:

> We have been having trouble for some time with Kisthard over the water, and he has repeatedly turned off the water from my place which I am entitled to. Shortly before 7 o'clock I saw the Dutchman [Kisthard] sneaking up through the field with a shovel on his shoulder. I suspected that he was going to tamper with the ditch and sent my man, Jack Phillips, out with instructions to ask him to desist. Phillips left in that direction and I saw McCall and McKenna, who had been playing quoits in the yard, follow him, presumably to see if anything should occur. The next I heard was five shots, and looking across the field I saw McCall lying dead and McKenna running unsteadily towards the house. Several of the crowd which was about the place ran out to the spot where McCall had fallen, about 400 yards away, and met McKenna, who told them Sam had been killed.

Joe denied that he fired any shots in reprisal and said no serious trouble with Kisthard had occurred previously. McCall, he said, had been spending the day at the place and McKenna had only arrived in the afternoon.

Jack Phillips was questioned closely and said he could find no reason why McCall and McKenna should have been shot:

> I walked up to where Kisthard was and found that he had dammed up the place where our ditch tapped dry creek completely. I asked him if he intended to take all the water, and he said he did. I walked up the ditch a few paces and saw that he had made preparations to do as he said. When I was near the spot where Kisthard was standing I saw another person approach on the opposite side of the fence and at the same moment Kisthard whipped out a revolver and shot McKenna. I saw McCall fall afterwards, but he was too bewildered to perceive from whence the shots that killed him came. They may have been fired by the other person who came up.

Phillips said he had carried a shovel to the spot but abandoned it to assist the men who were shot.

Among those questioned who had been at the Lowe house were several who witnessed the shooting, and they all considered that a man hidden behind a tree near the spot had fired several shots at McCall. McCall's roommate, William Hays, declared that he had seen Phillips and the other two cross the field, had seen Kisthard deliberately fire at McKenna, and had seen the latter running. It was then that the man hidden behind the tree rose up and ran out, firing at McCall. By the time people from Lowe's property reached the scene, McCall was dead.

Other people made similar statements, and Dr. Wilson removed from McKenna a .45-caliber bullet which had entered just below the heart and plowed its way toward the kidneys. It was removed near his back, the whole time McKenna suffering excruciating pain. He was a recent arrival from New York and had bad health, whereas McCall was well known about the city as a gambler and had worked at the Murphy Exchange for a long time.

Jacob Kisthard had been farming for only a few months, having taken the place over in payment of a debt. His two sons were not farmers but machinists employed in the McCarland foundry. In custody, the Kisthards talked freely of the shooting, maintaining that they had been having trouble with Joe Lowe for some time and intended to give themselves up after the shooting.

The irrigation ditch that had caused all the trouble actually belonged to a man named Jones, but Kisthard and Lowe had rights in it. Lowe, however, had cut the ditch so that the Kisthards could get no water at all. When they protested, Lowe ignored them. Finally, in desperation, Kisthard decided to build the flume, but Joe, "with an oath," had declared that they should do no such thing.

Naturally, Kisthard's version of events differed considerably from that put forward by Joe Lowe and his friends. Kisthard claimed that McCall was armed with a revolver and that McKenna was carrying a long-handled shovel. Both sides kept to their respective properties, separated by a wire fence. After a brief altercation, McCall suddenly said ("with a foul oath"), "Kill him!" McKenna then struck the old man with the shovel, and Jacob took the force of the blow on his upraised hands, turning the edge of the blade so that he was struck with the flat side, the force knocking him to his knees. At that moment McCall fired at him. Kisthard's son promptly shot twice at McCall in the belief that his father had been killed. The Kisthards then claimed that "twelve or fifteen shots were fired from the direction of Lowe's house which was 500 feet away." The Kisthards turned and ran toward their house, firing several shots toward the Lowe property as they did so.

Assistant District Attorney T. E. McLelland visited McKenna in the hospital to take his statement and found him sedated and unable to converse intelligibly. McKenna was reticent about the affair but did say:

> I walked with the man whom I afterwards found out to be McCall to a patch of ground where we met another party, who was also unknown to me. The man I was with and the one we met engaged in an altercation over a ditch. The argument lasted for some little time, during which I heard my companion called McCall. That's how I know his identity. Well, during this altercation I heard some shots, and the next thing I knew I fell to the grounding pierced by bullets.

McLelland said McKenna vowed that he had no idea who fired the shots, and neither did he know from which direction they came. In fact, the shooting came as a complete surprise. Later, when a newspaperman visited him in the hospital, he found McKenna to be in great pain and unable to talk. His "appeal for poultices to be applied to his side and back was pitiful," the newsman said. The medical staff said McKenna's condition was very serious. The Kisthards were charged with murder, but the authorities announced that they were still investigating the incident. It was popularly believed that some of the shots that were fired did come from the Lowe property.[17]

The outcome of the hearing and its aftermath is confusing, but two years later it was reported that the Kisthards had acted in self-defense and that Joe Lowe was the real aggressor, urging McCall and McKenna to cause trouble. It was also claimed that "Lowe behaved in a most cowardly manner, standing on his porch some hundred yards away and firing at the Kisthards with a Winchester. The Kisthards felt that right was on their side and they fought desperately. . . . Joe Lowe was arrested for causing the trouble, but the indictment was quashed. He boasted of his part in the fight, and thought himself clever for having got other people to do his fighting. Since then he has managed to escape the police, but his road house maintained its reputation for troublesome brawls." As for the unfortunate McKenna, some alleged that Lowe deserted him and he was "compelled to ask [for] public charity some time ago."[18]

The passing of time and the lack of conclusive evidence that Joe Lowe was indeed the aggressor precludes a firm judgment, but we would question the statement that he boasted of getting others to do his fighting. On the contrary, throughout his career Joe Lowe threw his own punches or fired his own weapons. We have no cause to think that, rightly or wrongly, he acted otherwise on this or other occasions.

Almost a year after the Kisthard incident, Joe's place was raided by the police when it was learned that he had been organizing dogfights. The full story was published in the *Rocky Mountain News* on April 28, 1898:

DOG FIGHT WAS RAIDED

Canine Go at Joe Lowe's Resort
Broken Up by The Police Force

A dog fight in progress at Joe Lowe's resort on South Broadway was stopped by the police last night and eleven men were captured and locked up in the city jail. Complaint was made to Chief Farley and the latter ordered Captain Phillips to conduct the raid. The captain took five officers, Slick, McDonald, Southard, Gordon and Putney with him. About 100 men were watching the dogs when the officers arrived. A grand rush took place when the alarm was given. Officer McDonald chased Joe Mosconi nearly half a mile and fired three shots at him, Mosconi then surrendered. Those who were arrested gave their names as follows; Jake Brown, Harry Davis, John Martin, Jim Cook, William Thompson, John Hardin, Harry Clark, John Lamont, Tom Thompson, and Joe Lowe. Brown was charged with dog fighting, and the others with aiding and abetting a dog fight. Some prominent officials connected with the fire and police departments are believed to have been interested in the affair but they escaped in the grand rush.

The following morning, the *News* reported that some believed that the police had exceeded their authority and that lawsuits might result from the raid on Joe's place, adding:

> A large number of men who attended the dogfight at Joe Lowe's resort last Wednesday night are congratulating themselves on the fact that they escaped the flying squadron under Capt. Phillips. The police managed to arrest only eleven participants and the two fighting dogs. Yesterday afternoon, W. L. Bowers, a clerk, was arrested by Officer Southard on a warrant charging him with dogfighting. Secretary Whitehead, of the Colorado Humane Society, took possession of the two dogs yesterday and will hold them for evidence. Lowe's resort is outside the city limits and a good deal of comment has been caused by the fact that the police conducted the raid. It is claimed that if the police have a right to stop a dogfight at Lowe's they have also the authority to stop the sale of liquor on Sunday at that place and nearby resorts. Secretary Whitehead, it is understood, will prosecute the dogfighting cases to the end.

Joe Lowe was charged with aiding and abetting the violation of the law and was bound over to district court by Justice Crane in the sum of five hundred dollars. For some reason, the press later noted, the case was "lost in the shuffle and never came to light in the District Court."[19]

Joe Lowe continued to make news and on Ocrober 23, 1898, was featured in a Denver *Daily News* article that originally had been published in the Chicago *Chronicle*. Considering that its author, E. D. Cowen, was an old Denver newspaperman, we find it strange that he should commit his comments to print before checking with Joe Lowe personally. Under the heading "Happy Bad Men of the West," Mr. Cowen recounted some of the stories then current about such notables as Wild Bill Hickok, Billy Thompson (Ben's homicidal younger brother), Jim Curry, Doc Holliday, Bat Masterson, and Joe Lowe. Joe, Cowen alleged, had avenged a brother murdered at Alder Gulch, Montana. "Disease robbed him of two victims and an accident of one; the others he caught, boots and all." Having dispatched his enemies (which took him many years), Joe finally settled down "near Denver and is there today, as content as an innkeeper on the Rhine. His deeds are now a myth, and he would be, perhaps, the last person in the world to rehearse them, because it would not be in accordance with the spirit of the times." What Joe thought about his reported exploits apparently was not recorded.

Joe continued his "contented" existence amongst the "sporting elite," and to avoid further problems with Denver ordinances, he hung this sign outside his Cottage Grove establishment: "No liquor served except to members of the Cottage Grove Club." He entertained lavishly, it is reported, and laid on an occasional prizefight. Joe and Lena had problems, and for a time she left — it was claimed because of his rough treatment of her — but by 1899 they were back together. His two daughters were now four and ten and enjoyed being the center of attention when their father's many friends came to visit. Most of the callers were customers who regarded Joe Lowe as a kind of hero, probably because of his reactionary attitude toward authority, taxation and restrictive city ordinances. Some even thought Joe Lowe was "slowing up." Indeed, he had given some thought to the future. On August 29, 1890, he tried, unsuccessfully, to secure a pension from the U.S. government on grounds of "advancing years [he gave his age as forty-eight] and growing infirmities" that were not the result of "vicious habits." His application probably was prompted by an act of Congress on June 2, 1890, concerning invalid pensions, and he apparently filed another unsuccessful application for the benefit on December 18, 1897.[20] It was during this rare period of complacency that Joe Lowe kept his date with a destiny that many felt was inevitable.

Notes

1. *Rocky Mountain News*, February 13, 1899.
2. William F. Cody, *The Life of Hon. William F. Cody, Known as Buffalo Bill*, 229–42; San Francisco *Call*, August 1, 1877; Nebraska City *News-Press*, June 16, 1930; *Rocky Mountain News*, December 5, 1915.
3. *Rocky Mountain News*, February 13, 1899.
4. Ibid.
5. Denver *Times*, May 16, 1883.
6. Kansas City *Evening Star*, May 15–16, 1883.
7. Rosa, *The Gunfighter*, 77–79.
8. *Rocky Mountain News*, August 20 and 22, 1883.
9. *Rocky Mountain Daily News*, February 13, 1884.
10. Thomas J. Noel, *The City and the Saloon: Denver, 1858–1916*, 35.

11. Case No. 8621, Mary Lowe vs. Joseph Lowe, copy supplied by Philip Panum.
12. Marriage License No. 5795, issued at Denver, February 10, 1888. The marriage was solemnized by Judge George W. Miller on the eleventh (copy supplied by the Arapahoe County District Court). In his December 18, 1897, application for an invalid pension, Joe gave the date of his marriage to Lena as March 10, 1888, but this may have been his slip or one on the clerk's part. In an affidavit dated September 11, 1934, concerning her pension, Lena Lowe stated that she was born on August 10, 1864, at Weinge, Hollands, Sweden, and was christened Carolina. She dropped the name when she came to the United States and adopted the name Lena instead. Joe's grandson recalled that she once criticized his mother, Anna, for sewing on a Sunday. Lena told her daughter that she had sewn a suit for her son Thomas on a Sunday and "buried him in it the following Sunday." *Rocky Mountain News,* February 13, 1899; Joseph Lowe's Pension File, National Archives, Washington, D.C.; Affidavit of Lena Lowe, made at San Pedro, Calif., September 11, 1934, Records of the Widows Subdivision, Section C, Pensions, National Archives, Washington, D.C.; Edward Dunbar to Joseph W. Snell, undated, ca. 1970, Manuscripts Department, KSHS.
13. Noel, *The City and the Saloon,* 74; *Rocky Mountain News,* February 13, 1899.
14. *Rocky Mountain News,* February 13, 1899.
15. Copy supplied by the National Archives, Kansas City Branch, Kansas City, Mo.
16. *Rocky Mountain News,* February 13, 1899.
17. Ibid., May 24, 1897.
18. Ibid., February 12, 1899.
19. Ibid.
20. Joseph Lowe's Pension File.

9

With His Boots On

Joe Lowe must have known that the odds were against his reaching old age, but he evidently accepted the situation philosophically. On September 5, 1898, he was one of the spectators when Buffalo Bill Cody's Wild West and Congress of Rough Riders of the World paid yet another one-day visit to Denver. Joe stood on the platform of a Broadway tramcar that had been stopped at a street corner. He watched the aging scout lead the parade past, turned to a policeman who stood beside him, and remarked, "I have often thought that Buffalo Bill would bite the dust some day, but I guess he won't, I guess I'll be the one to die with my boots on." Joe was not to know that Cody almost did precede him. Within days of his Denver appearance at Kansas City, the old showman contracted typhoid fever but recovered. Joe's reaction when he saw Cody may have been premonition, or perhaps he was being nostalgic. His alleged claim to have been associated with Cody as an army scout has not been verified, but we do not doubt that Joe had known Cody when both lived at Ellsworth or worked at Fort Harker during the late 1860s.[1]

On February 11, 1899, his eleventh wedding anniversary, Joe hitched up his horse and set out on the eight-mile trip into Denver. He spent about an hour or so driving around town, then left his horse on the Arapahoe Street side of the post office. Here the animal remained without being fed or watered until about five-thirty in the evening, when policeman John Johnson found it. He led it away to the police station, where it was fed and watered; at that time no one had any idea who its owner was. About an hour later, Joe Lowe suddenly appeared at the police station and demanded the return of his property. He angrily denied cruelty to the animal and verbally abused the police for being "too fresh." They ignored his outburst and, when he had calmed down, told him that if he wanted the horse returned, it would cost him $2. Grudgingly, Joe paid up and departed, "a curse upon his lips." He went to George Walker's saloon on Curtis Street, where he had words with former policeman Emmanuel A. Kimmel. Then, just before 11 P.M., followed by Kimmel, Joe walked into Mart. H. Watrous's saloon at 1527 Curtis Street. George Watrous described what happened next:

> Lowe came in first and Kimmel followed him shortly after. I was standing behind the bar, not paying much attention to either of them. In a few minutes I heard Lowe commence roasting Kimmel for making an arrest. It seems that Kimmel arrested one of Lowe's friends and Lowe was just in the right mood and had just enough whiskey to make him ugly enough for anybody. He called Kimmel all sorts of names and Kimmel was fast getting mad. Lowe wound up cussing the police in general although Kimmel has been off the force for some time. Well, finally I saw that the argument and abuse would do no good and might result in trouble, so I called Joe to one side and told him to let up on his abuse. Kimmel went out shortly after this and Lowe followed him.
>
> Just before midnight, when I was preparing to close up for the night, Lowe came in the front door. Kimmel next appeared. They had some words together, but I did not think they were as bad as before and didn't pay very much attention to them. I did hear, however, Lowe jumping on Kimmel for the arrest of one of Lowe's friends. Matters quieted down somewhat and then I saw them go into the backroom and sit down to a table. Kimmel asked Lowe to have a drink, but Lowe refused to take it. By this time I thought the whole thing had blown over and kept at my work in the front of the saloon. I was determined to fire them both if they kept up the fight. But I believed the whole matter was squared and that they were friends again. A little while after midnight while I had my back to the counter in the front of the saloon, I heard three shots. I turned like a flash then saw Lowe rush from the backroom. He was as white as a sheet, and staggered back of the lunch counter. Just then I started for him and before I had proceeded two feet, I saw Kimmel emerge from the backroom and start after Lowe. I reached Kimmel before he got to Lowe and I at once realized that it would be all off with Lowe if Kimmel was not stopped where he was. I seized Kimmel just as he was about to fire the revolver and the gun went off

for the fourth time, the bullet striking the glass box in which we kept some of the food for the lunch counter. I did not hold Kimmel and he started out the door. I have not seen him since. I do not know what led up to the shooting unless it was abuse which Lowe gave Kimmel about the arrest. One of the bullets, either the first or the second one fired, struck Lowe in the left side four inches below the armit and in a line with the heart. There is a bullet hole in the casement of the rear or dining room, a bullet hole in the woodwork back of the lunch counter and another large one in the glass lunch case. Kimmel's third shot must have been fired while his victim was struggling to gain the front room, because it struck behind the lunch counter towards which Lowe was staggering.

The reporter for the *Rocky Mountain News* described the odd behavior of one of the waiters and the efforts to revive Joe:

F. Heitler, a young waiter, who may know more than he cares to state, was in the rear of the room at the time of the shooting. He declares that he did not witness the tragedy. He heard three shots but before the echo of the last one had died away, Heitler had skipped out by the backway, fearing he might get mixed up. "I was back in that curtained apartment," said he, pointing to the only individual drinking room in that establishment, "when the shooting occurred I did not serve any drinks to the party. The three men, Lowe, Kimmel and a gentleman [Daniel J. Seaman] who wore a light overcoat and carried a cane, came in together. It was about 12:05 as nearly as I can remember. They seemed to be friendly but did not indulge in any loud talking and I paid no attention to them. Not caring to go near them until they called for me, I went into that rear room to fix up my bed and other things for the night for it was after closing time you know. The trio had been seated but a short time when I was startled by hearing the report of a pistol. That was enough for me. I bolted for the rear door and did not even look back, as I ran. Quick as a flash I opened the door rushed out into the enclosure in the rear of the saloon and stayed there until I believe the trouble was over. Just as I was opening the door, I heard another shot and a third as I closed it. But for the fact that the gate opening onto the alley was closed, I probably would have been running yet. I was thoroughly frightened. There was one thing that I noticed and that was that Lowe was very drunk. The others did not seem to be under the influence of liquor to any great extent. Lowe was gesticulating rather wildly when he came in, and the other two appeared to be rather sullen. The man with the light overcoat I had never seen before. I do not remember his description, and did not notice whether he wore a beard. The lights were not very bright. I heard no very loud talking. The men were arguing about something, but being in the rear of that section of the saloon, I was unable to catch the drift of their conversation. I never pay much attention to what the men who come in here are talking about, and did not vary from that custom this time. When I aroused sufficient courage to return, I saw Lowe lying on the floor in the front division. That's all I know."

After the Shooting

As soon as Kimmel had departed, Watrouse placed Lowe at full length on the floor and propped up his head. The police and the police surgeon were notified at once. Shortly after the officers arrived, Dr. Dulin's assistant made his appearance. A hasty examination of the clean-cut, almost stab-like wounds in the victim's left side convinced the surgeon that Lowe was beyond the hope of recovery. However, he was given several injections of nitroglycerin in order to encourage the circulation of the blood. No sooner had this operation been completed than Lowe, who had been breathing slowly, almost in gasps, died. He expired at 12:55 o'clock.[2]

It was reported that the wound "was between the fifth and sixth ribs in the immediate region of the heart. The bullet hole was unusually large, as if the revolver had been of large caliber, or the ball had struck sideways. There was but one wound inflicted, and Watrous could not say whether it was the first shot which struck the victim or not. Most likely it was the first shot, which was fired while the men were sitting not five feet apart."[3]

Initial investigation of the shooting concluded that both men were intoxicated at the time. Kimmel in particular was disheveled and lacked a necktie. He disappeared soon after the shooting and the alarm was raised. He ran into the Windsor Hotel, telephoned his wife (they lived at 2858 Grant Avenue), and told her that he had shot and killed Joe Lowe in self-defense, that she was not to worry over anything she heard. He replaced the receiver and turned to find himself confronted by Officer J. C. Lindsey, who placed him under arrest. Kimmel remarked that he was on his way to the police station anyway to give himself up.

By the time Kimmel and Constable Lindsey arrived at the station, Kimmel was in control of himself. He greeted his former companions cheerfully and said he was sorry to appear as a prisoner instead of accompanying one as he had done in the past. Captain Phillips interviewed him and Kimmel said he was willing to make a statement to the press. The *Time*'s reporter, who was on hand, was allowed to record Kimmel's comments, which contradicted some of the other witnesses' statements:

> I was at the Orpheum theater and staid [*sic*] until about 10 o'clock. After I left the theater I went to Walker's saloon on Curtis street, just back of the opera house. Lowe was there and began abusing me as soon as he saw me. He called me all the vile names he could think of, and promised he would get me some time, and he had it in for me and for every other man who was on the police force or had ever been on the force. I was in Walker's place for some time and Lowe was abusing me all the time I was there. During our talking I put my hand in my overcoat pocket. Lowe asked: "What have you got there?" I replied that I had nothing but my pocket handkerchief. He put his hands in his hip pocket and said he had something, too.
>
> I knew Lowe's reputation and was afraid of him. In order to avoid trouble with him I left the place and went into Watrous's saloon. I took a seat in the office and was there several minutes when Lowe came in. He had some man with him that I didn't know. The barkeeper told me to keep still, as he had heard of the trouble I had had with Lowe. Lowe saw me in the office and came and pulled me out. He called me vile names and insisted that I take a drink with him and call it square. We sent out to the bar and then Lowe said to the barkeeper, "This big —— —— —— can't have a drink on me." I replied that I did not care to drink, anyway. I turned to a man I knew and asked him to take a drink. We went over to a table and Lowe followed us. We walked back to the office and I told Watrous that I was sorry I had caused any trouble in the place. Lowe followed me again and I told him that he was mistaken, that I had never done him any harm. He said that neither I nor Charley Sanders [*sic* – the man in the brown overcoat] had ever caused him any trouble, but that our friends had, and he would get us all. The man with me – I can't think of his name – and I walked to the back of the room and took a seat at the table. Lowe followed us and began abusing me. He finally reached for his hip pocket and I thought he was going to shoot me. I drew my revolver and shot him. That's the truth and all there is to the story.[4]

Bat Masterson, photographed when he was sheriff of Ford County, Kansas, in 1878. Bat regarded Joe Lowe as a friend and bitterly condemned Kimmel for shooting him down while Joe was drunk and unarmed. Courtesy Kansas State Historical Society.

Joe's body was removed to Coroner Rollins' office, where an examination revealed that there were three bullet holes in him. The fatal bullet had entered his right side in line with his kidney and had ranged upward, indicating that he had probably been leaning over and away from the pistol. It exited on his left side just above the fifth rib, entered his left arm about halfway between the elbow and shoulder, then ranged upward, which suggested that his arm had been resting on the table at the time. It came out at the shoulder joint but did not touch the bone. The second ball entered his right arm in the front some three inches below the shoulder, shattering the humerus, and exited almost at the armpit. A search of Lowe's body revealed no sign of a pistol, but he did have a small pocket knife. A gold watch, a diamond stud, and some small change were also found, together with some papers or business correspondence.[5]

The news of Joe's murder aroused strong feelings, particularly the manner of his "taking off." General Cook was saddened and disgusted: "Although Joe may have been a bad man, I look upon his killing as a most cowardly caper. Kimmel thinks he will get a chromo for ridding the world of such a man as Lowe, but I tell you the public opinion will react in a few days and the cruelty of the killing will then draw upon the people. The very act shows cowardice. He had no more right to kill him than I had. It was unnecessary. I knew Kimmel and Lowe. I thought as much of one as the other, but it wasn't fair. No matter how bad a man Lowe was, he should have had a chance for his life."

Bat Masterson, who was staying at the St. James Hotel when Joe Lowe was shot, was equally outspoken: "Why can't men fight fair when they fight? . . . I have no sympathy for a man who goes into a square fight and gets killed, and no censure for the man who kills him, but this one wasn't square. Everybody, Kimmel as well as others, knew that Joe Lowe never went armed, and it would have been easy for that stalwart young man to punish the old fellow without killing him."[6]

Others expressed similar reactions, and several of the newspapers resurrected the story that Joe had once avenged a brother shot down at Alder Gulch. The more perceptive noted that he had spent much of his life at odds with authority — that, at least, was true — but it was Joe's reputation as a killer that received the most attention. In Denver it was reported:

> About ten years ago, he went after John Murphy, the Larimer street saloon man, and came very near getting him. Lowe had some words with Murphy in the latter's place and reached for his gun. Murphy got away, but Lowe was on the warpath for several weeks, friends finally getting the difficulty settled.
>
> At another time he went after Jim Moon, the faro dealer, but it is not believed he was very anxious to find the gambler. Moon had a reputation of being mighty handy with shooting irons himself, and when he heard that Lowe was after him, he sent around a tip that the vicinity was full of dangerous germs of the lead variety and Mr. Lowe might save some repairs to his hide by keeping out of reach. It was currently believed that this message completely bluffed the avenger of the vigilantes for he suddenly expressed a desire to make terms with Moon.[7]

It was Kansas, however, scene of so many of Joe's confrontations and misdeeds, that mourned him most. Under the banner headline "ROWDY JOE KILLED . . . DIES WITH HIS BOOTS ON — History of a Man Who Had No Equal of His Kind," it was declared:

> This was the death of one of Wichita's earliest citizens, of a man more or less prominent in his career while a habitat of this place in the days when Wichita's banners were hung on the outer walls having printed thereon in letters of scarlet the motto: "Everything goes." . . . Joe Lowe, known here as "Rowdy Joe," was perhaps one of the indifferent sort. He possessed many splendid traits of character and then accumulated others which did not add any luster to his name or career . . . he located his dance house just at the west end of the Big River Bridge, which location put it in the vicinity of where the old building now stands, which was used in after years as a mattress factory. West Wichita, at that time known as Delano, was something of a Monte Carlo sort of a place; that is, there was a great variety of things going over there; and Joe was to some extent a king in that element. . . . In 1878 [sic] Rowdy Joe, having dropped that name appeared in Leadville. . . . In 1882 [sic] he moved to Denver. The Cripple Creek papers say, "He had a family and was devotedly attached to his children." At the time of his death he ran a roadhouse about five miles south of Denver. . . . Occasionally a Wichitan would go out to see him, but he was reticent and never talked about his Wichita experiences.[8]

Similar reminiscences appeared in Ellsworth and other places that had known Joe Lowe. There were many who vilified Joe Lowe's name and reputation, doubtless some had good cause, but others sought to strike a balance. Among these was Phil Golding, manager of the Tortoni in Denver, who had known Joe Lowe back in Leadville:

> Joe was inoffensive to people who knew him, but to a stranger his language when drunk was awfully insulting. When he would get drunk and ugly of temper, all that would be necessary to recall him to his senses was a sharp tug at his coat, and he would become quiet at once. He got drunk frequently and carried a gun in those days, as everybody did, but I never saw him make an effort to use it. About the time of the conventions that nominated [Major General Winfield Scott] Hancock for the presidency [1880] Lowe was running his first saloon in Denver. The Leadville delegation of Democrats that came here to attend the state convention visited his place. I was with the party. Lowe plainly said at that time that he had not carried a gun for years, and never would again. I believe he carried out his intentions.
>
> He was never considered a man of quarrelsome disposition. He was good-hearted and would do anything for a friend, and I cannot understand why anybody should kill him. He was good to his family, but seldom spoke of his early life to anybody. He was connected to the army in the early days . . . and the rough life of the plains made him fearless, but he was not a bad man.[9]

Once word of Joe's death reached the ears of his cronies, there were many who could not accept that he had been unarmed, for it was "the opinion of some that Lowe really had a gun with him, and that it was removed by the unknown man before he fled." The "unknown man" was later identified as Daniel J. Seaman. He had been present during the shooting and promptly disappeared before the police arrived. A search lasting three days, part of it spent trying to establish his identity, finally led Deputy District Attorney S. S. Abbott to Seaman, who was well known in the city, especially by the sporting set, among whom he had a reputation as a former faro dealer. When questioned by the police, Seaman said he had gone into Watrous's saloon late Saturday night on his own. Here he met Kimmel, who invited him for a drink. Joe Lowe then appeared and Kimmel invited Joe to have a drink. The three men then adjourned to the dining room at the rear of the barroom and sat at a table. Seaman sat opposite Joe, while Kimmel and Lowe sat facing each other, their chairs so placed that the corner of the table was between them. Lowe sat near the rear door, which led into the saloon.

Seaman stated that Joe used abusive language but made no moves towards a weapon. Kimmel grew very angry over Joe's continued abuse. Seaman could not remember the exact position of Lowe's hands when the shooting started, but he was positive that Lowe made no move to draw a pistol. Kimmel, however, drew his pistol very quickly and shot at Joe, who was still seated. The pistol misfired. Had he wished, Seaman said, Joe could have reached across and grabbed the gun and probably saved his life. Instead, his brain befuddled by alcohol, he just pushed himself back in his chair. Before Joe could get out of his chair, Kimmel then fired twice more, both shots taking effect. Seaman's version of the shooting (which was not recorded at the inquest because he was still being sought at the time) differed from Kimmel's, but the coroner's jury returned a verdict of felonious killing.[10]

The *News* reported on the thirteenth that Joe's two sisters, Mrs. B. F. Dietrich of Cheyenne, Wyoming, and Mrs. Annie Rita of Ogden, Utah, had been informed by telegraph of their brother's death. Recent research has failed to verify the presence of Annie Rita at Ogden, and according to local records at Cheyenne, Mrs. B. F. Dietrich was named Jennie, not Elizabeth.

Lena was informed of Joe's death in the early hours of February 12. That afternoon she appeared at the mortuary, where she identified his body and left soon afterward. With scarcely a word to anyone (many of Joe's old friends had also viewed his remains), she returned home in the buggy that Joe had driven into town the day before. Joe's funeral was conducted on February 15. A large crowd accompanied the casket from McGovern's undertaking parlors to Riverside Cemetery, where he was buried beside his son. The service was conducted by the Reverend Charles Marshall. The large turnout and the many floral tributes surprised the residents of Denver. Even his pallbearers included some of the city's most respected residents: Martin Welch, Con Featherly, Barney Slack, General David Cook, Phil Golding,

The undertaker's bill for burying Joe Lowe. Courtesy Kansas State Historical Society.

James Leonard, Charles Smith, and Richard Roe. For Lena, it was a time of much strain and unwanted publicity. Joe's daughters were still too young to understand why their father would never come home again, and with this came the additional burden of never being told why. In later years, Elizabeth recalled things she had heard about her father, but never from her mother, and she managed to acquire a few mementos of him. For Anna, scarcely old enough to have even known him, he remained a dim and distant figure.[11]

Anticipating a sudden departure, Joe had taken the precaution of deeding all his property to Lena just in case Mollie (or Mary) Lowe were to cause her any problems. His former wife was reported to have "judgement amounting to ten thousand dollars against her former husband," but a search of available records has turned up no proof of this. We suspect that some provision for a division of property was ordered in the original divorce settlement, and there may have been problems over alimony payments. Therefore, Joe's concern for his wife and family is understandable. The property in question was his roadhouse cum ranch on Cherry Creek, eight miles from the city. The "diamond stud" was valued at only forty dollars and his "gold watch" and chain at only ten, so that by the time the estate was settled Lena had very little to live on. She was a hardworking woman who put her young family first. She never remarried and went to great pains to play down her late husband's past. Lena died in 1938, her daughter Elizabeth in 1965. Anna lived long enough to learn who her father was and to understand why his exploits had been kept secret.[12]

Emmanuel A. Kimmel, generally called Charley Kimmel, was said to be a hard case, a man with many enemies, particularly in the sporting set. There were rumors that some of Joe's cronies might take it upon themselves to avenge him in true frontier tradition, for during his service as a police patrolman Kimmel had incurred the wrath of many of them. But no attempts were made on his life. It was recalled that he had been dropped from the city's payroll in 1897 when the new Fire and Police Board went into office, but the reason was obscure. About twenty-eight years old, he had no full-time occupation after he left the police

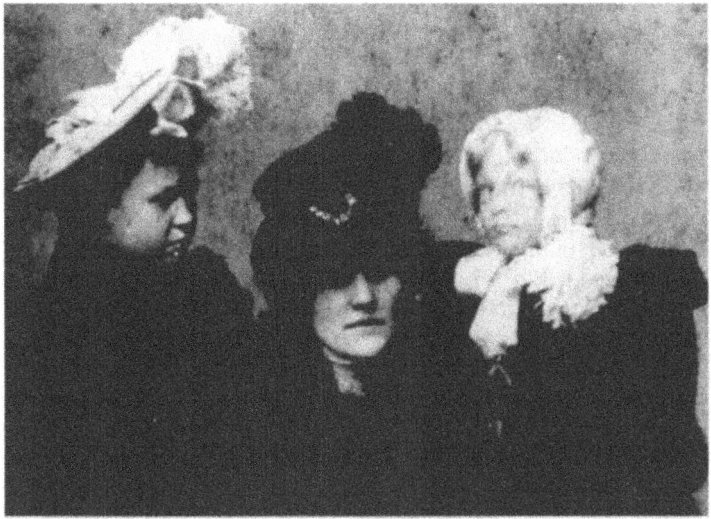

Joe Lowe's daughters, Elizabeth (left) and Anna (right), photographed several years after his death. The attractive lady in the center has not been identified. Courtesy Kansas State Historical Society.

force. He served for a brief period as a "special policeman" at the Bachelor Club and had a reputation for being a very dangerous man when drunk, but he was said to have "an agreeable disposition" and had "many friends," some of whom visited him in jail. Little else had emerged about the man by the time he came to trial.[13]

Kimmel's trial for murder took place at the West Side Court in Denver on June 12, 1899, where he was defended by attorney Thomas Ward. Ward made an initial plea for a continuance in the hope of producing a witness, D. C. Webber, who, it was claimed, could testify that the previous December Lowe had said he would one day kill Kimmel. However, the judge refused to grant such a request on hearsay evidence. For the prosecution, Messrs. Prescott and Elliott of the district attorney's office were assisted by E. A. Ballard, who had made himself a reputation in a murder case some years before. Shortly after the jury was impaneled, Mrs. Kimmel, accompanied by six other women, appeared in court. Embarrassed by the publicity, she blushed but went and sat beside her husband, who smiled and clasped her hand. Almost unnoticed by the rest of the court, Lena Lowe, described as "blonde, tall, serious of face and dressed in deep black, came in late and sat down near Attorney Ballard. She has large hands and a face which is not handsome, but which has a determined set."[14]

Questions put to the would-be jury members to establish any acquaintanceship with the deceased were revealing. Charles Smith claimed that he never read newspapers anyway and knew nothing of the shooting or, indeed, of Joe Lowe, answering "with a superior smile." W. C. Blay, asked if he were native born, replied: "No sir, I am a Missourian." Another man was excused because he was sixty-six, over the age limit for jury duty, and another claimed that although he paid taxes in Denver he was now a resident of Alamosa. Much emphasis was placed upon the birthplaces of potential jurors, their age and nationality, and whether they were married or single. But the overriding object was to establish any sort of relationship with the deceased. Only one black man, G. W. Smith was called. He was challenged, as were a schoolteacher, a salesman, and a member of the militia. Of the thirty-five members of the venire, twenty were challenged. The jury consisted of Calvin Boyer, Charles Smith, Richard H. Brown, W. C. Blay, W. E. Greenlee, Theodore F. Freland, A. A. Ebersole, S. W. Chaney, C. H. Wells, T. D. Jones, John Prothro, and Harry Ketcham.[15]

During most of the preliminary proceedings, Kimmel remained calm and smiling, but he did not miss a thing. "Kimmel is a remarkable prisoner in many ways," wrote the *Post*'s reporter. "He is quite stout, which is a very unusual thing in prisoners charged with murder. He is clean shaven, and with good, free color and bright eyes. Although exhibiting little emotion he is evidently closely, if not intensely interested in every detail, listening to every question minutely, and he follows the accepted men from the witness seat to the jury box with his eyes studying them closely, if furtively."[16]

In his opening statement for the prosecution, attorney Daniel Prescott told the jury: "On the night of February 11 Emmanuel Kimmel followed Joe Lowe from Walker's saloon to Watrous's saloon, there telephoned for his revolver, and then followed Lowe into the back room and killed him without provocation, Kimmel being sober and Lowe helplessly drunk. Hemphill, the waiter who was in the lunch room and saw the midnight shooting, is now in Texas and will not appear at the trial." This was the first intimation that Kimmel had not been armed during the earlier row. The defense promptly complained that the prosecution was acting as if there was no such thing as self-defense and a man must endure all things before defending himself. Mr. Ward then claimed that the trouble between Lowe and Kimmel could be traced back to 1896, when Kimmel was a policeman and arrested a number of Lowe's friends, thus incurring Lowe's hatred.[17]

Jacob W. McCausland, a farmer who lived eight miles out on Broadway and who was a friend of Joe Lowe for many years, stated that he was with Joe Lowe and Joseph N. Taylor on February 11. The trio began drinking at Greenbaum's Fifteenth Street saloon about 4 P.M. They drank beer until they joined Kimmel in Walker's saloon at 11 P.M. Lowe was by now quite drunk, and he began cursing Kimmel, who drank with them, Joe Lowe paying for the drinks. McCausland worried that there might be trouble and asked Joe to stop abusing Kimmel, who had done nothing to harm him. Lowe retorted that Kimmel had harmed his friends, which was why he was so angry. Kimmel denied the allegation, and the row continued for about fifteen minutes. McCausland then paid for a second drink, and leaving Kimmel at Walker's saloon, went on to Watrous's saloon, where they found Kimmel already there.[18]

George Watrous's testimony at the trial as a principal witness was similar to his original statement, quoted by the *News,* after the shooting and before the coroner's hearing. In court, however, the most damning evidence came to light when he described Lowe's abuse of himself and Kimmel:

When Kimmel and his friend named Harry came back, Kimmel came up to the bar and said to me, "I got quite a roast tonight." I told him he was not especially picked on, as Lowe was roasting everybody and I came in for my little bit.

Kimmel said: "You know you wouldn't stand and take what I did tonight."

I said, "I certainly would, being sober, as you are and knowing Joe was drunk."

I asked Kimmel why in the world he didn't go away, go home, or anywhere, but he didn't answer me.

Soon after this, when Kimmel had gone out and come back again, the waiter came and told me that Lowe and Kimmel were sitting together in a back room. I asked if there was any trouble and he said no. I listened and could not hear what the two men were talking about, although I stood within five feet of where they were sitting. I then went back and sat down and in a minute or two I heard the first shot.

Watrous later testified:

The first thing I saw was a hand and a gun sticking out from the open door of the back room and pointing toward the cook's steam table. Then I saw Lowe just in front of the pistol, holding the end of the table. He was leaning over, and fell immediately — fell behind the table.

Kimmel then came out from the back room, the gun still in his hand. He leaned over the table, resting on his left hand and pointing the gun downward. I rushed from behind the bar and caught Kimmel around the waist, pulling him backward, and the gun went off, the bullet striking the mirror above the table and sending the pieces of glass clattering to the floor.

"This is a pretty piece of work you have done tonight," I said to him. He turned and went out, the pistol still in his hand.

Since he was the only eyewitness apart from Seaman, Watrous's statement was crucial to the prosecution's case, and during his testimony it was noticed that Kimmel's face "suffused with blood and then paled again, white and rigid." The defense, however, was quick to point out contradictions in the testimony.[19]

The third day of the trial opened with the prosecution's claim that Kimmel had deliberately armed himself and had lain in wait for Joe Lowe. Joseph Taylor testified concerning Joe's conduct before the shooting, while Daniel Seaman "could not swear that

Lowe made a motion as though he intended to draw a revolver," but he did agree that Joe had verbally abused Kimmel.

Evidence that Kimmel might have lain in wait for Lowe was given by William H. Green [William Hamilton Green?], an officer at the state penitentiary, who testified that he saw Kimmel standing in front of Burpee's real estate office, next door to the St. James Hotel. This was at 1:45 A.M. "I passed very close to him," said Green. "He was looking across the street. It was a very cold night and I was wondering who he was watching at that time of night."

Walker's bartender, Gus Cavanaugh, stated that Kimmel was on his way out of the place at ten o'clock when Lowe and his friends came in and that it was McCausland who asked him to join them. "Lowe, however, called out, 'Hello, there's that —— stiff of an ex-policeman. He's as dirty a —— as ever walked the earth.'" Ten minutes later, Lowe and his friends left. Kimmel then turned to Cavanaugh and remarked, "Well, what do you think of that? That's the dirtiest roast I ever got in my life."

Harry William Hogan, a "weak-voiced youth of 14," stated that he had been by the A.D.T. on February 11 and had been asked by a man resembling Kimmel to carry a note to Twenty-ninth and Champs and also to carry a telegram to the Western Union office. But he could not swear positively that Kimmel was the man who hired him.

C. W. Wilhelm testified that he saw Kimmel fire the first and second shots before he fled from the saloon, and policeman W. E. Griffiths, the first officer on the scene, stated that he searched Lowe's clothing and found no trace of a revolver.[20]

"Why did you shoot Joe Lowe?" attorney Ward demanded when Kimmel took the stand in his own defense on June 16. "I shot him," Kimmel replied, "because I thought my life was in danger." But why more than once? "I was afraid he would kill me."

Kimmel was very cool and collected, and his replies to questions were slow and concise. He thought Lowe had left Watrous's saloon by the time he walked over there to talk to George Watrous, and he was surprised to find Lowe still there. He denied that he had hired a messenger or armed himself for the purpose of shooting Joe Lowe. In fact, he had been carrying his revolver in his waistband all the time. He met Daniel Seaman in the bar and invited him back to the restaurant for a drink. While they sat drinking, Lowe suddenly appeared and Kimmel said, "Are you going to continue to abuse me?" Lowe replied, "You ——— I guess I'll get you now." Joe's hand dropped down to his pocket, and "then I fired."

Kimmel said he had been warned by D. C. Webber, former president of the Fire and Police Board, that Lowe intended to kill him and had made similar threats on several occasions. Witnesses Robert Cunningham and D. G. Bradt (the latter said he had known Joe Lowe for ten yers) also testified that as late as January Joe had threatened Kimmel's life. Joseph Kerr, a reporter, confirmed George Watrous's statement. Ada M. Hale of 637 Twenty-second Street testified that she had heard Joe Lowe declare: "I'll get that man some day. I'll give him a walnut overcoat."

When Lena Lowe was called to the stand, she displayed no emotion and answered questions in a firm voice. She testified that her late husband had not been in the habit of carrying a revolver. In fact, his pistol was still in their bedroom on the night of the tragedy. Indeed, the day after the shooting, the *Rocky Mountain News* had carried a crude sketch of Joe's holstered pistol hanging over the bedpost (presumably where it was normally kept). The weapon was not identified or produced during the trial and remains in the family's possession today. In 1969 it was lent to the Kansas State Historical Society for photographing and examination. It was found to be a .45-caliber Colt double-action 1878 Army model. The Colt company confirmed that the pistol, serial number 2655, was shipped from its factory on March 1, 1880, along with twenty similar pistols, to a New York dealer, Hartley & Graham. Originally, the pistol had a 7 1/2-inch barrel, but either Joe or a previous owner had had it shortened to 5 1/2 inches.[21]

In its closing argument, the prosecution laid great stress upon the allegation that Kimmel had lain in wait for Joe Lowe and had taken advantage of Joe's intoxicated condition. Furthermore, Kimmel was "young, strong and sober," whereas the "man who

Joe Lowe's double-action Colt 1878 Army revolver. On the day he was killed, it was in its customary place — holstered and hanging from his bedpost. Courtesy Kansas State Historical Society.

was killed was old [sic], drunk and garrulous. If he was abusive it was only with his mouth. If he was vile in his conversations it was the result of an early life full of hardships. We are not here to praise Joe Lowe. We are here to inquire into the manner of his taking off." Warming to his subject, Prescott then summed up:

Kimmel waited in Walker's saloon ten or fifteen minutes after Lowe left, and although the roasting Lowe had given him rankled in his heart deeply enough to cause him to mention that to the bartender, not a word about his fears escaped his lips. Then he too left and instead of going home at that hour of the night, for some unaccountable reason found his way into the very place whither his antagonist had gone, and when he found him there instead of leaving, waited for him again to ask him to drink. And then he went across the street and watched and waited, not as he says for Lowe to go away but to be sure that the time was ripe to put his plans into execution. His home was far away, the cars would soon stop, the night was bitter cold, and yet he watched and waited.

And so here we have the plan. Then he put it into execution. He went across to Watrous' met Lowe coming out, and asked him back into the room to drink a glass with him, chose the table at which he was to sit and waited pistol in hand, for him to be seated at it, with his hospitable liquor on the table, and then opened fire on him. If this was a fair fight I do not know what could be called foul. Those clothes that Joe Lowe wore, filled with bullet holes tell too plainly what was done. They are dumb mouths but they are eloquent with condemnation of this cowardly murder.

In his closing remarks for the defense, Ward dwelt upon Joe Lowe's "bad record," spending half an hour on it before concluding:

Kimmel had before him in his mind the record of Lowe and the knowledge of what a desperate, vindictive man he had been. The hostile movement of Lowe justified Kimmel in acting not slowly but quickly. I don't care whether Lowe had a pistol or not. I don't care whether he intended to harm and injure Kimmel or not. Kimmel was justified. If Kimmel was not guilty of murder he was not guilty of manslaughter or involuntary manslaughter. It is either acquittal or murder in the first degree. If you believe that Kimmel lay in wait as the state promised to show you, if you believe that he sent for a messenger boy and that the messenger brought him a revolver with which to kill Lowe, then Kimmel is guilty of murder. Otherwise he should be acquitted. There is no middle ground.

Ward then drew the jury's attention to the instructions of the court concerning self-defense and also to George Watrous's testimony, in which Watrous had contradicted himself. He said the state had not proved that Kimmel had obtained a revolver after his meeting with Lowe in Walker's saloon and noted that a pawnbroker had testified that the pistol used by Kimmel had been sold by him to the defendant the previous December. To strengthen the defense's case that Lowe was a thoroughly bad and vicious individual, a number of witnesses had been called, but only statements regarding the general character of the deceased were admitted.

On the twentieth the jury retired at 3:20 P.M. to consider its verdict, which it reached at seven o'clock. Kimmel was brought from the county jail to the courthouse shortly before 8 P.M. It was reported:

He did not appear very anxious as the general opinion seemed to be that there would either be [an] acquittal or a hung jury. After the verdict had been read [he was acquitted] Judge Allen ordered the court adjourned. Kimmel shook hands with all the jurors. He had been locked up in the county jail since the day after the shooting.[22]

In reviewing all the evidence, we have reached the conclusion that the verdict went in Kimmel's favor primarily because of the character assassination launched against Joe Lowe rather than Kimmel's motive. The impassioned plea by Mr. Ward that he did not care if Lowe was armed or not, that Lowe's actions entitled Kimmel to react as he did in self-defense, must have carried much weight with the jury. In truth, Joe Lowe had been his own worst enemy, but that Kimmel was, after all, the man of violence described by the defense can be gleaned from the following, which was published in 1901:

> E. A. Kimmel, ex-policeman and slayer of Joe Lowe about a year ago, was arrested at his home, Gray and Twenty-seventh Avenue, on a warrant sworn out before Justice Rice, charging him with assault and battery. Kimmel was locked up in the city jail.
>
> His wife was afraid of him, because of his dissipation and threat to kill her if she carried out her pupose to leave him. Kimmel went home drunk last night and began to abuse her, she says. She was brought down in a cab by a neighbor to the police station, and secured the warrant from Justice Rice.[23]

Joe Lowe was very much a product of his time. He was not a gunfighter in the manner of Wild Bill Hickok or as homicidally inclined as John Wesley Hardin, but when Joe pulled a gun on another man he meant to use it. On occasion Joe Lowe was rowdy, uncouth, ill-mannered and vindictive, yet he could also be kind, considerate, and a man of his word — traits that highlight his enigmatic character, which is the stuff of legend. Yet for anyone to suggest that Rowdy Joe Lowe was a Wild West hero would be stretching credibility to its limit. Rather, we think he was a likable rogue, for whatever history may make of him, Joe Lowe was a character, undoubtedly a character.

Notes

1. Nellie Snyder Yost, *Buffalo Bill: His Family, Friends, Failures and Fortunes,* 281; *Rocky Mountain News,* February 13, 1899.
2. *Rocky Mountain News,* February 12, 1899.
3. Denver *Sunday Times,* February 12, 1899.
4. Denver *Times,* February 12, 1899.
5. Ibid.
6. *Rocky Mountain News,* February 13, 1899.
7. Ibid., February 12, 1899.
8. Wichita *Eagle,* February 15, 1899.
9. *Rocky Mountain News,* February 13, 1899.
10. Ibid., February 15, 1899.
11. Ibid., February 16, 1899; conversation with Edward Dunbar, 1969; Joe had purchased a plot — space for three graves — in Lot 35, Block 24, northwest quarter of the Riverside Cemetery.
12. Clerk of the Denver District Court to Waldo E. Koop, July 30, 1970; Case No. 548, In the Matter of the Estate of Joseph Lowe, Deceased. Joseph Lowe's Pension File.
13. Denver *Sunday Times,* February 12, 1899; Leadville *News-Reporter,* February 14, 1899.
14. Denver *Post,* June 14, 1899.
15. Ibid., June 13, 1899.
16. Ibid.
17. Ibid., June 13, 1899.
18. Denver *Post,* June 14, 1899.
19. *Rocky Mountain News,* June 16, 1899.
20. Denver *Post,* June 16, 1899.
21. Colt Industries to Joseph W. Snell, KSHS, February 11, 1970.
22. *Rocky Mountain News,* June 21, 1899.
23. Ibid., February 24, 1921.

Bibliography

I. Books and Pamphlets

Andreas, A. T. *History of the State of Kansas.* Chicago, 1883.
Armes, Colonel George A. *Ups and Downs of an Army Officer.* Washington, D.C., 1900.
Beebe, Henry S. *History of Peru*, n.p., 1858.
Biographical History of Barton County, Kansas. n.p., 1912.
Burns, Robert T. *A Link to the Past: The Saga of La Salle County, Illinois.* LaSalle, Ill., 1968.
Bushick, Frank H. *Glamorous Days.* San Antonio, Tex., 1934.
Cody, William F. *The Life of Hon. William F. Cody, Known as Buffalo Bill, the Famous Hunter, Scout and Guide: An Autobiography.* Hartford, Conn., 1879.
DeArment, Robert K. *Knights of the Green Cloth: The Saga of the Frontier Gamblers.* Norman, Okla., 1982.
Dykstra, Robert C. *The Cattle Towns.* New York, 1968.
Gard, Wayne. *The Chisholm Trail.* Norman, Okla., 1954.
Hardin, John Wesley. *The Life of John Wesley Hardin.* Seguin, Tex., 1896.
Heitman, Francis B. *Historical Register and Dictionary of the United States Army, 1789–1903.* Washington, D.C., 1903.
Jelinek, George. *Ellsworth, Kansas, 1867–1947.* Salina, Kans., 1947.
―――. *The Ellsworth Story: 90 Years of Ellsworth County History.* Ellsworth, Kans., 1957.
Knight, Oliver. *Fort Worth, Outpost on the Trinity.* Norman, Okla., 1955.
Koop, Waldo E. *Billy The Kid: The Trail of a Kansas Legend.* Kansas City, Mo., 1965.
Lake, Stuart N. *Wyatt Earp, Frontier Marshal.* Boston, 1931.
Lamar, Howard R., ed. *The Reader's Encyclopedia of the American West.* New York, 1977.
Logan, Herschel C. *Buckskin and Satin.* Harrisburg, Pa., 1954.

McCoy, Joseph G. *Historic Sketches of the Cattle Trade of the West and Southwest.* Kansas City, Mo., 1874.
Masterson, V. V. *The Katy Railroad and the Last Frontier.* Norman, Okla., 1952.
Miller, Nyle H., and Joseph W. Snell. *Why the West Was Wild.* Topeka, Kans., 1963.
Miner, H. Craig. *Wichita: The Early Years, 1865–1880.* Lincoln, Nebr., 1982.
Noel, Thomas J. *The City and the Saloon: Denver, 1858–1916.* Lincoln, Nebr., 1982.
Plenn, J. H. *Texas Hellion: The True Story of Ben Thompson.* New York, 1955.
Rosa, Joseph G. *They Called Him Wild Bill: The Life and Adventures of James Butler Hickok.* 2d ed. Norman, Okla., 1974.
– – – *The Gunfighter: Man or Myth?* Norman, Okla., 1969.
Sonnichsen, C. L. *Billy King's Tombstone.* Caldwell, Idaho, 1951.
Streeter, Floyd Benjamin. *Prairie Trails & Cowtowns.* New York, 1963.
Vestal, Stanley. *Dodge City: Queen of the Cowtowns.* London, 1955.
Webb, Walter Prescott. *The Texas Rangers: A Century of Frontier Defense.* Austin, Tex., 1965.
Willison, George F. *Here They Dug the Gold.* New York, 1931.
Yost, Nellie Snyder. *Buffalo Bill: His Family, Friends, Failures and Fortunes.* Chicago, 1979.

II. Magazines and Articles

Elliott, Bishop Robert. "Letters from Bishop Elliott," in *The Spirit of Missions.* Corpus Christi, Tex., 1875.
General Statutes of the State of Kansas The. Lawrence, Kansas, 1868.
Hunter, Martin, Sr. "Reminiscences of Colonel Lewis Ginger," *Frontier Times,* Vol. XXX, No. 2 (April–June 1953).
Ostrander, Major A. B. "Old Days in Denison," *Frontier Times,* Vol. VII, No. 9 (June 1930).
Publication No. 23, Illinois State Historical Library, 1917.
Rickards, Colin W. "Vengeance, Kansas 1870's Style." English Westerners Society *Brand Book,* Vol. IV, No. 1 (October 1961).
Roberts, Gary L. "From Tin Star to Hanging Tree: The Short Career and Violent Times of Billy Brooks." In *The Prairie Scout,* Vol. III. Abilene, Kans., 1975.
Rosa, Joseph G. "J. B. Hickok, Deputy U.S. Marshal." *Kansas History,* Vol. 2, No. 4 (Winter 1979).
"Stories of Wichita," Scrapbook of news clippings from unidentified sources. Wichita Public Library, Wichita, Kansas.
Texas Writers' Project. *Fort Worth and Tarrant County.* 26 vols. Typescript, Fort Worth Public Library.

Thompson, W. F. "Peter Robidoux: A Real Kansas Pioneer." *Collections of the Kansas State Historical Society*, Vol. XVII (1926–28). Topeka, Kans., 1928.

III. Newspapers

Abilene (Kansas) *Chronicle*
Denison (Texas) *Daily News*
Denver (Colorado) *Daily News*
Denver (Colorado) *Daily Times*
Denver (Colorado) *Post*
Denver (Colorado) *Rocky Mountain Daily News*
Denver (Colorado) *Rocky Mountain News*
Denver (Colorado) *Sunday Times*
Dodge City (Kansas) *Ford County Globe*
Dodge City (Kansas) *Times*
Ellsworth (Kansas) *Reporter*
El Paso (Texas) *Lone Star*
Emporia (Kansas) *Ledger*
Emporia (Kansas) *News*
Fort Worth (Texas) *Daily Democrat*
Fort Worth (Texas) *Gazette*
Galveston (Texas) *Daily News*
Hays City (Kansas) *Sentinel*
Jacksboro (Texas) *Frontier Echo*
Junction City (Kansas) *Union*
Junction City (Kansas) *Weekly Union*
Kansas City (Missouri) *Evening Star*
Kansas City (Missouri) *Times*
Lawrence (Kansas) *Daily Tribune*
Lawrence (Kansas) *Weekly Tribune*
Leadville (Colorado) *Daily Democrat*
Leadville (Colorado) *Daily Herald*
Leadville (Colorado) *News-Reporter*
Leadville (Colorado) *Weekly Herald*
Leavenworth (Kansas) *Daily Commercial*
Leavenworth (Kansas) *Daily Conservative*
Leavenworth (Kansas) *Daily Times*
Leavenworth (Kansas) *Times and Conservative*
Nebraska City (Nebraska) *News-Press*
Newton (Kansas) *Kansan*
Osage Mission (Kansas) *Mission Transcript*
St. Louis (Missouri) *Democrat*
St. Louis (Missouri) *Republican*

San Angelo (Texas) *Standard-Times*
Topeka (Kansas) *Daily Commonwealth*
Topeka (Kansas) *State Record*
Weatherford (Texas) *Exponent*
Wichita (Kansas) *Beacon*
Wichita (Kansas) *City Eagle*
Wichita (Kansas) *Eagle*
Wichita (Kansas) *Tribune*
Wichita (Kansas) *Weekly Beacon*
Wichita (Kansas) *Weekly Eagle*

IV. Manuscripts and Other Materials

Annual Reports of the Adjutant General of Missouri (1864–1865). Microfilm copy, Kansas State Historical Society (cited hereafter as KSHS).
Cappelle, Mrs. Anna, to Joseph W. Snell, May 13, 1969. Manuscripts Department, KSHS.
Case No. 91, Estate of E. T. Beard, Records of the Sedgwick County, Kansas, Probate Court.
Case No. 548, In the Matter of the Estate of Joseph Lowe, Deceased. Arapahoe County Court Records, Denver, Colo.
Case No. 690, State of Kansas vs. Joseph Lowe, Indictment for Murder. Records of the Sedgwick County District Court. Microfilm copy, Manuscripts Department, KSHS.
Case no. 828, U.S. vs. Manley B. Gilman and James Stitt, Topeka District Court Records (1869). Federal Records Center, Kansas City, Mo.
Case No. 8621, Mary Lowe vs. Joseph Lowe, Petition for a Divorce. Denver District Court Records, Colorado State Archives.
Census of Dimmick Township, LaSalle County, Illinois, 1850.
Clerk of the District Court, Ellsworth County, Kansas to Joseph G. Rosa, September 1987.
Clerk of the District Court, Tarrant County, Texas, to Joseph G. Rosa, April–September 1987.
Colt Industries, Hartford, Conn., to Joseph W. Snell, February 11, 1970. Manuscripts Department, KSHS.
Deed Record Books, Office of the Registrar of Deeds, Sedgwick County, Kansas.
Docket Book, Justice of the Peace, Ellsworth Kansas. Microfilm copy, KSHS.
Dodson, J. E., to Hon. W. C. Perry, U.S. Attorney, Topeka, Kansas, July 30, 1888, relative to a "Rowdy Joe." Copy supplied by Federal Records Center, Kansas City, Mo.
Dunbar, Edward, to Joseph G. Rosa (1969–1973). Author's Collection.
Ellsworth County Commissioners Record Book A, Vol. 1, 1867 and 1868. Microfilm copy, KSHS.

Ellsworth County Ordinances for Ellsworth, 1870. Microfilm copy, KSHS.
Everly, Elaine C., Navy and Old Army Branch, Military Archives Division, National Archives, Washington, D.C., to Joseph G. Rosa, May 18, 1981.
Fauquet, L. C. Scrapbook, Wichita Public Library.
Governor's Correspondence Files, "Crime and Criminals." Manuscripts Department, KSHS.
Grand Central Hotel Register, Ellsworth, Kansas (1873). Microfilm copy, KSHS.
Kate Lowe vs. State of Texas, 4, Ct. App. 34 (1878). Records of the Court of Appeal, Austin, Texas, 1878.
Lowe, Joseph. Civil War Service Record and Pension File. National Archives, Washington, D.C.
Marriage Records (Vol. 1, 1876–1885), 2. Tarrant County Court Records, Fort Worth, Texas.
Marriage License No. 5795, issued to Joseph Lowe and Lena Larson, Denver, February 10, 1888. Records of the Arapahoe County District Court.
Muster Roll, Battery B, Second (New) Missouri Regiment of Light Artillery. National Archives, Washington, D.C.
Parker, Elmer O., Assistant Director, Old Military Records Division, National Archives, Washington, D.C., to Joseph G. Rosa, December 18, 1969.
Police Judge Returns, City of Wichita, 1873 and 1874. Microfilm copy, KSHS.
Post Sutler's Journal, Fort Harker, Kansas (1867–68). Microfilm copy, KSHS.
Proceedings of the Governing Body, City of Wichita, Journal A. Microfilm copy, Archives Department, KSHS.
Records of the City of Wichita. Microfilm copy, Manuscripts Department, KSHS.
Records of the District Court, Harvey County, Kansas.
Schattner, Fred, to Leon Fouquet, January 21, 1913. Copy on file, Manuscripts Department, KSHS.
Secretary of State, Memorials and Petitions, File 19, No. 296, Letter C. Texas State Library, Austin, Texas.
Secretary of War: Habeas Corpus, *Opinions of the Attorney General.* Washington, D.C., 1869.
State of Kansas vs. Joseph Brennan, Indictment for Murder, Justice of the Peace Records, Ellsworth County. Microfilm copy, KSHS.
State of Kansas vs. Richard Cavanagh, Records of the District Court, Ellsworth County, Kansas.
State of Texas vs. James Courtright, Case No. 1476, Tarrant County Court, Criminal Case Index.
State of Texas vs. Joel Collins, Case No. 1266, Records of the Caldwell County Courts, Lockhart, Texas.

State of Texas vs. Joseph Lowe, Case Nos. 1250, 1276, and 1249, Records of the Caldwell County Courts, Lockhart, Texas.

Tuttle, Perry C. Civil War Service Record and Pension File. National Archives, Washington, D.C.

Warford, Sherrill, Historical Research Cooperative, Leadville, Colorado, to Joseph G. Rosa, September 26, 1987.

Index

Abbott, S. S.: 159
Abilene, Kans.: 38, 44, 54, 65, 66, 73, 98
Age Saloon, Newton, Kans.: 57
Alamo, Tex.: 105
Alder Gulch, Mont.: 148, 157
Aley, M.: 65
"Allegro" (newspaperman): 43ff., 45, 51, 59n., 64
Allen (judge): 171
Allen, Henry: 21
Allen, Tom: 96
Allen's Grocery: 75
Almond, Frankie (prostitute): 107
Anderson, Bill: 42ff.
Anderson, James H.: 54
Anderson, John: 42ff.
Anderson, William ("Billie"): blinded by Joe Lowe, 80; sues Lowe, 91
Andrews, J. H.: 75
Armes, Maj. George: 23
Armour, James: 56
Armstrong, William: 51
Atchison, Kans.: 60n.
Atchison, Topeka & Santa Fe Railroad: 65, 100
Atkins, Thomas.: killed by Joe Brennan, 21–22

Bachelor Club, Denver, Colo.: 163
Bailey, Billy: *see* McCluskie, Michael
Ballard, E. A.: 164
Bass, Sam, killed by Texas Rangers: 104
Battery B Second Missouri Artillery: 8–10
Baumann, Charles (policeman): 54, 56
Beach, Sumner: 61–62
Beard, Amos: 74
Beard, Caroline ("Red's" sister): 74
Beard, Clara ("Red's" daughter): 91, 92n.
Beard, Deborah (Mrs. E. T.): 84–85, 92n.
Beard, Edward T. ("Red"): 5, 12, 56, 71, 73; origins, 74; fight with printer, 75; saloon burned down, 77; saloon rebuilt, 78; showdown with Lowe, 78–88; killed, 84
Beard, Illian ("Red's" daughter): 91
Beard, Inez ("Red's" daughter): 91
Beardstown, Ill.: 74
Becker, A. A. (Lowe's alias): 93ff.
Beckwith, Dan: 39
Beebe, Carrie: 75; takes over Lowe's dance hall, 90
Beebe, Henry S.: 8

Beebe, Walter: 75; testifies at Lowe's trial, 79–81; aids in Lowe jailbreak, 88; jailed and later pardoned, 88, 90; murdered, 91
Beehive Saloon, Denison, Tex.: 98
Belknap, William W. (secretary of war): 30
Bennett, H. W.: 104
Berry, Harrison: 51
Berry, Mort: 51
Bideno, Juan: 44
Big Tree (Kiowa): 98
Billings (saloon owner): 126
Billy the Kid: 91
Black Hawk (Sac and Fox): 7
Black Hawk War: 7
Black Hills, Dak.T.: 99, 104
Blay, W. C. (juror): 164
Booth, George: 28
Booth, Lewis: 28
Bowers, W. L.: 148
Bowie, Jim: 105
Boyd, Alexander: 23
Boyer, Calvin (juror): 164
Boyle (soldier): 76
Bradt, D. G.: 168
Brennan, Joseph: 21–22
Brennan, Miles: 22
Bristow, B. H. (solicitor general): 30
Brockett, J. W.: 98, 100
Brooks, William L. ("Billy"): 54ff.
Brookville, Kans.: 29
Brown, Jake: 147
Brown, Judge Richard H.: 164
Brown, "Trick" (gambler): 48
Buffalo Bill: *see* Cody, William F.
Buffalo Bill's Wild West and Congress of Rough Riders of the World: 151
Bush, James S.: 23
Bush, William ("Billy"): 36n.

Caldwell, Kans.: 64
Calhoun, Jim: 133
Campbell, Bill (sheriff): 99
Campbell, Judge W.: 86
Campbell (runner): 126
Can-Can (dance): 101
Carbonate Rifles: 121
Carbondale, Kans.: 100
Carson, Tom (policeman): 45, 46
Cattle: shipping pens for, 38–39; numbers shipped, 66
Cavanaugh, Gus: 167
Cavanaugh, Richard: 31
Centennial Hotel, Leadville, Colo.: 112
Centennial Theater, Leadville, Colo.: 112, 114
Chaney, S. W. (juror): 164
Chaves (Mexican): 18
Cheyenne Indians: 9
Cheyenne, Wyo.: 9, 160
Chisholm, Jesse: 38, 61
Chisholm Trail, origin of: 38, 61, 105
Chisholm Trail bridge, Wichita, Kans.: 69
Cincinnati Home for Friendless Women: 50
Clarendon barroom, Leadville, Colo.: 124
Clark, Dick (gambler): 48
Cody, William F. ("Buffalo Bill"): 12, 15, 119–20, 151
Cohron, William: 44
Collins, Joel: 103, partner of Joe Lowe, 104; killed, 104–106
Collins ("Shotgun"): 133
Committee of Public Safety, Leadville, Colo.: 122
Colorado Humane Society: 148
Colorado Militia: 121–22
Colvin (Judge): 95–97
Connor, Gen. Patrick: 9
Connors, John.: 134
Cook, Gen. David: 4, 121ff.; describes Lowe, 129; saddened by his death, 157; pallbearer at his funeral, 160

Index   181

Cook, Jim: 147
Corbin, Jack (scout), lynched: 28
Cottage Grove (roadhouse): 5, 137, 143, 149
Courtright, Timothy Isaiah ("Long-haired Jim"): 113ff.
Cowen, E. D., writes about Joe Lowe: 148
Crafts, W. A.: 106
Craig (lynched): 17
Craine (justice): 148
Crawford, Gov. Samuel: 14
Cregier, Billy, killed: 114
Creston, Iowa: 44
Crockett, Davy: 105
Cronk, William: 51
Cunningham, Robert: 168
Curry, Jim: 148
Cusick, Patrick, 134
Custom House Saloon, Wichita, Kans.: 53

Darlington Township, Kans.: 39
Davis, Harry: 147
Davis (saloon owner): 64
Day, H. H.: 114
Deitrich, Mrs. B. F.: *see* Lowe, Elizabeth (Joe Lowe's sister)
Delano (West Wichita), Kans.: 62ff., 73ff., 97, 100, 158
Delany, George: *see* McCluskie, Michael
Del Norte, Colo.: 65
DeMerritt, Josephine: 51; mistress of Red Beard, 75; shot at by Red, 81; takes over Red's saloon, 85; jailed for forgery and pardoned, 87, 89
Denison, George: 97
Denison, Tex.: 97; description of, 98, 100
Denver, Colo.: 4, 5, 38, 107, 126–29ff., 158ff.
Denver, James W.: 129

Denver and Rio Grande Railroad: 119
Department of the Missouri: 78
Devere, Harry: 112
Dickerman, Mrs. Nancy C.: 74
Dickerman, Willard A.: 74
Dimmick Township, Ill.: 6
Dodge, Edward Judson: 26–27
Dodge City, Kans.: 56, 98, 111, 131
Dodge City Gang: 131
Dodge City Peace Commission: 134
Doley (soldier): 76
Dow, William ("Rattlesnake Bill"): 50
Dowd, Thomas: 26
Drought, Fred (policeman): 16
Duckworth (policeman): 94; arrests Joe Lowe, 95, 95ff.

Earp, Wyatt: 82–84, 132–34
Ebersole, A. A. (juror): 164
Edwards, Thomas: 46
Eleventh Kansas Cavalry: 44
Elgin, Kans.: *see* Delano, Kans.
Elliott (attorney): 163
Elliott, Bishop Robert: 101
Ellsworth, 2d Lt. Allen: 12
Ellsworth, Kans.: 5, 12, 14, 16–19, 21–23, 35, 38ff.; cowtown, 66, 97, 121, 151, 159
El Paso, Tex.: 116
Emporia, Kans.: 39, 56
Entertainments: at Newton, Kans., 48, 51; at Wichita, Kans., 67; at Fort Worth, Tex., 112
Erlick, Ben: 23

Farley (police chief): 147
Featherly, Con: 160
Field, Mollie: *see* Lowe, Mollie
Fifth Infantry: 29
Fisher, B. H.: 86
Fisher, George: 73
Fisher (judge): 87

Fitzpatrick, Michael, kills George Halliday: 57
Fort Dodge, Kans.: 27
Fort Griffin, Tex.: 111
Fort Harker, Kans.: 11–14; cholera at, 16, 18–20, 29, 30, 151
Fort Harker post sutler's journal: 19
Fort Hays, Kans.: 78
Fort Laramie, Wyo.: 9
Fort Leavenworth, Kans.: 9, 11, 13
Fort Riley, Kans.: 11, 13, 76
Fort Sam Houston, Tex.: 105
Fort Sill, I.T.: 62
Fort Worth, Tex.: 106ff.
Foster, Lottie (prostitute): 50
Fouquet, L. C.: 67
Franklin, Annie (prostitute): 85–86
Franklin, Mo.: 9
Freeland, Theodore F. (juror): 164
French, Capt. A. R.: 42

Gainsford, James (policeman): 46
Gallagher, John: 48
Gambling: description of characters, 47–48; at Wichita, Kans., 67, 70; at Newton, Kans., 95
Gardner, Alexander (photographer): 13
Gilman, Manley B. (horse thief): 27
Ginger, Col. Lewis: 103–104
Glinn, Annie (prostitute): 49–50
Golding, Phil: 159; pallbearer at Lowe's funeral, 160
Gold Room Saloon, Denison, Tex.: 98
Gold Room Saloon, Newton, Kans.: 48ff., 57
Gordon (policeman): 147
Grand Central Hotel, Leadville, Colo.: 97
Grand Central Theater, Leadville, Colo.: 123, 127
Gray, Fannie (prostitute): 53
Green, William H.: 129–30, 167

Greenbaum's saloon, Denver, Colo.: 165
Greenlee, W. E. (juror): 164
Green Room Saloon, Dodge City, Kans.: 111
Griffiths, W. E.: 167
Grotto Saloon, Denison, Tex.: 98
Guns: ammunition issued to Wichita police, 68–69; 1851 Colt navy revolver, 18, 32ff., 54, 99; 1860 Colt army revolver, 32ff.; Henry rifle, 57; sawed-off shotguns, 78; Joe Lowe's shotgun, 78ff.; Webley .45 "Bulldog," 126; Winchester rifle, 146–47

Hale, Adam: 168
Hallett, C. H. (deputy U.S. marshal): 93–95
Halliday, George: 56–57
Hancock, John: 17
Hancock, Maj. Gen. W. S.: 159
Hardin, John Wesley: 44–45, 101, 171
Harker, Maj. Gen. Chas.: 12
Harrigan (policeman): 94
Harrington, F. J.: *see* "Allegro"
Harris, W. H.: 132
Hartley & Graham (gun dealers): 168
Hartman, L. C.: 132
Hawkes, John: 21
Hays City, Kans.: 17
Heath, Lewis: 90
Heitler, F.: 153
Hemphill (waiter): 165
Hendrickson, Dr. W. T.: 63
Hickok, Howard: 7
Hickok, James B. ("Wild Bill"): 7, 15, 16, 18, 19; as a fighter, 51; offered post as marshal of Newton, 54; drives prostitutes out of Abilene, 73, 104, 118n., 148, 171
Hicks, Dan ("Cherokee Dan"): 54

Hide Park (brothel district at Newton): 39; sold off, 58
Hill (saloon owner): 19
Hogan, Harry William: 167
Hohner, Mrs.: 22
Holland, George: 116
Holliday, Bert: 129
Holliday, Dr. John ("Doc"): 132, 148
Homer, Ill.: 7
Hope, Mayor James: 91
Houston, Harrisburg & San Antonio Railroad: 100
Houston, Gen. Samuel: 105
Houter, Al: 114–15
Hudson, J. E. (policeman): 16
Humboldt Creek, Kans.: 28
Hunt, James: 56
Huntsville State Prison, Tex.: 98

Illinois-Michigan Canal: 6

Jackson (stable hand): 29
Jackson, A. (printer), fight with Red Beard: 75
Jefferson City, Mo.: 8, 9
Jennison, Charles: 64–65
Jewett, E. B.: 86
Johnson (saloonkeeper): 39
Johnson, Charles: 17
Johnson, Jack (policeman): 51, 60 n.
Johnson, Jake (saloonkeeper): 39
Jones, A. E.: 128
Jones, Charles B. (deputy sheriff): 84
Jones, Ed: 51
Jones, T. D. (juror): 164
Junction City, Kans.: 13, 22, 26, 28, 129

Kansas City, Mo.: 18, 19, 35, 62, 132
Kansas City Railroad: 42, 151
Kansas Pacific Railway: 65ff.
Kansas Supreme Court: 90

Kelley, James H. ("Dog"): 131
Kelly, James: 74
Kelly, John: 26
Keogh, Capt. Myles: 19
Kerwin, Jack: 137–38
Kesler, Sheriff E. A.: 22
Ketcham, Harry (juror): 164
Kimmel, Emmanuel A.: 152ff.; kills Joe Lowe, 154–55; tried for Joe Lowe's murder, 163–71
Kimmel, Mrs.: 154, 171
King, Carlos B. (policeman): 45; murdered, 45–47
King, William A. ("Billy"): 111
Kingsbury, Sheriff George W.: 14, 16, 18
Kisthard, Daniel: 143ff.
Kisthard, Jacob: 143ff.

Land Grant Railway Trust Co.: 98
Lane, Joseph: 19
Lanham, S. W. T.: 109
Larkin House Hotel, Ellsworth, Kans.: 32
LaSalle, Ill.: 6, 8
Lathrop, Dolly (waitress): 123
Lauster (doctor): 135
Lawrence, Kans.: 17, 21, 100
Leadville, Colo.: 15, 109, 115, 119ff., 137, 159
Leadville Guards: 121
Leavenworth, Kans.: 14, 17, 53
Lee, Patrick: 42
Lentz, Nick (saloonkeeper): 26
Leonard, James: 162
Leshart, Charles: 77
Levy, M. W.: 90
Lewis, Jack: 124–25
Lindsey, J. C.: 154–55
Liquor licenses: 16–17, 19, 71
Lisle, David: 46
Little Jake's Saloon: 32
Long Branch Saloon, Denison, Tex.: 98

Long Branch Saloon, Dodge City, Kans.: 133
Lovett, Harry: 54
Lowe, Anna (Joe Lowe's sister): 7, 160
Lowe, Anna (Joe Lowe's daughter): 6, 7, 137, 149, 150n., 163
Lowe, Col. Charlie: 127
Lowe, Elizabeth (Joe Lowe's sister): 7, 160
Lowe, Elizabeth (Joe Lowe's daughter): 4, 7, 137, 149, 163
Lowe, J. (horse thief): 142
Lowe, John W., killed in Black Hills: 99–100
Lowe, Joseph ("Rowdy Joe"): 3; character and reputation, 4, 66–67, 133, 142; love affairs, and treatment of Kate, 5, 53, 105, 131; origin of nickname, 8; enlists in Union Army, 8; on Powder River Expedition, 9; honorable discharge, 9; at Fort Harker, 12; saloonkeeper, 20; as "Rowdy Joe," 21, 22; brothel keeper, 24, 58, 116; accused of theft, 25; at Topeka, 26; witness to shoot-out at Ellsworth, 31–35, 99; leaves Ellsworth, 35; at Newton, 38ff.; relationship with gamblers, 49; leaves Newton, 59; at Wichita, 61ff.; beats up Joseph Walters, 63; integrity of, 68; thrown from horse, 68, 134; saloon saved from fire, 77; showdown with Red Beard, 77–78; blinds Billie Anderson, 80; tried for murder, 86–89; escape from Wichita, 88–91; arrested, 93–96; gone to Texas, 97ff.; at Denison, 99ff., 103; charged with illegal gambling, 103; at San Antonio, 105ff.; at Fort Worth, 105ff.; leaves Kate, 107; first marriage, 107; theater owner, 112; at Leadville, 119ff.; sergeant in Old Tabor Guards, 122; shoots John Timms, 125; involved in footrace scandal, 126; claims to have given up guns, 130; at Denver, 129ff.; involved in dispute over ranch, 142; organizes dogfights, 147–48; last days, 149ff.; dispute with Kimmel, 152ff.; murdered, 154; shootout over ditch, 155ff.; remembered at Wichita, 158; burial of, 160, 172 n.
Lowe, Kate ("Rowdy Kate"): 5, 25; description of, 63–64; intervenes between Red Beard and Joe Lowe, 80; helps Joe escape, 88; follows Joe to St. Louis, 93; gone to Texas, 103ff.; leaves Joe, 107; charged with keeping a disorderly house, 110–14, 129
Lowe, Lena (Joe Lowe's second wife): 5–6; marries Joe, 137; temporary separation from Joe, 149, 150n.; learns of Joe's death, 160; gives evidence at Kimmel trial, 168; devotes life to daughters, 162; death of, 162
Lowe, Mollie (Mary) (Joe Lowe's first wife): 6, 107–108; divorces Joe, 108, 112, 123, 127, 137, 162
Lowe, Samuel (scout): 12
Lowe, Susan (Joe Lowe's mother): 6
Lowe, Thomas (Joe Lowe's father): 6, 8, 107
Lowe, Thomas (Joe Lowe's son): 137, 160
Luhn, Peter (Pioneer Store): 39
Luling, Tex.: 100; description of, 100–101, 106
Lynchings: at Ellsworth, 19; Joe Lowe's alleged involvement in, 27

Index   185

McAdams, T. C.: 25
McAdams, T. J.: 25
McCall, Jack: 118
McCall, Samuel: 142–43; killed, 143
McClury & Co.: 78
McCluskie, Arthur: 43
McCluskie, Michael, killed at Newton: 41ff.
McCoy, Joseph G., influence on cattle industry: 38–39ff.
McCoy's Addition (brothel district): 73
McCoy's Extension (of the Chisholm Trail): 38
McDonald (policeman): 147
McDonald, James H. (policeman): 45–46
McDonald, R. S.: 95–96
McDonough, James (policeman): 94–96
McGivern, E. P. (undertaker): 161
McKenna, John: 143–46
McLelland, T. E.: 146
Madden, Capt. Daniel: 76–78
"Mark" (newspaperman): 88
Marshall, Rev. Thomas: 160
Marshall, Tex.: 97
Martin, John: 147
Martin, William ("Hurricane Bill"): 61–62
Massey, Sheriff Pleasant H.: 97
Masterson, Bartholomew ("Bat"): visits Leadville, 120; recalls Joe Lowe, 121; member of the Dodge City Peace Commission, 131–32; condemns Kimmel, 157
Mead, A. W.: 95–96
Mead, James R.: 61
Meagher, Michael (town marshal): 61, 83–84
Meagher, Sheriff John: 77–78, 82–83
Medicine Lodge, Kans.: 43

Medlin, Dr. P. A.: 65
Menafee, Jim: 67
Mexicans: at Ellsworth, Kans., 18; as vaqueroes, 18
Miller, James: 21
Miller, Joseph: 56
Miller, Judge George W.: 150n.
Milner (policeman): 125
Milner, Moses E. ("California Joe"): 28
Missouri, Kansas, Texas Railroad: 97
Monte, Joe (gambler): 101
Mooar, Josiah Wright, recalls Rowdy Kate: 111
Moon, Jim (gambler): 48–59, 158
Moscony, Joe: 147
Murphy, Capt.: 123
Murphy, John: 137
Muse, Judge R. W. P.: 39
Musgrave, H.: 142
Musick, C. E.: 22
My Theater, Leadville, Colo.: 116

Nasmyth, Capt. Clarence E.: 76
Neville, Harry (deputy U.S. marshal): 43
Newton, Michael (magistrate): 21, 22, 32ff.
Newton, Kans.: origin, 38ff., 45ff., 54, 64, 103, 120, 121, 133
Newton, Mass.: 38
Newton General Massacre: 43
New York, N.Y.: 30
Nugent, John: 90
Nuttall, Billy: 123–24

Ohmert, E. A.: 79–81
Old Tabor Tigers: 122
Omaha, Nebr.: 9
Omohundro, John B. ("Texas Jack"): 15, 119–20; death of, 120
Ordinances: against firearms, 24–25, 68; against gambling,

186 Rowdy Joe Lowe

Ordinances (*continued*)
  69–71; against prostitution, 71;
  against saloonkeepers, 71, 135
Orpheum Theater, Denver, Colo.:
  155
Osage Indians: 78
Osage Mission, Kans.: 89, 93
Osborn, Gov. Thomas A.: 87
Osbourne, Frank: 33
Ostrander, Maj. A. B., describes Joe
  and Kate Lowe: 100
Overlin, Sam: 51
Owens, Dr. H.: 65, 84

Park, John S.: 21
Park City, Kans.: 65
Pendleton, Enoch: 33, 35
Pendleton, P. I. (county attorney):
  35
Perry, W. C.: 142
Peru, Ill.: 7–8
Phillips, Capt. (policeman): 147,
  148, 155
Phillips, Jack: 143
Pitkin, Gov. Fred W.: 121
Platte River, Nebr.T.: 9
Pleasant Hill, Mo.: 100
Police: at Ellsworth, 14, 16; at
  Newton, 41, 45ff., 54ff.; at
  Wichita, 62, 64; ammunition supplied to, 68–69, 83
Pond Creek, Kans.: 78
Pope, Gen. John S.: 30, 31
Potawatomi Indians: 7
Powder River, Wyo.: 9
Powder River Expedition: 9
Prescott, Daniel: 163ff.
Price, Gen. Sterling: 8
Prostitution: at Ellsworth, Kans.,
  14, 25; at Newton, Kans., 49
Prothro, John (juror): 164
Prouty, S. S.: 66–67
Putney (policeman): 147

Quimby, Lt. Henry: 29

Reid, Pony (gambler): 48
Reynolds, Thomas: 28
Riley (friend of Mike McCluskie's):
  43
Ritter Jake (musician): 51
Riverside Cemetery, Denver, Colo.:
  137, 160, 172 n.
Rocheport, Mo.: 8
Roe, Richard: 162
Rolla, Mo.: 8, 9
Rollins (coroner): 157
Round Rock, Tex.: 104
Rowdy Joe: *see* Lowe, Joseph
Rucker, 2d Lt. John A.: 76
Rupp, W. W.: 120

Sac and Fox Indians: 7
St. James Hotel, Denver, Colo.: 167
St. Louis, Mo.: 9, 11, 42, 49, 73, 93
St. Louis, Lawrence & Western
  Railroad: 100
St. Louis Saloon, Ellsworth, Kans.:
  21
Saloons: licensing, 16, 25, 26; description of Lowe's at Ellsworth,
  20; fights in, 21–22, 31–35,
  41–45, 56, 57, 64, 76–77, 78–82,
  99, 125–27, 152–55; at Wichita,
  67, 75–76; taxation of, at
  Wichita, 71; and Red Beard's,
  75–76; other keepers protest at
  cost of Lowe's murder trial, 88;
  crackdown on, at Fort Worth,
  114; at Denver, 135
San Angelo, Tex.: 111
San Antonio, Tex.: 104–105
Sanderson, George: 28–29
Sanderson, Mrs. George: 29
Sanderson, John: 28
Sanderson, Jonathan: 28
San Francisco, Calif.: 51

San Francisco Saloon, Denison, Tex.: 98
Santa Fe, N.Mex.: 14
Santa Fe Stage Road: 12
Satanta (Kiowa): 98
Sazarac Saloon, Denison, Tex.: 98
Schattner, Charles: 53
Schattner, Fred: 52-53
Schooler, John: 28
Seaman, Daniel: 153ff., 159, 166, 168
Seamens, William ("Apache Bill"): 23
Searcy, B. (deputy U.S. marshal): 16
Second (New) Missouri Regiment of Light Artillery: 8-9
Seguin, Tex.: 101
Seiber, Sheriff J. Charles: 22, 26, 28
Senate Saloon, Fort Worth, Tex.: 113
Seventh U.S. Cavalry: 12, 19, 28
Shabonna (Potawatomi): 7
Shellabarger, Lt. Jacob H.: 23
Short, Luke (gambler): kills Courtright, 113; dispute at Dodge City, 131-34
Silsby, Edward (musician): 51
Simmons (saloon bouncer allegedly killed by Lowe): 127
Sioux Indians: 9
Sixteenth Michigan Infantry: 47
Sixth U.S. Cavalry: 76ff.
Skiddy, Francis: 98
Skiddy Street, Denison, Tex. (brothel district): 98, 99
Slack, Bernard M.: 123, 128, 131; pallbearer at Lowe's funeral, 160
Slick (policeman): 147
Sloss, H. C.: 86-87
Smith, Charles ("One Arm Charlie"): 81ff., 86
Smith, Charles (juror): 162, 164

Smith, G. W.: 164
Smith, J. T.: 48
Smith, Sheriff William ("Bill"): 83-84; offers reward for Lowe, 89; attempts to extradite Lowe from Missouri, 94-97, 106
Smith, William: 143
Smokey Hill Trail: 12
Snyder, Capt. J. A.: 30-31
Snyder, John T. (deputy sheriff): 31-35
Southard (policeman): 147, 148
Stanley, Emma (prostitute): 76
Stanley, W. E.: 70
Stewart (judge): 96
Stitt, James (horse thief): 27, 28
Stockwell & Walton (merchants): 39
Storms, Charlie, killed by Luke Short: 132
Sumner City, Kans.: 44
Sutton, Mike (lawyer): 131
Sweet, A. M.: 5; shot by Joe Lowe, 53-54

Tabor, Horace: 119, 122
Tabor Light Cavalry: 120, 121
Tabor Opera House, Leadville, Colo.: 119
Taylor, Joseph N.: 165-67
Taylor-Sutton Feud: 101
Teft House Hotel, Topeka, Kans.: 26
Templeton, Fay (singer): 112
Texas Central Railroad: 43
Texas & Pacific Railroad: 106, 111
Texas Rangers: 104
Thayer, Isaac N. (gambler): 69-70
Thompson, Benjamin ("Ben"): 103, 148
Thompson, Court (runner): 126-27
Thompson, William ("Billy"): 148

Thompson, William: 147
Through Ticket Saloon, Newton, Kans.: 53
Thurman, U. E. (policeman): 16
Timms, John: 124; shot by Joe Lowe, 125–26
Tombstone, Ariz.: 48, 111, 132
Topeka, Kans.: 26, 28, 30, 44, 133
Tucker, S. M. (lawyer): 86–87, 90
Tuttle, Perry (saloonkeeper): 40ff.; his saloon scene of Newton General Massacre, 41–44

Union Pacific Railway Co. (Eastern Division): 12, 14, 38, 65
U.S. Saloon, Ellsworth, Kans.: 19; taken over by Joe Lowe, 20

Vigilance Committee: 18, 22

Wade, Tommy: 124
Walker, George (saloonkeeper): 152, 155
Walker (partner of Joseph Lane): 65
Walker, Sheriff W. N.: 26
Wallace (thief): 46
Wallace, Thomas, stabbed at Ellsworth, Kans.: 14
Ward, Thomas (attorney): 163ff.
Weatherford, Tex.: 109
Webber, D. C.: 163, 168
Webster, Alonzo B.: 131–32
Welch, Martin: 160
Wellington, Kans.: 64
Wells, C. H. (juror): 160
Western Union Telegraph Co.: 100
West Wichita: *see* Delano (West Wichita, Kans.)

West Wichita Town Co.: 89
Wheeler, Col. Homer: 44
Whipple, Gen. W. D.: 30
White, James R.: 29
White Elephant Saloon, Fort Worth, Tex.: 113
Whitehead (secretary, Colorado Humane Society): 148
Whitehouse Saloon, Denver, Colo.: 53
Wichita, Kans.: 4, 12, 23, 43, 54, 58, 61ff.; cowtown, 65ff., 71ff., 93, 98, 99, 103, 106, 120
Wichita Saloon, Wichita, Kans.: 53
Wichita & Southwestern Railroad: 38ff., 75, 77
Wilcoxon, John E.: *see* Moon, Jim
Wild Bill: *see* Hickok, James B.
Wilde, Oscar (playwright): 119
Wild Joe: *see* Lowe, Joseph
Wilhelm, C. W.: 167
Williams, John: 46
Wilson, N. H.: 113–14
Wilson, William: 41
Winchester, Lt. Homer F.: 76, 78
Windsor Hotel, Denver, Colo.: 154
Wolf Tone Guards: 121
Woodbury, S. S.: 143
Woods Opera House, Leadville, Colo.: 107
Worth, Gen. William J.: 106
Wyman ("Pap" saloon owner): 135

York (saloonkeeper): 135
York Cottage Saloon, Denver, Colo.: 135

www.ingramcontent.com/pod-product-compliance
Lightning Source LLC
Chambersburg PA
CBHW050758160426
43192CB00010B/1567